THE POLITICS OF COMMUNITY ACTION

A Decade of Struggle in Notting Hill

by

Jan O'Malley

Spokesman

First published in 1977
This edition published in 2020
Spokesman Books
5 Churchill Park
Nottingham
NG4 2HF
England

Phone 0115 9708318
www.spokesmanbooks.com

Copyright Jan O'Malley

All rights reserved. No part of this book may be reprinted or reproduced or utilised in any form or by any electronic, mechanical or other means, now known or hereafter invented, including photocopying and recording, or in any information storage or retrieval system, without permission in writing from the publishers.

A catalogue record is available from the British Library.

ISBN 978 0 85124 8875

THE POLITICS
OF
COMMUNITY ACTION

Contents

Foreword to the 2020 edition	
Introduction	7
The Political Economy of North Kensington	9
The Political Vacuum	21
The Growth of Local Organisation	26
The Notting Hill Summer Project 1967	43
The Problems of Organisation	59
Planning, Play and Motorway Space	75
Housing Struggles Against Private Capital	100
The Fight to Change Council Housing Policy	119
Housing Shifts 1966–1974	140
Lessons for the Future	164

Preface to 2020 edition

The Politics of Community Action focuses on community struggles in a small neighbourhood in West London over a period of eight years from 1966 to 1974. So, 50 years on, is it still relevant?

Today, similar struggles are going on in London against major regeneration schemes driven by local councils which will have the same effect of driving out many of the original inhabitants as rents in the new properties will be higher and leaseholders will be scattered. This is taking place in Lambeth, Southwark and Tower Hamlets. The constraints on local councils over building council housing have resulted in them teaming up with developers to build more homes at greater density on existing council estates, demolishing the existing homes. The current battles of local residents are not against gentrification by private landlords but by some local councils.

Whereas in the 1960s, the Council and Housing Associations were seen as sources of non-profit housing, the Right to Buy and the transformation of Housing Associations into mainstream developers have ended this simplistic view.

New organisations were forged in North Kensington such as the North Kensington Amenity Trust (running the land under Westway) and the North Kensington Law Centre. The process of institutionalisation which has taken place, as the radical edge is lost, is an important lesson that still applies. The Amenity Trust became another institution with which local people still have to battle.

The Politics of Community Action shows how the traditional Left organisations failed to provide an effective organisation through which local people could express their needs politically and how new organisations were forged to fill the vacuum. The Labour Party, in the main, focused its electioneering work on council estates where the vote could be relied on and ignored the much worse conditions in which private tenants lived. They did individual casework but did not develop collective action from the lessons learned from individual cases.

The growth of the Notting Hill People's Association from the crisis faced by the tenants of one block into an organisation focused on the needs of the wider community shows the real sense of solidarity of those tenants who looked beyond their own individual situation. As fresh needs were identified, new groups were set up to encompass playspace, traffic dangers, police harassment, benefits issues as well as housing. The energy that was unleashed by weekly meetings led to a speed of response when a fresh demand led to prompt action and engagement with the authorities.

Today there is a similar creative spontaneity in groups such as Extinction Rebellion and the new unions organising those working in the gig economy as they develop new semi-autonomous working groups to fill the gaps left by traditional political parties and unions.

Both the Labour Party and Momentum have started to employ community organisers to feed in skills to support activists in local communities to fight for what their community needs, replicating in a way the Notting Hill Community Workshop initiative in North Kensington. The Workshop's aim was to build local community organisations through which a local force of people could 'fight to wrest from the authorities whatever they decide their community requires'.

Strong community leaders developed and the book gives a voice to the working class heroines who led these struggles: Pat MacDonald, Maggie O'Shannon and Merle Major. They deserve to be remembered and celebrated for having the strength to widen their individual struggle to include demands for the whole neighbourhood despite the very difficult conditions they were living in.

The Politics of Community Action makes the case for the need to integrate industrial and community struggles and that socialists should take community struggles seriously as an equally valid arena to the workplace. Trades Councils and unions such as Unite Community provide examples of how this has become an accepted part of organisation on the Left.

The book demonstrates that victories can be won despite the resistance of a very entrenched Conservative Council. In housing, Council policy was opened up to public debate both locally and nationally, and plans for two major areas of North Kensington developed by the Council as a result. These involved massive shifts from private to non-profit ownership in areas for which the Council had no plans at all.

The vital need for playspace was established in the area and space and resources were won for play for years to come. The future use of the land under Westway for a car park was challenged and a decision forced to use the space for community facilities.

Such victories are important to feed hope that change is possible and to help generate fresh struggles in the here and now.

Jan O'Malley
London, March 2020

3 areas covered by Housing Survey and on which housing struggles focussed.

Map of North Kensington

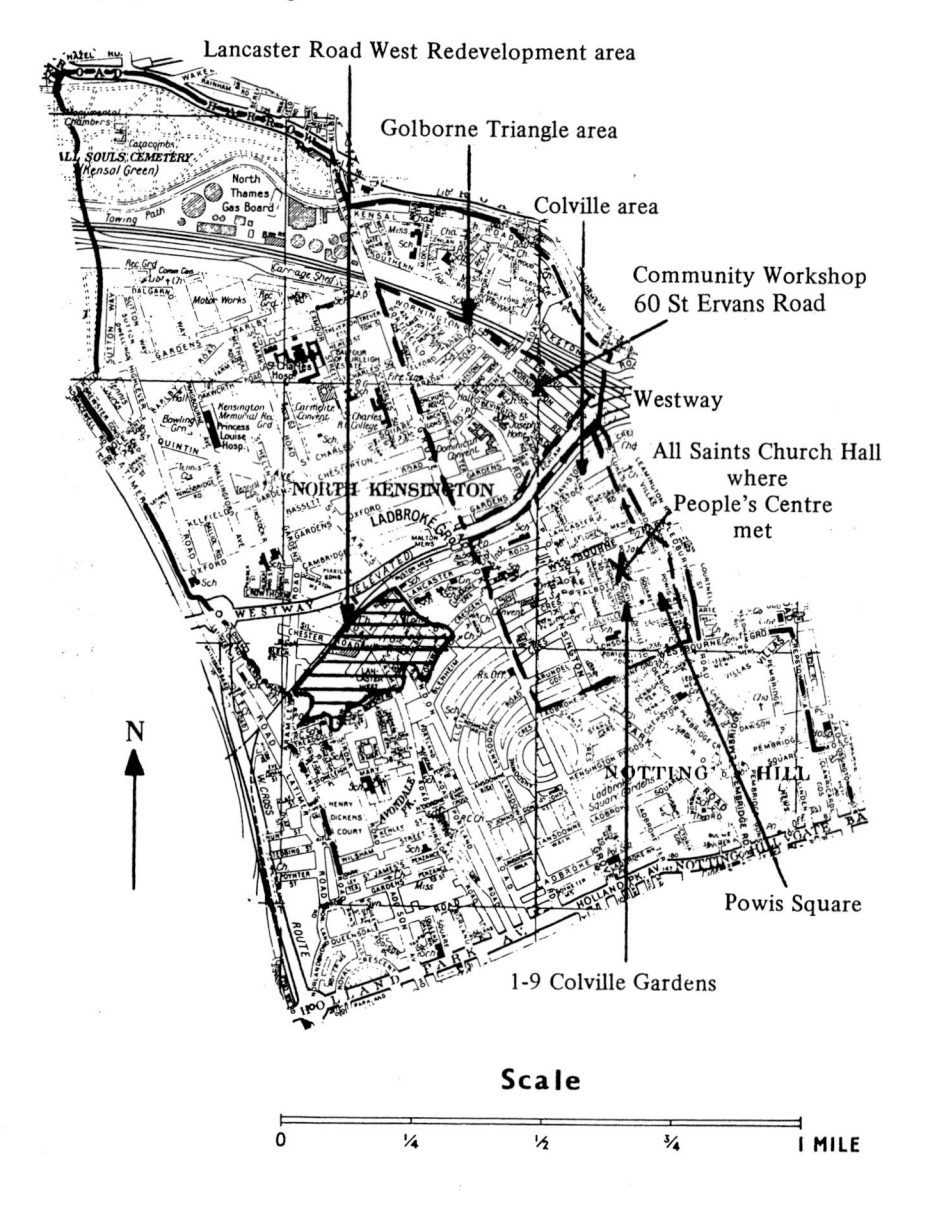

- Lancaster Road West Redevelopment area
- Golborne Triangle area
- Colville area
- Community Workshop 60 St Ervans Road
- Westway
- All Saints Church Hall where People's Centre met
- Powis Square
- 1-9 Colville Gardens

Scale

0   ¼   ½   ¾   1 MILE

Introduction

The focus of this book is on the struggles of the working class for survival in the North Kensington area, and for control over the resources and decisions which determine their living conditions, in the years between 1966 and 1974.

In order to take part in these struggles hundreds of ordinary working people broke with the routines of the daily grind and took steps into the void and became involved in actions which had no guarantee of success, but which they saw as a means of regaining some degree of power and self-determination.

This is a partisan view of what happened in Notting Hill, but it is worth examining the experience on which it is based. This book is an attempt to explore the dynamic of community struggle in Notting Hill over this period, focussing on the activities and organisational developments of the groups with which I have been most closely involved — those which made up the Notting Hill People's Association.

This has meant certain omissions. No attempt has been made to touch on the developments around the Golborne Neighbourhood Council since there are others who are bound to write it up. Also no attempt has been made to document the development and struggles of black groups in North Kensington. This is partly because, being white, I was necessarily not part of them, but also because I was never aware of local black groups pursuing a political strategy which related to the needs of the working class people of the area, black or white, in a coherent way. There were a series of well organised defence groups which arose to counter police harassment but when cases were won against the police, as in the Mangrove trial in 1971, there was no attempt to shift from the defensive to the offensive and expand a political strategy on a wider front.

The structure of this book is in four main sections. The first attempts to provide a context in which the developments over this period can be understood. The conflicts of interest built into the economic and political structure of the area are explained, as well as the inadequacy of the Labour Party as a channel through which the working class of North Kensington could mount any serious resistance. The second section covers the form local organisation took and the kinds of struggles which developed over this period, against bad planning, for play and for the control of the motorway space. Housing struggles are looked at in greater detail in the third section and a detailed attempt is made to evaluate the effects of these struggles against private capital and the local state in terms of the shifts which resulted in Council policy, in ownership and in resources. The housing struggles are looked at in the greatest detail since they are crucial to the working class people being able to continue to live in the area. All the other struggles over play and motorway space are secondary in that they are only part of working class struggles so long as working people continue to live in the area and so be able to make use of whatever amenities are won. Without the housing struggle the struggle for more amenities would just increase the pace at which the area was transformed into an upper income residential area. The final section attempts to weigh up the strengths and weaknesses of community struggles in terms of a socialist perspective and on the basis of this to formulate strategic ideas about the way in which community struggle could lead to more fundamental political change in future.

I have written primarily for two groups of people: for socialists involved in community based struggles and those involved in industrial struggle in the hope that much greater integration will be forged between these two forms of struggle in the future.

ACKNOWLEDGEMENTS:

The book is the product of all the people of Notting Hill who have been involved in the struggles of the last ten years. However, I would especially like to thank those friends who spent time reading and criticising the drafts in the light of their memories of the struggles as they had experienced them: Eddie Adams, Sean Baine, Beryl Foster, R.A. Gilmore, Chris Holmes, Peter Kandler, Brenda Laing, Pat McDonald, Rose Morrell, John O'Malley, Dave Perry, Bill Richardson, Adam Ritchie and Kate Truscott.

Helpful criticism was also given by others who had not been involved in any of the struggles and read the drafts as interested outsiders. They shared with me their experience of writing and helped me to structure the mass of material I had to draw on: Cynthia Cockburn, David Donnison, Keith Jackson, Peter Marris, Marj Mayo, Shelagh Rowbotham, Ralph Samuel and Edward Thompson.

Chapter 1

The Political Economy of North Kensington

The origins of the struggles which have taken place in North Kensington throughout its history and in recent years, lie in the political economy of the area itself, and in its relationship with the economy of London as a whole.

Both the land and the labour of the people in the area have been used in a continuous process of capital accumulation. Sometimes this involved a new production process as, for instance, farming was replaced by brick-making which was in turn replaced by building, as the development potential of the land increased its value, so leading to a fresh flow of investment. At other times capital accumulation took place by speculative developments within the same sector. This happened when houses built for single family occupation were bought up in the 1880s and 1890s for sub-division into flats for several families, and in the 1950s and 1960s when these houses were sub-divided yet again, four families filling the space in each flat where just one family had lived before. Each shift was a result of speculative investment based on the estimation of the low income demand for private rented housing and the increased rate of return which could be gained by aiming to alter the nature of the use of the housing to meet the demand. Over the last ten years the strategy of property owners has changed again and their interest has revived in the upper income groups as tenants or buyers. It was by catering for this sector of the market that profits could be maximised and be subject to the least governmental controls.

In this continuing process of capital accumulation the owners of capital were always at an advantage as a result of the constant immigration to the area from central London and towards the end of the 19th century from the rest of England, and from the world over the rest of the period. This decreased the bargaining power of workers in the area so depressing wages, and increased the competition between workers for the supply of privately rented houses, so increasing the rents which the owners could charge.

Perhaps the most important process through which this area was used as a source of capital accumulation was through the building of both working class and upper class housing, by private capital.

The main areas of working class housing were built in Kensal, in the north of the area in the 1830s, in the Silchester and Notting Dale areas in the west and south-west of the area in the 1860s, and in parts of St. Charles and Golborne in the 1870s. There were two important factors which led to the development of parts of North Kensington as working class residential areas: the eviction of the working class from central London, and the expansion of the railway network.

The forcible eviction of the working class from central London over the period between 1830 and 1880 meant that thousands of working class people had to find homes outside the central London area, so creating a ready demand for working class housing in areas like North Kensington. This process of evicting the working class from central London was a result of the growth of the infrastructure of the expanding capital city, of the offices to house the expanding government and of the conversion of residential to commercial premises. All this expansion took place at the expense of the working class population which was evicted to make more room. Despite the Metropolitan Street Improvement Acts of 1872 and 1877 which gave the Board of Works limited rehousing responsibilities, the Board continued to avoid these at all costs, and the norm was compensation of £1.50 and one week's notice. So between 1830 and 1880 it has been estimated that street clearance and urban improvement alone evicted 100,000 people from central London, and whereas in the 1830s most workers in central London lived within walking distance of their work, by the 1880s this was no longer the case.[1]

However the workforce was still needed in central London and in order to enable the working class both to get to work in central London while living outside the area, the railway network was expanded to cover areas like North Kensington. In 1838 the Great Western Railway was opened due west out of Paddington, passing right through the northern tip of North Kensington. Then in 1869 the Metropolitan Railway was expanded from Paddington to Hammersmith and finally in 1899 the Central Line Railway was completed. This railway network, together with the introduction of cheap fares in the 1860s, meant that workers living in North Kensington were within a half hour journey of workplaces in the City.

The railways also contributed to the growth of working class residential areas in another way. The process of building the railways extended over a period of several years and was often subject to long delays when investment capital was short. This meant that for years the surrounding areas were subjected to noise and dirt which was likely to put off the upper classes from wanting to live there. The builders involved in house building in these areas predicted this, and so both the Silchester area to the north of the railways and the Notting Dale area to the south, were covered with densely packed rows of 3-storey houses and artisans' cottages to meet working class housing demand.

However there were some builders with interests in North Kensington who had much more lofty ambitions than merely building terrace upon terrace of 3 or 4 storey houses for the working class. They aimed at higher rates of return by catering for a very different sort of demand for housing — the wealthy citizens of London who were not forced out of central London by demolition, but who chose to live away from the dirt, noise and bustle of the centre.

Building on the land north of Notting Hill Gate began in the 1820s when Notting Hill Farm was sold for building land and an early terrace of Ladbroke Grove Nos. 11-19 was built on the site. These houses were on a far grander scale than the small terraces built for the working class further north. Then in 1827 James Weller Ladbroke took over as ground landlord for the whole area north of Notting Hill Gate to Portobello Farm, at the north end of Portobello Road.

He commissioned an architect, Allom, to draw up a design for the development of the whole of what came to be known as the Kensington Park Estate. The plans were for gracious terraces, squares and crescents with gardens alternating with rows of houses. Ladbroke proceeded to lease individual building plots on condition that they were built on in accordance with the overall plan.

One of the first purchasers was the Reverend Walker who had come from Cornwall with £½ million to invest in property. He started building on the west side of Clarendon Road, but he misjudged the market and built houses intended for the upper classes but much nearer to the pig-keepers, brick kiln workers, gypsies and laundresses than they were prepared to live. The result was rows of unfinished, uninhabited houses — "He was not long in causing hundreds of carcases of houses to be built" was the way an old inhabitant put it in 1882.[2]

But Reverend Walker was obviously not daunted by this experience and went on in 1852 to buy more land — 51 acres of what is now the Colville area. There was at this time no buildings north of Westbourne Grove except for Portobello Farm. Walker had a grandiose plan to build a 'new town' and erect an elaborate church. But again his plans did not work out as he had hoped. The symbol of his failure to make the area attractive to the upper classes can still be seen in the stunted stump of All Saints Church Tower which Rev. Walker had intended to have a spire as high as Salisbury Cathedral. It soon became known as 'Walker's Folly' and 'All Sinners in the Mud'.

South of the church at this time in the Colville and Powis Square area were brickfields owned by the Tippet family who later built terraces on the land of 5 and 6 storey houses. They too failed to attract the upper classes, for which they were intended. By 1885 Tippett was bankrupt because he had underestimated the upper class resistance to living in an area surrounded by working class homes. Even before Tippett went bankrupt, in 1881 the houses he had built as single family homes were being sub-divided for many more families. By 1888 the vicar of All Saints declared, "There is no wealth or even moderate means in the parish."

Yet just half a mile from All Saints Church was St. John's, the church on the top of the hill, around which the gracious curving terraces of the Kensington Park Estate were developed. These were built for the upper classes, and it was the upper classes who retained firm hold of them, undaunted by the goings-on in nearby Notting Dale, with its piggeries, its laundries and its brick kilns.

By 1900 private landlords had built up most of North Kensington. The only open land still open was in the north west of the area between the railway in the north and Bassett Road in the south. Since 1900 private capital has continued to be centrally involved in North Kensington housing, and its interests have never been fundamentally threatened by the new agencies which have developed since then, the local authority and the housing trusts.

Council inaction meant that private landlords have been given a free hand to maximise their profits subject to national legislation. Rent control, introduced in 1913 and not released till the 1957 Rent Act, was one of the real constraints on private profits, which had limited speculation in property. However as soon as the return of a Conservative government in 1951 heralded the decontrol of rented property, property speculators had started buying in North Kensington, and held onto their property till the 1957 Rent Act gave them the opportunity they had been waiting for. This Rent Act, by decontrolling rents without giving tenants security of tenure, ushered in an era of intimidation and strong arm tactics aimed at getting rid of any tenants who stood in the way of an increasing flow of rent income from the houses. If letting the room to a prostitute guaranteed a higher rent income than letting it to a family, then the family had to be got out, even if it meant just dumping their possessions on the street. Peter Rachman became one of the best known names around North Kensington in the late 1950s and early 1960s because of his rapidly expanding property empire, based on the more lucrative returns from using property for gambling and prostitution at the expense of ordinary tenants.

The 1965 Rent Act, by introducing greater security of tenure and control of rents put a stop to most of this kind of activity and introduced a new phase in the way in which housing was used as a source of profit. The high income tenant or buyer gradually became the main focus of the property owner's interest, as the source of maximum profits most likely to evade legislative controls. And again, just as in the previous phase, there were the casualties — all tenants who obstructed plans to convert the large houses into luxury flats.

The interests of the local authority have never been in conflict with the property owners, and throughout its history the local authority has always tried to deflect blame for the conditions from the profit making process to the tenants themselves. In 1893 a national newspaper attacked the housing conditions in part of Notting Dale, which it called a *West End Avernus*. The attack was sufficient to force the Works Committee of the Vestry (the forerunner of the Borough Council) to call a public meeting which ended up inspecting the area en masse. The Vestry however concluded at the end of the visit that any defects were "of constant recurrence in houses occupied by the lowest classes and are largely brought about by the dirty and careless or mischievous habits of the people themselves".[3]

However the infant mortality rate continued to be 432 per 1000, four times as high as the rate in the rest of the parish and a committee was set up in 1896 to decide what was to be done. Their dramatic conclusion was that "the necessity for frequent sanitary inspection can hardly be overstated" but the Vestry went ahead and reduced the health inspection staff from seven to six. This gave each health inspector the responsibility for 28,000 inhabitants, the highest number in London. Yet even then the Medical Officer of Health was urging the Vestry to buy up the houses and let them as decent homes, since the inspection programme was totally ineffective. "Houses have been registered, surprise visits are paid to check overcrowding . . . Yet at the end of it all the medical officer reports that the evil conditions still continue, much overcrowding remains, and the locality is much the same as formerly when it was described as being as 'godforsaken as anything in London'. The problem is now left to the new Borough Council to solve."[4]

Kensington Borough Council came into being in 1899. In the same year Octavia Hill started managing property in the area for private landlords, the forerunner of the housing trust movement which has become of central importance in the Borough housing policy. (Housing trusts are charitable bodies which provide rented housing on a non-profit basis.) So the growth of housing trust and Borough housing activity began together. The Borough realised early on that the trusts could be absorbed into official housing strategy. The historical records show how the Borough came to rely on the trusts for rehabilitation and redevelopment work wherever possible. The Council even built the charitable element of housing trust work into the first attempt at house building in 1904. The Mayor made a large interest free loan for a small redevelopment scheme in Kenley Street. It was finished in 1906 but rents were too high for the casually employed unskilled poor who lived in the street before. So only one fifth of the original residents were rehoused in the new buildings. The rest had to move to more crowded, cheaper rented rooms elsewhere in the borough.

Meanwhile the housing trust ownership of housing had started in 1900 with the formation of the Improved Tenements Association, set up with the aim of providing better housing for the poor. They bought houses with money borrowed from well off individuals at low interest rates and repaired them. In 1926 they were joined by the Kensington Housing Trust (KHT) and throughout the 1920s and 1930s the Council policy was to encourage the expansion of these and other trusts.

The Housing Act of 1930 required the Council to prepare a five year slum clearance plan. Extensive plans were laid for Council schemes but the only extensive schemes to proceed were done by the housing trusts, with the Council acquiring the land for them — the land initially designated as the sites for Council schemes. So that by the time the Second World War broke out in 1939 the ownership score in North Kensington was under 500 tenancies to the Council and around 2,000 tenancies to the trusts. For new building and acquiring older badly managed property, the Borough Council had relied primarily on the energy of the trusts.

It was only after the Second World War that the council took the housing shortage seriously enough to engage in extensive building projects itself while the trusts played a very minor role.

However, the housing crisis precipitated by the 1957 Rent Act restored the trusts to the centre of the housing scene. The Council response was to give a loan of £½ million to Kensington Housing Trust on condition they agreed to take the 'fall-out' from the 1957 Housing Act, or in plain words — the casualties. Also the fresh sense of crisis created by the race riots, the scandals of Rachmanism and the persistent neglect of the Borough Council set the scene for the intervention of the Notting Hill Housing Trust (NHHT) in 1963. From the late 1950s onwards the Council has relied on the trusts in North Kensington for all the rehabilitation of old property for those in housing need, and has turned to the trusts whenever possible to take responsibility for redevelopment as well. So this left the Council with exclusive responsibility for only one major redevelopment scheme in North Kensington — the Lancaster Road West scheme with 1058 dwellings. This was planned in the mid-1950s and yet not even the first stage was completed by 1974.

The Council/Trust relationship has not only involved interdependent activity but also a considerable overlap of personnel. For instance, Lord Burleigh was active in the KHT and the Council in the 1920s and 30s and from 1954 Mrs Paul was active in both Trust and Council and was to become in 1969 both the Trust's Vice Chairman as well as being the Chairman of the Council's Town Planning Committee.

Why did such a close relationship between the trusts and the Council develop? Perhaps the most important reason is that, given the Council's commitment to a Conservative philosophy of minimal intervention in the private market and given the anger and publicity arising from the conditions produced by that same private housing market, something had to be done.

The trusts were there and were eager to do the job of providing homes for the poor and badly housed. They combined a kind of unaccountable private enterprise with the provision of non-profit low rent homes. Since they were non-profit institutions having to pay market prices for houses, they were easily outbid by other private buyers who based the price they would pay on the profits they expected to make. So the trusts offered no serious threat to the private market in housing. The trusts were just the agency the Council needed since they removed the necessity of any consideration of large scale municipalisation. Ideologically and practically, the Council had no alternative but to use the trusts.

The Council must also have seen the trusts as offering them housing on the cheap. John Dearlove quotes the Chairman of Housing in 1968[5] –

"Housing trusts and property companies are experts at reconditioning, we are not, and we should leave it to them, as if we do it we have to provide higher standards and that only pushes the cost up."

The actual cost to the Council of housing trust building and conversion work over the century has varied tremendously. During the first 30 years of the century there was virtually no cost to the Council at all, since the trusts raised all their own money as loans from wealthy individuals. But then the Council did buy the land on which the trust developments of the 1930s were built. However, it was not till 1957 that the first sizeable loan was given to a housing trust and that was just the beginning of a flow of resources which was to end up in 1973 by exceeding the capital expenditure of the Council on its own building schemes. But even now with loans of £millions flowing to the trusts for new building and purchase and conversion of property, they still rely on a large amount of charitable money to cover welfare and administrative expenses which the greatly increased subsidies still do not cover.

It is not just money which the Council saves by parcelling out its housing schemes, it also saves a huge amount of effort and administration and staff expansion. The Council overheads can be kept at a minimum and the trusts are left to cope with all the complexities of coordinating many different sorts of specialists which any major redevelopment or conversion scheme entails.

A final reason why the Council absorbed the trusts into their housing policy can be seen in terms of the way they house the poor, and its contribution to the social control of the working class.

The essence of the trust approach is the regular, intimate, and formal relationship with each tenant. The management ratio of the Kensington Housing Trust is five times that of the Council's Housing Department. Much stress is placed on the regular weekly collection of rent and the avoiding of arrears.

However the Council's heavy reliance on the housing trusts was just one element of their housing policy. The underlying philosophy of the housing policy was one of non-intervention in the private market and the policy aimed at minimising Council responsibility for housing in every possible way by building as little as possible, by spending as little as possible and relying as much as possible on private landlords.

According to whichever measure you take — annual completions of Council houses, or total stock of Council dwellings to date — Kensington Council have shown how little building you can get away with. They have a stock of Council housing and a rate of building lower than any other Inner London Borough.

By the end of the financial year in 1966 Kensington and Chelsea had a stock of only 5,381 Council dwellings whereas their neighbour Westminster, had 11,880 and at the other extreme, Southwark had 22,391.

The Council's argument has always been that they are a land-locked borough with no open land to build on, having to clear every bit of new building land by the demolition of existing homes. However in the two years immediately following 1966 the figures show that private developers found land to build twice as many dwellings as the Council itself. In 1967 and 1968 the Council built a total of 158 dwellings and the private developer 343.[6]

But it is not just in comparison with the private developers that the Council's record is low. While the Council only completed 68 dwellings in 1967 the average for the rest of the Inner London boroughs was around 500. (Table 7.11 Public sector completions GLC Annual Abstract of Statistics 1967.) The result of such low rates of building over the years meant that by 1966 only 7.6% of households lived in Council housing as compared with over 20% in Greater London as a whole.[7]

So far as spending money on housing is concerned the Tory view over the years is well summed up by the Housing Committee Chairman in 1968:

"Our view is that it is quite wrong to deflect money into an area which is quite capable of pulling itself up by its own bootstraps, and if we do, then we are loading the housing account with unnecessary expense. Hillgate Village — just behind Notting Hill Gate — was awful just after the war, but now it's looked up fantastically — the area improved not at our cost but we get an improved rate return."[8]

The dominant view of local government taken by the Councillors in 1968 was that the local Council is primarily a spender of the ratepayers' money and only secondarily a provider of services. This was coupled with an image of the traditional ratepayer as an old person on a fixed income, providing for him/herself, despite inflation and with no reliance on the public services. This meant that policy was seen as restricted to statutory obligations as far as possible with permissive legislation being virtually ignored. As one of the Chief Officers said:

"We don't make much use of permissive legislation and that's policy."[9]

If this is put in the context of housing legislation, the bulk of which is

permissive, it explains perfectly the nature of the Council's housing policy.
The Council's meanness in housing expenditure can only be fully appreciated if seen in relation to its wealth. In terms of the yield of a 1d rate Kensington and Chelsea was the third richest of the Inner London boroughs. For the financial year ending in March 1969 the league table reads:

Westminster	£417,000
Camden	£134,800
Kensington & Chelsea	£102,000

Despite this wealth the Council only chose to levy a rate of 9s.10d in the £ in 1966, next to lowest of all Inner London boroughs. Of the money raised in rates only an amount equivalent to a rate of 3.69d in the £ went to housing as compared to figures of 1s.5.99d in the £ in Camden and 3s.3.13d in the £ in Southwark. (GLC Annual Abstract of Statistics 1966 Table 241). This meant that in terms of total housing revenue account expenditure Kensington and Chelsea were right at the bottom of the league in 1966 spending £144,639.

The necessary counterpart to the Council building so little and spending so little on housing themselves was the Council's reliance on private landlords to provide housing for the majority of the households in the borough. In 1966 nearly 75% of all households in the borough and in North Kensington lived in privately rented accommodation.

Throughout its history the Council has been prepared to go to extraordinary lengths to avoid using any compulsion in their dealings with private landlords. Instead the Council has used endless persuasion, with the public health inspectors as their agents, and improvement grants as bribes, to try to help landlords to see that it is in their interest to improve their property. Interspersed with this persuasion campaign have been a long series of surveys, which were used as stalling devices whenever it looked as if the Council might be under pressure to intervene more in the private market.

The most recent inspection programme was begun in January 1963 as a result of a report by the Medical Officer of Health on two areas in North Kensington where the houses were over 100 years old and according to the report not worth converting. The main properties concerned were the 1,900 houses of the Colville and Golborne areas. The MOH stated that the best solution would be to demolish and redevelop these areas but he realised that the Council's slum clearance commitments made this impossible. So it was agreed to use the powers under the 1961 and 1957 Housing Acts to get the houses repaired and provided with the basic facilities like baths, toilets and hot and cold water. The staff of Public Health Inspectors was increased to make up a team of six to work in the two areas.

As a result of problems the inspectors found in enforcing the 1961 Housing Act, the Council made representations to the Ministry which they saw as leading to the additional powers provided by the 1964 Housing Act.

Yet by 1966 little had changed. The Census figures for that year showed that overcrowding and shared facilities were facts of life for a very large number of the people. In two of the wards, Colville and Golborne the percentage of persons living at over 1.5 persons per room was as high as 25% and 37%. Multi-occupation — the sharing of basic facilities, affected an even larger number: 66% of persons in Colville and 80% in Golborne.

The ineffectiveness of this programme was evident for all but the Council to see and in 1966 the Greater London Council offered help to Kensington. However by November no response had been received. The GLC followed this up in 1967 by suggesting that what was needed was a private bill to give London boroughs like Kensington simpler powers to compulsory purchase the houses of all landlords who would not rehabilitate their property. Kensington's response was to emphasise the administrative problems, and the technical problems of the Council getting builders to rehabilitate property. The Council reply ended complacently:

> "The Royal Borough's twilight areas are predominantly those concerning houses in multi-occupation for which existing legislation is reasonably adequate and which in practice is succeeding fairly well."

So these were the main elements in the housing situation in the borough in 1966. However, it is not enough to consider the people who live in the houses of North Kensington simply as units of investment. They are also workers and it is necessary to take a brief look at where the residents of the area work. In 1966 the Census showed that of the resident working population of around 36,000 in North Kensington 30% were manual workers and 70% worked in service industries, taken in a broad sense to include gas, electricity, water, transport, distribution, banking and public administration.

Many of both types of worker did not work within the borough of Kensington and Chelsea. In 1966 85% of the manual workers worked outside the area and this proportion was increasing due to the decline of manufacturing industry in the Borough. Between 1951 and 1966 the number of manual jobs declined by over a third, this loss of jobs being counteracted to a large extent by the increase in service employment. But though the decline of manufacturing industry was affecting all areas of Greater London, the borough of Kensington and Chelsea stands out from the other boroughs as having the lowest proportion of manufacturing employment.

So far as North Kensington was concerned, in 1974, the largest employers were Fidelity Radio, manufacturing radio and audio equipment, St. Charles Hospital, the Council Cleansing Department and Sir William Halcrow, a consultant engineers. These four each employed between 500 and 1,000 workers. Next in order of size came 12 employers of between 100 and 500 workers. These covered the manufacturing of records, catering equipment, rubber goods, printing, a hospital, an employment agency, film lighting contractors and several involved in distribution. Then there were about 30 employers of between 25 and 100 workers including large chain stores, British Rail, the Council Social Service Department and miscellaneous services like laundries, and film processors. At the bottom of the ranks of employers came the small workshops doing car repairs, light engineering, printing and upholstery, as well as shops and banks with under 25 workers.

The high proportion of residents working in service industries meant that instead of producing profit for industrial capital, they were manning the essential services which are crucial to the profit-making sectors of the economy. In the period from 1966 onwards this included not just industrial capital but increasingly the finance capital agencies like property companies, insurance companies and banks, which all had direct financial interests in the property they own — including the homes of the North Kensington workers they employed. So the working people of North Kensington were enmeshed in a circular process of exploitation both at work and at home. However, the physical distance between home and work for the majority of workers has meant that political organisation in North Kensington has focussed on their housing and living conditions, and the fusion of industrial and community struggles has proved rare and hard to achieve.

Before coming on to consider the form community struggles took and the issues over which the Council was challenged, it is necessary to explain the electoral invulnerability of the Council which made the prospect of challenging Council policy in this area that much more daunting.

The Conservatives had controlled Kensington Council since it was formed in 1899 and when Kensington was linked with Chelsea in 1963 the position of the Conservatives was even further strengthened so that they enjoyed an invulnerable electoral position. South Kensington and Chelsea made up over two thirds of the electorate leaving North Kensington with just under one third. In the 1964 local elections the Conservatives had around 75% of the vote in the twelve southern and central wards they controlled, while the Labour Party had around 65% of the vote in the three northern wards they controlled. This has meant that the interests of the Council have consistently been those of the landowner, the stockbroker, and the businessman, and so indissolubly linked with the exploiting class. This class was involved in capital accumulation in both housing and employment and so responsible for the low wages, high rents and bad housing in North Kensington.

However, inherent in the Council's position was a fundamental inconsistency. Reliance on the uncontrolled operations of private capital in housing meant the houses would be improved, but for high income buyers and not the original low income tenants. In December 1968 Sir Malby Crofton, the stockbroker leader of the Council recognised this clearly:

"Kensington is *bound* to become a middle class community . . . the lower income people are bound to be excluded."[10]

Yet these same low income people were in the main essential workers in keeping the service sector running both in the local Council area and in London as a whole.

But within two months of declaring the inevitability of the exclusion of low income workers, Crofton was recanting and he announced he deplored the process which was pushing the low income people out.

> "After all, the people who live in these communities service not just the part in which they live but the whole of London and the tourist trade ... Special government funds are needed to bridge the financial gap between the cost of land, the level of rent which lower income people can afford to pay. I believe that a possible solution may well be found in making available much greater funds at low rates of interest to Housing Trusts." [11]

So this was the dilemma which faced the Council. Their housing policy relied on essential workers being treated as units of investment, to be dispensed with when no longer profitable. The Council's shifts over the years since 1966 must be seen as efforts to modify their non-intervention housing policies in order to try and resolve this inconsistency.

However this inconsistency in the Council policies was dependent on the more fundamental inconsistency between two processes of capital accumulation: one based on land and property and the other on the employment of workers. Over the last 20 years in North Kensington, capital has flowed into property speculation at the expense of industry either in the area or elsewhere in London. This has intensified the economic pressures on low income workers to move out of North Kensington, yet it is not in the long term interest of either finance capital or industrial capital in London to lose the labour power of these workers since they perform a vital role in the maintaining of the essential services which allow London to continue to function as the capital of the country and as a world financial centre.

FOOTNOTES

1. *Outcast London* 1971 Gareth Steadman-Jones, page 169.
2. Florence Glastone — *Notting Hill in Bygone Days*.
3. *Survey of London*, Vol.37 N. Kensington 1973, GLC.
4. Booth, *Life and Labour of People of London*, 1903.
5. *The Politics of local government policy*, J. Dearlove.
6. All figures are taken from the GLC *Annual Abstracts*.
7. 1966 Census.
8. *The Politics of Policy*, John Dearlove, page 217.
9. *Ibid.*
10. 'A Royal Borough's Way with the Poor: Push them out,' J. Bugler, *Nova* December 1968.
11. *Kensington Post*, February 21st 1969.

Chapter 2

The Political Vacuum

Some elements of the political economy of North Kensington have been explained so as to provide some context within which the growth of local organisation and struggle between 1966 and 1974 can be understood. The policies of the electorally invulnerable Conservative Council have been shown to reinforce the economic forces which produced the high rents, bad housing and low wages which were facts of life for the working class of the area.

However, before being able to understand the form local organisation took in this period, it is necessary to look at the nature of the local branch of the party which was traditionally the representative of the working class interest — the Labour Party. It was because the local Labour Party had not provided a real channel' through which people could effectively challenge the controlling class interests of the Council and private capital, that a political vacuum had developed in the 20 years of the post-war period, which was a necessary condition for the growth of a strong political life outside the traditional party structure.

In a formal sense, the local Labour Party had a substantial hold on the area of North Kensington. The Labour Party first gained control of a ward in the area in 1906; the whole constituency went Labour for two years in the 1930s and became a solid Labour preserve in 1945. This meant that while the Labour Councillors from the area always faced an invulnerable Conservative majority within the Council, they still had a Labour Member of Parliament to represent their interests at national level. (This was the case till 1974 when the boundaries were changed and North Kensington was merged with South Kensington and Chelsea, and a Conservative MP was elected.)

However, the electoral victory in 1945 never led to the North Kensington Labour Party becoming the effective political instrument of the working class in the area. The Party's emphasis was on three types of activity: electioneering, the discrediting of any groups which challenged the Party's position as sole representative of the working class, and individual casework. This meant that no effective organisation was developed through which local people could express their needs politically. As a result the local Party was unresponsive to developments in local conditions and the political climate and left itself no resources with which to fight back when its right as sole representative of working class interests was seriously challenged in the period following 1966.

It is ironical that in an area where the Parliamentary seat was safe for the Labour Party, and where a Labour majority on the local Council was unimaginable, the local Party should have been so preoccupied with electioneering techniques. By the mid-1960s the Party had a full-time agent and an electioneering strategy with two main components: one, of concentrating effort on polling districts which showed a high number of Labour voters on canvas returns, and the other, of reducing the campaigning to the shortest possible period. It was believed that people were bored with politics and so during general elections the largely inactive member, George Rogers, was kept out of sight till the last week of the campaign, when the voters were suddenly bombarded with the Labour Party case. The concentration of attention on the traditional Labour strongholds of the public housing estates meant that the high canvas returns became a self-fulfilling prophecy. Recruiting drives too were focussed on this sector, leaving tenants experiencing more severe pressures in private rented housing largely untouched. Practically no effort was made to take up issues which local people thought important and none was expended on political education. The result of this electioneering strategy was to divorce the Party more and more from the sections of the population experiencing the brunt of the economic pressures – the private tenants and especially the immigrants. So by stressing the electioneering aim so heavily, the local Party failed to build up a live political base and the Labour Councillors who were supposed to represent the people in their wards, became detached and isolated.

The second way in which the North Kensington Labour Party sought to consolidate its position in the post-war period was by discrediting any groups which challenged its position as sole representative of the working class interest. The atmosphere of the Cold War provided an opportunity to intensify this form of political protectionism. The technique was simple. Spontaneous groups developed on issues like housing or food prices and initially attracted Labour Party supporters and people from other political parties particularly the Communist Party. Once the group was established and Communists were identified among its members, the Labour Party instructed its own members to withdraw. The withdrawal of central activists at an early stage often resulted in the group foundering and the political initiative withering. The local press contains many examples of tenants associations, peace groups and even the British Legion Subcommittee on housing, which were short-lived because of this kind of manoeuvring by the Labour Party. Once the boundary had been defined between the Labour Party and other groups further left, any member who tried to cross that boundary could expect no tolerance. This was made clear in March 1956 when three senior Labour Party members, including one Councillor, were expelled for continuing to associate with the North Kensington Tenants Association, a federation of tenants associations in the area which was organising resistance to the Conservative Government proposals to decontrol rents. The Labour Party had decided the group was a Communist front organisation and so those in the Party who ignored the Party decision to withdraw from the group, had to go.

The Labour Party withdrawal from a whole series of local groups over the years would not have been quite as destructive of local political initiative if it had been counterbalanced by Labour Party encouragement for a number of other local groups. However an examination of the local press over the 20 year period reveals no such groups.

The final strand of the Labour Party consolidation strategy in the post-war years was the organising of a casework service in the area, taking up legal, housing and social problems. A small group of Councillors and the MP manned the service and performed a mediating role by interceding with the relevant authorities to put right particular problems. This sort of activity had deep roots in the Labour Party in the Fabian tradition of doing things for the working class, but did little to build up or sustain a vital political organisation in the area. Nothing appears to have been done to develop the idea that the majority of pressures bearing down on the local people have their origins in the economic and political structure of the area and so have to be tackled by collective action.

Linked with this casework approach to the problems of the area was an initiative of a prominent Labour Party member which resulted in the setting up of the Notting Hill Social Council in November 1960. The Social Council was a forum set up for all those who worked in the statutory or voluntary social service agencies in the area, so that they could gain a more integrated idea of the problems faced in the area and so perform their social service function more effectively. One of the early actions of the Social Council was to organise a housing petition, urging the Council to buy up every house which came on the market for letting at reasonable rents. This was backed up by a long list of Kensington notables and provoked a furore in the Council who branded the organisers, who were in fact in the Labour Party, as Communists. In the face of Council refusal to change their policy the Social Council dropped the issue of housing and concentrated on less contentious issues like experimental youth and education projects. Just as in individual casework the Labour Councillors acted as mediators between the individual and the authorities, so the Social Council developed into a mediator between the Council and the local groups which developed after 1966. The

Council came to regard the Social Council as a 'responsible' body with which it could talk instead of having to have direct contact with the less 'responsible' new groups. Both the individual casework and involvement in the Social Council were bound up with the personal advancement of Labour politicians. The justification of gaining higher and higher office was seen as the increased capacity to do more and more good. There are many Labour politicians who have used the local Party apparatus as a springboard for higher office. Wedgwood Benn, Crosland, and Jenkins are just some of the better known who are members of the North Kensington Labour Party.

Perhaps the clearest indicator of the state of the Party and its mean posturing in defence of the status quo, is the Party's response to the race riots in the summer of 1958. Within a week of the riots, George Rogers, the MP, issued a press statement which called for increased controls on immigrants. He called for the restriction of entry of immigrants into overcrowded areas, for the government direction of immigrants into accommodation and jobs, for the deportation of all immigrants convicted of crimes of vice and violence, increased powers to restrict prostitution, and the introduction of a black section of the CID to restrict crime in black areas. The local Labour Party put out a press statement which claimed proudly that they had advocated controls on the entry of immigrants into areas like North Kensington for the last three years. It went on to call for Government control of the flow of immigrants into the country as a whole if a policy of dispersal proved impossible to achieve; for no immigration of those with criminal records and for instant deportation of any immigrant convicted of a crime. In fact, the Labour Party went along with Oswald Mosley who was building up support in the area at the time, in blaming all the bad housing, crime and prostitution of the country on the black immigrant population. When, in 1959, Mosley stood for Parliament in North Kensington, it was left to the Liberal candidate to take him on on the hustings, with the Labour candidate, George Rogers, staying out of the fight right up to the last week of the campaign. The Party's response to the political situation in 1958 and 1959 in no way provided an effective challenge to the growing racism or facism in the area.

So the North Kensington Labour Party in the 20 years after the war was a limited electoral organisation, defensive, inward-looking and unprepared to take up the real issues of the area, surviving mainly as an instrument for personal advancement for aspiring politicians, and hardly at all as a substantial political force in the area, contributing to the expansion of a socialist consciousness.

It was because of the nature of the local Labour Party that a political vacuum existed on the left which was filled in the years after 1966 by new groups which developed outside the structure of the Labour Party and not within it. As a result of this the local Labour Party became just one of a number of local organisations through which the working class were taking political action and certainly not the sole representative of the working class.

The Labour Party was affected by these developments in various ways. An influx of new members including former members of the New Left, community activists and Methodists in 1963 resulted in a purging of the old guard, who had controlled the local party since the war. The growth of new organisations outside the party structure, which commanded the support of large numbers of local people, was a clear demonstration of alternative power bases in the neighbourhood which the Labour Party could not ignore and from which its members could not exclude themselves. This meant that the defensive protectionism of the Party could no longer operate and the left boundary which had previously been so clearly defined, became meaningless. Labour Party members were free to involve themselves in the new groupings without fear of reprisals from the Party.

Another component of the local Party consolidation strategy was also challenged by developments in the years after 1966. The growth of advice services in the neighbourhood centres culminating in the setting up of the Neighbourhood Law Centre, a full time legal service, in 1970, made the Labour Party advice sessions redundant, and so decreased the capacity of the Councillors and the MP to play their individualising mediating role.

Alongside these changes there was a growing awareness within the Labour Party that a more open, responsive perspective was needed, if the Party was to retain any credibility as a political agency. The new Chairman in 1968 who eventually succeeded to the Parliamentary seat in 1970, showed himself aware of the constituencies in the area which the Party had hitherto ignored. As a Labour Party member and a solicitor, he gave assistance to private tenants, black groups and the developing community activities. As Chairman of the Party he used the Party machine to change the Labour Party policy on furnished tenants, giving them equal security with unfurnished tenants. Other individual members of the Party got involved with the new groupings and committed time, and energy to working with them, so that gradually the Party developed greater responsiveness to immediate local issues.

However these changes occurred in response to the development of political groupings outside the Party, which succeeded in opening up channels for working class political action which the Labour Party had allowed to atrophy. Whereas in the 1950s groupings which established themselves outside the Labour Party were seen to be committing political suicide, by the late 1960s the situation was very different. The growth of political organising outside the Labour Party in North Kensington and elsewhere expanded considerably and revealed a political immediacy which the Labour Party had long since lost.

It is now necessary to examine the development of the organisations in North Kensington which grew up to fill the political vacuum which had developed by 1966 as a result of the state of the local Labour Party and its failure to challenge effectively the class interests of the Council and private capital.

Chapter 3

The Growth of Local Organisation

There were three major bursts of local organisation in North Kensington in the 1950s which can be seen as the forerunners of the expansion of local organisation after 1966.

The first started early in 1956 in resistance to the proposed bill which was to become the 1957 Rent Act, and decontrolled private rents. While Council tenants associations were folding up over 1956 and in the early part of 1957, the private tenants, who were most threatened by the threat of decontrol, built up their own organisation, the North Kensington Tenants Association. Monthly bulletins were put out examining how the Act would affect each of the streets in the area. In January 1957 the Association linked up with a newly formed West London Rent Bill Action Committee which was made up of 41 delegates from 17 organisations in West London. The campaign was stepped up in North Kensington and large street meetings held in Portobello Road involving up to 400 people at times during the early part of the year. As the date of enactment of the bill approached the tempo of activity hotted up. The Association attended a Council meeting in force to find out the Council's plans for the people who would be made homeless by the Act. The Council had no answer except to call the police to clear the public gallery. The South Kensington Tenants Association got together a large stock of war surplus bell tents and talked of encampments for the homeless in the private garden squares. Squatting in empty houses was also seen as a practical possibility. The Act became law in July 1957 and North Kensington Tenants Association continued to pressurise the Council to provide for the homeless, by marches and meetings well into 1958.

Alongside the increasing pressure on private tenants in their homes caused by the 1957 Rent Act, there were additional pressures on tenants who happened to be black as well. In March 1956 the Union Movement had announced the start of a campaign to reintroduce their movement to active politics in the area, with their slogan 'The Blackshirts are on the march again'. Small public meetings were held in 1956 and 1957. Over the summer months of 1958 attacks by white groups on black people intensified, provoking a few retaliatory attacks by black groups on white. These attacks reached a peak on the last two weekends in August. In the early hours of Sunday, August 25 nine white youths were arrested and later gaoled for driving round the area on what they called a 'nigger hunt' and beating up four black men, all total strangers. The situation reached near riot proportions the next weekend when a white crowd of 200 swelled to 700 and surged round the area from Bramley Road to Blenheim Crescent and Westbourne Park Road, smashing the windows of black people's homes, and attacking any black people they happened to meet en route. Throughout they were urged on by Union Movement members shouting 'kill the niggers'. Situations like this continued to erupt into the first week of September and by September 5th 150 arrests had been made. In October the Union Movement tried to exploit the situation by announcing they would contest the next local election and would start a monthly distribution of their newsheet the *North Kensington Leader* into every house in the area. In April 1959 Mosley announced he would stand for North Kensington in the General Election in the autumn. Over the summer months Mosley held often twice weekly street meetings attracting crowds of up to 800. Deliberate provocation motivated the siting of one of these meetings. Kelso Cochrane, a West Indian, had been murdered by white youths in May 1959 in Golborne Road, and Mosley chose the exact spot for a meeting in July, attracting a crowd of over 500.

All this did not happen without a local organisational response. At the first news that Mosley was to start organising public meetings in March 1957 a West London Anti-Fascist Youth Committee had been formed. Then immediately after the race riots in September 1958 three local black groups were formed in North Kensington: the Racial Brotherhood Movement, the Coloured People's Progressive Association and the Afro Asian Club. The Racial Brotherhood Movement was based at the North Kensington Community Centre and had come out of the centre passing a resolution against any restrictions being put on the movement of coloured people, in opposition to the Union Movement and the local Labour Party who were responding to the riots by calling for such restrictions. (The centre had also asked the Mayor to convene a meeting of representative citizens to see what could be done to prevent such outbursts of racial hostility occurring again.) The Coloured People's Progressive Association was based in Tavistock Crescent and aimed to provide a community centre where black people could band together and speak for themselves. The Afro Asian Club was in Bassett Road and run by the Association for the Advancement of Coloured People. By the end of the year a coordinating committee was set up, the Committee for Inter-racial Unity in West London including representatives from 18 Trade Union branches, six Labour Parties and several local black organisations. Before this the trade unionists had kept outside anti-racist and anti-fascist activity. Though the

Trades Council had attacked the Mayor for excluding working class representatives from the coordinating committee he set up in September after the riots, the Trades Council decided in June 1959 that they could not cooperate in organising opposition to Mosley since they were a non-political body.

It was in response to both the pressures on private tenants resulting from the 1957 Rent Act and the spread of racist and fascist ideas that the third burst of local organisation developed in the form of the Powis and Colville Residents Association and the St. Stephens Gardens Tenants Association. Both attempted to take up and fight all issues which were important to the people living in their immediate area.

The St. Stephens Gardens Tenants Association was set up in June 1959 at a meeting called to discuss how to get basic repairs done, but very soon started to take action over other issues felt important by the tenants. Injunctions were taken out against all night parties and clubs which disturbed people's sleep; resistance was organised to stop any fascist or racist meetings in the street, outings and social evenings were organised for old age pensioners and efforts were made to get prostitution stopped in the street. The association declared itself to be a 'non political organisation which serves the interests of all members irrespective of race, religion or complexion.' By April 1960 11 tenants had got so impatient with the landlord's refusal to do repairs that they went on rent strike, and demanded the Council compulsorily purchased their houses. Then in August 1963 the barricades were put up to defend a family who were facing eviction for complaining to the Council about the landlord's failure to do repairs. The barbed wire barricades were up for six days and a system of alarm bells was rigged up in case of eviction attempts. The family was finally evicted in the early hours of one morning but carried the struggle on to the Council's own doorstep by camping on the steps of the Town Hall.

The Powis and Colville Residents Association was set up about six months after the St. Stephens Gardens Tenants Association at a public meeting early in December 1959.

The aims of the association arising out of this first public meeting were to fight for better housing in the area; to get the private garden squares opened; to get the clubs shut down and to get better street lighting and rubbish collection in the area. From the start the association was determinedly multi-racial as was the St. Stephens Gardens Tenants Association. However very few black people attended the first meeting, allegedly because of threats of eviction if they attended.

The group responsible for organising this meeting included very different kinds of people. There was Bill Richardson who lived locally and had political experience in the Communist Party which he had recently left and also in trade union activities at his place of work as a toolmaker. There were two local West Indians Michael de Freitas and Lloyd Hunte with whom Donald

Chesworth (a London County Councillor) and Richard Hauser (from the Institute for Group Studies) had been working over the previous year. They had been meeting weekly since December 1958 on a course organised by Chesworth and Hauser for local West Indians who wanted to take a more active part in their own community. Donald Chesworth had introduced Bill Richardson, Michael de Freitas and Lloyd Hunte to a group of people from the London New Left Club[1] including Rachel Powell and George Clark. These members of the New Left had started coming to North Kensington in the summer of 1959 as part of a study group whose brief was to try and discover the causes of the race riots the year before, and of the support for Mosley at the time. During the summer they had followed Mosley around on his election campaign meetings, and had helped to organise a protection patrol for West Indians returning home late at night. However once they had been introduced to Bill Richardson and heard of the development of a tenants association they abandoned the study group and got involved in helping to build up the tenants association instead, since it was felt that housing problems were fundamental to the racism and fascism in the area.

At this meeting Bill Richardson was elected Chairman, Lloyd Hunte was elected Secretary and Michael de Freitas Treasurer. The allegations of intimidation keeping tenants away from the meeting led to a decision to canvass all the houses which were associated with Rachman, one of the largest landowners in the area. Michael de Freitas provided a list of over 100 houses owned by Rachman.

Soon after this canvass had started Lloyd Hunte reported to the Association that he had heard that there was a plan to evict all the current tenants in the Rachman houses and convert the houses into unfurnished flats so as to avoid the limited security provided by the law to furnished tenants. The association decided to counter this plan with an attempt to organise a mass application to the rent tribunal for security by all the tenants. Within the first month about 20 tenants had applied to the tribunal. Then in January 1960 Peter Davies, one of the Rachman's agents came to the tenants association's office in Powis Terrace and started trying to bargain with the members of the association in order to get the rent tribunal applications withdrawn. He even offered to buy Powis Square gardens for a playground if the applications were withdrawn. But the association would have none of it. However one by one most of the applications were withdrawn by the tenants, presumably as a result of pressure being put on them. Then an amazing discovery was made – the keys to lots of Rachman's houses were found in the office of the association which was Lloyd Hunte's flat in Powis Terrace. And suddenly unanswered questions and odd events began to tie up; Michael de Freitas' ability to provide a list of Rachman's houses; the fear on the face of tenants visited by members of the association when they realised Lloyde Hunte and Michael de Freitas were involved; the Alsatian dogs in the Hunte's flat, and now the keys. Hunte and de Freitas were obviously an integral part of the Rachman organisation which the association was trying to challenge. The picture gradually became clearer: Rachman at the top of the pyramid, with agents like Peter Davies and Edwards under him and below them men like Lloyd Hunte and Michael de Freitas and under them individuals in each house responsible for the rent collection. Each layer in the hierarchy took its cut of the rent and only intervened in the layer beneath when the money failed to flow smoothly for one reason or another. The involvement of both de Freitas and Hunte in organised prostitution also became clearer and by March 1960 both were excluded from the association.

It was at this stage that the workers from the London New Left Club withdrew because of their realisation of how deeply they had been involved in passing useful information to the Rachman ring. Being outsiders their feeling of impotence in the face of the Rachman organisation was probably increased. Rachel Powell explains her view of the situation at the time,[2]

> "There were violent evictions and everyone was too scared to do anything. Nobody ever appealed to the police. There was a general feeling that authority was against them and certainly the tenants were never given any sign that it was on their side. There were never any police around when anyone was beaten up. If the residents wouldn't let us help them to help themselves there wasn't much we could do . . . The only people with real power in the area were Rachman and his underlings and nothing we could do changed that."

Rachel Powell and a few others from the London New Left Club shifted the focus of their work to the Tavistock Crescent area where they tried unsuccessfully to get a tenants association going.

So far as the involvement of Hunte and de Freitas in the association was concerned there seem to have been three possible explanations. There was evidence that both were in a temporary state of dispute with Rachman at the time and were keen to gain additional types of leverage in their battles with him. It was also possible that they thought it as well to get in at the beginning of an organisation which might give trouble. The third possibility was that they thought that the London New Left Club was a rich organisation and that there might be pickings to be had.

Anyway whatever their strategies, the association decided to exclude them but continued to organise locally up to 1962. In mid 1961 they restated the nature of the association as "a non political, multi racial group of private citizens, who are simply demanding their right in law to live free from exploitation or abuse by their landlord or their neighbours." The association continued to campaign for noisy clubs to be closed down, and for prostitution to be clamped down on. An attempt was made to clean up Colville Square gardens and open it up for the children but this was countered by one of the local landlords of property adjoining the square fencing the square and padlocking it. In housing the association continued to get rents cut at the tribunal and also got landlords fined for charging tenants rents higher than the rent fixed by the rent tribunal.

So these were the main forms local organisation took in the years up to 1966: resistance to the 1957 Rent Act, resistance to facism and racism and the formation of local associations to fight on whatever issues were important to the local people. It is only in the context of this history of local organisation that the expansion of local organisation after 1966 can be understood.

The opportunity for a fresh burst of local organisation was created in 1966 by a group called the London Free School which was an anarchistic temporary coalition which came together in March 1966. It brought together a wide range of people including Bill Richardson, Michael Abdul Malik (formerly de Freitas and now a leader of the Racial Adjustment Action Society), George Clark, Richard Hauser, all of whom had been involved in the Powis and Colville Residents Association. The group also included John Hopkins who later became involved in International Times, Peter Jenner who became involved with the Pink Floyd pop group, as well as some students from the London School of Economics and Rhaune Laslett, who had been a social worker and lived in the area. The London Free School was based on the Free University idea from America and aimed to generate self-organised learning for adults in whatever subjects people needed.

Classes were set up on a wide range of subjects including, basic English, housing, immigration, trade unions and music. A fortnightly newspaper *The Grove* was produced carrying news of all the activities. The house of Rhaune Laslett was used as a Neighbourhood Service Centre for advice and as premises for a playgroup. In addition to the classes and the advice centre the group decided to start up an adventure playground on some waste land in Acklam Road, cleared of houses to make way for the elevated motorway to be built in the near future. This opened as a playground in early summer and the Free School followed this up by organising an amazingly vibrant carnival in the area at the end of August.

The Free School seemed to disintegrate soon after the carnival but some parts of its activities continued: the group working on the Acklam Road Playground became the North Kensington Playspace Group and the advice centre continued as the Neighbourhood Service. It was perhaps inevitable that the Free School was shortlived as there was little to hold its very diverse members together in that the basic ideas which had brought them together were anti-organisation, anti-sectarian and lacking in any shared analysis of the political problems in the area.

It was in September 1966, just after the carnival that a new group, the Notting Hill Community Workshop moved into North Kensington. Over that summer members of the Workshop group had taken part in discussions set up by former New Left members aimed at producing a socialist manifesto, as a counter-statement to the Labour Government's policies. The hope was that it would reunite the fragmented left. This resulted in the May Day Manifesto being published on May 1st 1967. This concluded that the only real choice for socialists lay in the building up of a political movement which would make "democratic practice effective throughout the society, by activity and locality rather than in some closed, centralised, ritualised place". It saw this as coming about through a more open and equal cooperation between all left wing groups, and through joint working at a local level.

But it was through involvement in the Campaign for Nuclear Disarmament movement in the late 1950s and early 1960s that many of the Workshop had built up their political organising experience. Out of this they developed a real scepticism of the type of political organising which relied heavily on ritualised leafleting, and on meetings of the converted. They developed a growing conviction of the need to work at the grass roots level, with all political activity growing out of the needs experienced by working people. It was also realised that the remoteness of decisions about nuclear disarmament would only be broken down and challenged if people gained some real confidence in their power to control decisions which affected them at much more immediate levels — their housing, schools and streets.

In coming to work in Notting Hill the Community Workshop group shared a commitment to helping to build local community organisations through which a local force of people could "fight to wrest from the authorities whatever they decide their community requires". (Community Workshop statement.)

The group included Peter Kandler, who had been involved through the London New Left Club in the Powis and Colville Residents Association in 1960, and George Clark, who had been involved both at that time and in the London Free School earlier that year. It was through this involvement in the London Free School that the Workshop was in touch with and initially worked with the Neighbourhood Service, which it saw as the first of many neighbourhood centres which would be needed in the area as a focus for organisation. The Workshop deliberately did not open up their own base as a neighbourhood centre because they neither wanted to be swamped by case work nor to become a local institution. Instead they wanted to set up their base as a local resource in the form of a full time worker, an office, typewriter and duplicator, which could be channelled into the local organisations which people decided they needed.

This was the organisational context within which the Notting Hill People's Association was formed early in 1967. But more important still were the conditions within one block, 1-9 Colville Gardens, which drove the tenants to take steps to organise themselves.

1-9 Colville Gardens is a terrace of six storey Victorian houses backing onto a square. Initially built as single family homes for the upper classes in the 1870s, this block was soon sub-divided into flats on each floor as it proved impossible to get the very rich to live in this part of the area. Fairly well-to-do business and professional people rented these flats though many moved away during the war to avoid the bombing. The long standing owner of the area, the Colville Estates sold off individual blocks to different owners, and in 1953 1-9 Colville Gardens was bought by Fernbank Investments Ltd., (a subsidiary of Davies Investments Ltd.) for £8,000. The 1957 Rent Act gave owners the break they had been waiting for since the return of the Conservative Government in 1951. The decontrol of rents meant that any owner who could persuade existing tenants to leave could relet at much higher rents so increasing the gross income from property and so its price by a considerable amount. Where persuasion failed the owners of 1-9 resorted to stronger methods. Late night callers, Alsatian dogs, the taking in of tinkers and prostitutes as tenants – all were used in attempts to dislodge sitting tenants. An anonymous letter, printed by the *Kensington News,* a local paper, in July 1963, making this sort of allegation led to libel proceedings against the paper, which resulted in an agreement to settle by withdrawing the allegations. Witnesses melted away, believed to have been intimidated. The strategy of the owners was clear – to sub-divide each flat into as many as six separate 'homes', charging about the same rent for each room, as was previously charged for the whole flat, which worked out at between £3 and £5.12.6 a room. The only extra cost this involved was the cost of a sink and cooker in each room and a few sticks of furniture. No extra bathrooms or toilets were added. Responsibility for letting the rooms was given to an old caretaker in the basement of one of the houses who chose to let them on a personal favour basis, demanding £20 or £30 key money when he felt like it. These changes were effective in doubling the rate of return on the property. Whereas in the eight years between 1954 and 1962 the nine houses produced a gross income of £78,000, they produced the same gross income in just four years from 1962 to 1966.

Henry Bowen Davies (Director of Davies Investments Ltd.) expanded his property and business empire. An increase in the gross rent income meant an increase in the market price of the property and so in the amount for which the property could be re-mortgaged to finance the purchase of other property. In this way Bowen Davies expanded from slum property like Colville Gardens to an empire including at least 40 other properties in the area and 98 shops, seven building firms, a car hire firm, a printing and publishing chain, an estate agents, and a timber business, worth a total of nearly £8 million.

But this was just one side of the picture. While Bowen Davies' profits were booming the tenants in 1-9 were living in progressively worsening conditions. By the beginning of 1967 there were 72 tenancies in the nine houses, and a total of 210 people living there, including 35 families with a total of 72 children under the age of ten. All these people experienced the social cost of Bowen Davies' expansion. This meant whole families living, eating, sleeping and playing in one room. In one room a mother, father and four children lived. You couldn't move for beds and cots. In another room a mother worked at washing up full time for £10 a week to pay over half of it in rent for one room for herself and her four children. In one basement room a man had lived for 23 years. For the last three there was no electric light. He lived by candlelight. The walls were running with damp. Basic repairs throughout the houses were left undone for years and complaints to the caretaker seemed to have no effect.

In the summer of 1966 the tenants started to act on two fronts. Two tenants Pat McDonald and R.A. Gilmore both went to the Rent Tribunal and got their rents cut. Gilmore had considered trying to get all the tenants to go on rent strike so as to force the landlords to do repairs. He talked to other tenants about the idea but there was not enough confidence to carry it through. But one tenant witheld his rent to pay for repairs and decorations he did himself, fed up with waiting for the landlord to do something.

However, also in the summer of 1966, some of the women from Colville Gardens, decided something had to be done to find somewhere for the children to play off the streets. In August one child from 1-9 was killed while playing in the street outside her home and in response to this a group of women, including Pat McDonald went to the Neighbourhood Service to get help to organise a petition to get the garden square their homes backed onto, opened for the children to play in. It was a huge garden square, the length of the block. It was full of trees, bushes and grass and ideal for children, but had been kept locked up by the landlord for years.

To get the square open meant getting in touch with the owner which presented a problem in itself since most of the rent books were inadequately filled in and the caretaker was evasive if questioned. However the name Fernbank Investments did appear on notices in the block and so two students who had got involved in the Neighbourhood Service through the London Free School, set to work to find out more about the owners by doing a search in Companies House. This revealed Fernbank Investments as a subsidiary of the Davies Investments empire and the accounts revealed the income from the property over the years.

Meanwhile the tenants continued to organise on the housing front. Pat McDonald together with some helpers from the Neighbourhood Service called on every tenant to see what complaints there were. Towards the end of 1966 a couple more tenants went to the rent tribunal, both women who had been active in the campaign to get the gardens opened. By the end of the year about half a dozen of the tenants had been actively involved in the first stages of organisation either on the play or on the housing front.

Then all of a sudden on January 20 1967 the newspapers were full of headlines that Bowen Davies, the Director of Davies Investments Ltd., was declared a bankrupt. His realisable assets of £7,700,000 and contracts worth £19 million were set against his liabilities of £10,750,000. The tenants made use of the ensuing publicity by pointing to the slum conditions on which the whole empire had been based. While Davies' fortunes had boomed and plummeted the conditions they lived in had just got worse. The bankruptcy produced a strong determination amongst the tenants "not to be screwed again" as one tenant put it. It was felt that it was time the tables were turned for once, and an effort made to stop anyone else making a profit out of their basic need for housing. The tenants decided they wanted a public meeting. So with the help of members of the Community Workshop and the Neighbourhood Service a huge public meeting was organised on February 2. All the tenants living in Davies property in the area were invited and 400 people packed the All Saints Church Hall. Experiences of what it meant to be a tenant in Davies property were pooled and a decision taken to hold another meeting the following week to decide what form the tenants' organisation should take. At this meeting it was agreed that an organisation should be formed to continue and expand the fight which the tenants of Colville Gardens had begun. However it was realised that the tenants of Colville Gardens were not alone in their fight against profits being made out of their most basic need for a home, and that the organisation should be open to all in the neighbourhood. So the Notting Hill People's Association was formed. Its aims were later laid down as:

1. To improve the living conditions of all tenants and to see fair play with both the landlords and the authorities;
2. To fight exploitation of and discrimination against people in the area, wherever it may occur;
3. To work for the adequate provision of playspace and recreational facilities for children;
4. To make Notting Hill a better place to live in.

A committee of 14 was elected including Pat McDonald and R.A. Gilmore as treasurer and secretary, Bill Richardson (former chairman of the Powis and Colville Residents Association) as chairman, two members of the Community Workshop, John O'Malley and George Clark as vice chairman and assistant secretary. From the start the Notting Hill People's Association pursued a strategy aimed both at strengthening the tenants' position in all possible ways and at forcing the need for the non-profit ownership of 1-9 into the consciousness of the Conservative Council.

The first prong of their strategy involved strengthening the tenants own organisation of the block. This meant visiting all of the 72 tenants and building up a complete picture of the rents paid, the repairs outstanding and the occupants of the nine houses. All tenants were notified of the weekly meetings of the People's Association held in the block and of the outcome of the meetings. At one of the early meetings it was agreed that all the 56 furnished tenants should apply to the Rent Tribunal both to get their rents cut and for six months security, since unlike the unfurnished tenants they had no legal protection in the long run from being evicted.

As soon as the notice of the hearing was received by the managing agents, most of the 56 tenants were immediately given notice to quit. But this of course could not take effect till the hearing of the tribunal. The mass hearing took place in April, with tenants being heard six at a time. The hearing went on for several days and was turned into a trial of the managing agents responsible for Davies' property. Evidence was produced to prove the extent of the mismanagement: the lack of rent books before October 1966; false entries in rent books since then; the difficulties of paying rent due to the rent office being seldom open; the indifference of the caretaker; the lack of repairs despite the frequent complaints of tenants and the falsification of inventories of the shabby furniture. At the end of the hearing the tribunal cut most rents by up to a quarter and gave most tenants the maximum of six months security. So the position of the tenants was strengthened while the battle was waged on another level with the Council.

The aim of the People's Association strategy on this second front was to force the Conservative Council to ensure Colville Gardens was taken out of private ownership and into non-profit hands. The Council's resistance to compulsory purchase was well known but despite this it was decided it was worth doing battle. The Council had obviously already been caught off guard by the news of Davies' bankruptcy back in January even before the People's Association was formed. They had passed an emergency resolution proposed by the Labour group instructing the Housing Committee " s a matter of urgency to prepare a detailed report of the properties owned by Davies Investments Ltd., and its subsidiaries and to take whatever action it deemed necessary."

Early in March the People's Association put out a report to the Council Housing Committee entitled "From private exploitation to public trust", to put the clear case for non-profit ownership. This explained the basic history of neglect and mismanagement of 1-9 and of the profits this had yielded to the owners. It argued that the sale of the property to another private landlord could not solve the problem faced by the tenants at all, since the only two options open to a private landlords if he were to make the same or larger profits, were to continue running the property in the same way, or else to convert the block into luxury flats for higher income tenants. Since all the furnished tenants were applying for their rents to be cut by the Rent Tribunal and cuts of up to 30% had already been made in cases that had been to the tribunal, the first option was extremely unlikely to be followed. But the second option would mean that all the existing tenants would be forced out of their homes. The report ended with the demand that all Davies owned properties should be removed from the private property market and used instead to provide decent housing at fair rents for the present tenants. The only realistic way this could be achieved was for either the Council or a housing trust to buy up the properties.

A People's Association deputation presented this report to the Council Housing Committee in March only to be countered by the Housing Committee's own report on 1-9 Colville Gardens. This report came out with the amazing double-edged conclusion that "the general standard of management was above average for the area", and that they could find "no real evidence of exploitation of the tenants" because of their right to apply to the Rent Tribunal or Rent Officer to have fair rents fixed. They concluded there was no crisis facing the tenants since they had the Rent Acts to protect them and, anyway, if they became homeless the Council would have to provide hostel accommodation. So there was no need for the Council to consider special action over the block. The position of the tenants was no worse and in some ways better than many in the area. However, the report did concede that it would be in the public interest for 1-9 to be acquired by a housing trust.

Since the Council seized on this report as an excuse to do nothing, the People's Association decided to produce yet another counter report exposing its inadequacies. This was presented to the full Council at their May meeting. It attacked the report for only looking at 1-9 Colville Gardens and ignoring all other properties owned by the Davies empire. It attacked the report for relying on the Health Inspectors' investigations and for accepting their view that they could find no 'exploitation' in the same way as you would accept their findings on dry rot or infestation by fleas and vermin. The People's Association restated their argument that Davies Investments had "sweated for profits" the properties they owned and the only way to investigate this was to look at the profit figures over the years, not by sending in a Health Inspector.

As for the tenants not facing a crisis in terms of their security of tenure — this was crazy in the light of the notices to quit which followed their application to the rent tribunal.

It was at the full Council meeting in May 1967 that the final decision over 1-9 Colville Gardens was made and the fate of the block sealed. First a petition was presented supporting the People's Association reports and making four clear demands:

— that the Council remove the Davies properties from private hands;
— that the Council set up a crisis committee including trusts to coordinate the purchase of Davies properties;
— that the Council make public money available for the Trusts to buy the properties;
— that the Council and trusts ensure no Davies tenants became homeless or went into a hostel.

Then the Housing Committee report and the two People's Association reports were considered. Finally the Council decision was made.

Their view was that it was unnecessary for the Council to buy 1-9 since the tenants had the Rent Acts to protect them and there were insufficient vacant units in the block to make Council purchase worthwhile. However, if the Kensington Housing Trust, who had expressed interest, were willing to buy and sought financial assistance from the Council 'it would be readily available'.

The Council tried to dismiss the matter finally:

> "In the light of the offer made by the Trust, the main cause of concern to the Association has been removed and no further action on the part of this Council is called for."

But then came 'Catch 22'. The Official Receivers offered 1-9 Colville Gardens to the Kensington Housing Trust for £52,000 in May. The District Valuer set the price the Council could lend the Trust at his valuation of the nine houses — £45,000. The Council had chosen not to use its compulsory purchase powers to take the block off the private market. Instead they chose to leave the Trust to buy on the open market but with finance restricted to the level that the Council would have paid under a Compulsory Purchase Order.

So what the People's Association predicted happened. In October 1967 1-9 Colville Gardens was sold on the open market for £65,000 to another property company, which proved to be even more remote than Davies Investments Ltd.

However, in May Bowen Davies had shot himself and his family. He explained the reasons just before he died:

> "My personal conflict is a terrible one. I have always considered the basis of morality is not to cause suffering. I have caused suffering — however inadvertently — to very many, and the burden on my conscience is intolerable."

But this did not change anything for the tenants. The new owners simply moved into the position he had vacated as owner of Colville Gardens, and the tenants had exactly the same threat hanging over their heads.

A last minute attempt was made to stop the sale going through. The Official Receiver was contacted by the People's Association and asked to call a shareholders' meeting to ask them to accept the District Valuer's price of £45,000 "on the basis that they have already made enough profit". Kensington Council were also reminded of their pledge, "to give every facility" to the Trust to buy 1-9. Both local newspapers came out with editorials arguing strongly that the Council should use its powers to take 1-9 out of private hands. The Housing Committee were forced to discuss again the possibility of using a Compulsory Purchase Order (CPO) on Colville Gardens. The

People's Associations held a picket outside the meeting but again the Committee decided to take no action. The Council meeting at the end of October was noisily disrupted by angry tenants from Colville Gardens and other members of the People's Association. The police were called to clear the public gallery and business was suspended. Even the MP George Rogers did his bit and fixed a meeting with the chairman of the Housing Committee to urge him to consider using a CPO. However, the Council did not move and bequeathed the responsibility of deciding the fate of the 210 residents of 1-9 Colville Gardens to another private property company.

This might well have been the end of the tenants struggle in Colville Gardens had they not decided early on to widen the struggle to all areas of life where people experienced exploitation or discrimination. This meant that when things looked bleak on one front they were still involved with struggles on other fronts which sustained their organisation and kept them together.

For instance, back in the summer of 1966 the idea of getting the garden square at the back of Colville Gardens opened up as playspace had been raised. This was not dropped as the housing struggle intensified and in the spring of 1967 the key was obtained and the gardens opened.

Then in May 1967 the tenants of Colville Gardens took up the issue of triple parking in the street at the front of their block. This happened on Saturdays with the influx of people into the area to visit the Portobello Road market, and it made it very dangerous for children to cross the road at all because of the parked cars restricting the motorists' field of vision. So for nearly a year on Saturday mornings, People's Association members were out on the street from 8 am onwards with home made bollards positioned in the centre of the road to stop the triple parking.

Another important factor which resulted in struggles continuing and not being dropped at the first sign of defeat was the formation of the Notting Hill People's Association early in February 1967 rather than a Colville Gardens Tenants Association. This meant that a wide range of political interests had become involved in the struggles: members of the Community Workshop, the Communist Party and the Labour Party.

Early in the summer of 1967 the People's Association was involved in the setting up of the Notting Hill Summer Project, with two of its members, Bill Richardson and R.A. Gilmore on the Organising Committee. A full account of the Project will be given later but what is important here is the way in which the People's Association, made use of the influx of energy and people which resulted from the Project to boost its ongoing campaigns.

However the relations between the People's Association and the Summer Project Organising Committee were by no means smooth. In May the Association was asked to set up a neighbourhood centre in their area as one of three local bases from which the Project could be organised. But the Association was not convinced of the urgency of setting up a base for the Project as a result of fundamental disagreements between its members and the Organising Committee as to the strategy of the Project. These disagreements were not resolved and the People's Association members were left with feelings of impotence over the direction the Project would take. So early in June the Organising Committee constructed a fresh committee, including a few members of the People's Association, and called it the People's Centre. For a short time the two committees existed side by side. But once the Organising Committee of the Project obtained All Saints Hall as a physical base in the area for the People's Centre, the People's Association saw this as an important development, moved in and put time and energy into decorating it and making it comfortable, and from then on the Association used it as their base. The People's Centre and the People's Association came together once they shared a physical base, and the joint organisation took over the name of the People's Centre which was seen as one of many possible centres of the Notting Hill People's Association.

Having gained a physical base with the rent for the time being paid by the Project Organising Committee, the People's Centre used it to organise their ongoing campaigns over housing, traffic and play, recruiting the extra help of the student volunteers whenever it was needed. The Centre decided to continue the campaign to get the remaining two closed garden squares Colville and Powis Square opened up for playspace, over the summer. It was decided to focus on Powis Square which had been locked up for nigh on 10 years. The Centre drew up a petition demanding the Council buy the square and open it up as a supervised play area, and took it round all the houses surrounding the square to rally support. Meanwhile the owner of the square, a Mr Shaw, was approached and asked to allow the square to be used as an emergency play area that summer, as part of the Summer Project. The Organising Committee of the Project was informed of these moves during the first week of the Project at the beginning of August, and they promised their support for whatever the People's Centre decided had to be done. A public meeting was held by the People's Centre a few days later to decide how and when Powis Square should be taken over. A surprise visit to Mr Shaw at the owner's suburban house was planned for Sunday morning and plans were made for a symbolic occupation of the square in two weeks time. The surprise visit to Mr Shaw's home in Surrey did not find him ready to negotiate. Instead he threatened to set the dogs on the delegation if they did not go away. So a poster parade was held outside his house with placards like: "Open the door Mr Shaw and let our children in".

The symbolic occupation of Powis Square was announced in a statement put out by the Project Organising Committee on August 17th. This gave details of the history of efforts which had been made to open it, and announced that "as a last resort and to draw attention to a situation which has lasted so long, we propose to go on to Powis Square this Saturday at 10.30 a.m. to start a play scheme".

But the next day George Clark, a member of the Community Workshop on the Project Organising Committee, tried to stop the planned action. He produced a statement arguing, "only gentle persuasion might change the minds of the owners . . . The neighbourhood might reasonably expect the space to be available, but since the owners do not take this view there are serious issues raised if we proceed on a course which wrests control from them illegally. In short we have no rights in the matter".

However the decision had been taken and the People's Centre were united and so the occupation took place on a wet Saturday morning.

About 60 people walked onto the square through a convenient hole in the chain link fencing, including people who lived round the square, members of the People's Centre, student volunteers and members of the Project Organising Committee. The more euphoric demonstrators played ball with the children and symbolically sheared the grass while the rest held a meeting on the square in the pouring rain. The determination was expressed to continue with actions of this sort till the square was bought by the Council and opened up for playspace. A picnic was planned for the following Sunday in Powis Square. It took place however not in Powis Square but in Colville Gardens because of the reluctance to take any further legal risks at this stage.

By the end of the Project those of the Organising Committee with reservations about illegal action forced a decision that the People's Centre be told that the committee would not support further acts of trespass, but that they were prepared to fix up a meeting between the People's Centre and the Council Amenities Committee to discuss the buying of the Square.

Over the summer People's Centre members were also involved in work with the Project in Lonsdale Road, a play street. The problem here was that though Lonsdale Road was officially a play street, its proximity to Portobello Road meant that it was full of parked cars especially on Saturdays. So approaches were made to the police to stop this illegal parking. Centre members also visited all the houses adjoining the play street to let them know about the play scheme in the street. After the Project finished the Centre decided to keep the street operating as a play street on Saturdays, to keep the cars out and to continue play activities in the street.

The Centre also got involved in the other play street in the area, McGregor Road, where a child was knocked down during the summer. The child's mother came to the Centre to get help to organise a petition to get the Council to close off one end of the road to stop through traffic.

By the end of the summer 1967 the People's Centre was firmly established with a permanent physical base, regular weekly meetings which provided a local political forum for the neighbourhood, at which local issues could be discussed and action planned. Two other neighbourhood centres had also come into existence by this time in the Golborne and Lancaster areas of

North Kensington. The Golborne Centre closed down in the early autumn of 1967 but the Lancaster Neighbourhood Centre continued to function for years after. However in a similar way that some of the seeds of the People's Centre can be traced back to the coalition generated by the London Free School in 1966 so the seeds of the Lancaster centre lie in the coalition generated by the Notting Hill Summer Project in 1967. But before looking at the Lancaster Neighbourhood Centre and at the development of the People's Centre it is necessary to examine what contribution the Notting Hill Summer Project made to the development of organisation in the area.

FOOTNOTES
1. The New Left was a grouping created by the two events of 1956, Suez and Hungary, including many of the 10,000 who left the Communist Party at that time. In 1957 they stated their aim as "to take socialism at full stretch" and to apply its values to "the total scale of man's activities". Local Left Clubs were set up in many areas, with the aim of acting as a focus for radical political discussion.
2. 'Lost in the Rachman Bog' Jean Stead. *Guardian* August 6th 1963.

Chapter 4

The Notting Hill Summer Project 1967

"Something must be done to relieve the desperate plight of families living in overcrowded inferior and highly rented accommodation . . . to meet some of these needs we are organising a summer project . . . both the housing and play projects are being used as a focus for community organising. This summer people living in Notting Hill will be encouraged to organise themselves into community groups, in order that work started can be continued . . . it is a challenging task . . . we cannot do it alone. Therefore we are appealing for 200 students to join us and make the summer project successful. Can you resist this call for help?"

These are the rousing words on the poster sent out to colleges and universities all over England to recruit workers on the Summer Project, the first venture of its kind in England. It was George Clark of the Community Workshop, who thought up the idea, building on his experience of summer campaigning in CND days, and recollections of talk in America about the Mississippi Summer Project in the early 1960's. The call for 200 students to come and pay £2 registration fee and all food costs for the privilege of working on the Project, produced a response.

On July 25th, over 100 volunteers arrived in Notting Hill, eager to get down to work — and work hard they did. By August 26th when the Project ended, around 5,000 households had been visited and interviewed in the three areas of the worst housing, and information gathered on the housing conditions, rents, ownership and management of the houses, and the household characteristics of the occupants. Two new play sites were opened up, a play street and a huge adventure play area on an overgrown building site. Both the housing and play activities were based on three neighbourhood centres which developed a working style of their own over the summer.

These were the bare bones of the Project, but in fact the Summer Project was much more than just this list of activities.

First and foremost it was a month long jamboree, bringing all kinds of people together with a sense of purpose and commitment. The short time, the concentration of energy and the radical rhetoric created a dynamic which no one was able to ignore. For many of the volunteers it was their first taste of living and working politically in a working class area, of talking on the doorstep to all kinds of people and of being confronted with all kinds of problems. For some it changed the course of their lives in that it opened up a very different set of political options to those previously considered. For all these reasons, to have been on the Summer Project still means a lot to many of the participants.

But it was not just the volunteers who were drawn into the jamboree. Hundreds of people with all kinds of connections with the area were drawn into the public meetings throughout the Project — from Michael Abdul Malik to members of the Methodist congregation, who had heard about the Project from the pulpit. The weekly newsletter went out to hundreds. Local people came up and volunteered meals, money, services, transport. Even the local convent opened its doors to house some of the volunteers. But it was not just a jamboree which took place at evening meetings. All day long throughout the summer the Project was visible on the streets — with volunteers knocking on every door, wearing and distributing 'Community Action' badges, relating as equals to the children on the play sites, with three neighbourhood centres extending their activities and opening their doors to all-comers who needed to make use of free legal advice and support of all kinds. All this was new at that time in North Kensington and was important in opening up people's minds to new possibilities and in clearing away political inhibitions.

Secondly the Project gave many people their first glimpse of how local action groups could work, through the developments at the neighbourhood centres: the People's Centre focussing on opening up closed garden squares and trying to fight the speculators over 1-9 Colville Gardens; the Lancaster Centre, focussing on the problems of the redevelopment area surrounding it, and the Golborne Centre concentrating on giving advice to individuals who called on them. Though the People's Centre had an independent existence long before the Project started, the stirring up of interest over the four weeks did bring a lot more local people into contact with the centre and the centre used the influx of energy and people to boost its ongoing campaigns.

Thirdly, the Project focussed attention on a number of issues in a way that left no doubt that organisation was necessary: on play and the unequal access to open space of the rich and poor in the area; and on the failure of the private landlord to provide decent homes for low income people. The four weeks of the Project had the effect of raising the expectations of many people in terms of what issues could and should be organised around. People took their experiences from the Project into political work in other areas of the country and also into the student activities in 1968.

It is because of these important contributions of the Summer Project to community struggle in Notting Hill that it is worth looking at the Project in some detail. These strengths of the Project uneasily co-existed with confusions, uncertainties and inconsistencies which all in part resulted from the nature of the coalition which organised the Project and from certain inconsistencies within the Community Workshop, the group responsible for putting together that coalition.

The Coalition Strategy

The Community Workshop had discussed earlier in the year following a coalition strategy, on the grounds that to enlist the support of long established liberal groups in the area would have a legitimising function and would widen the influence of Community Workshop programmes. The other Workshop members fell in with this proposal but only on condition that this was seen as a transitional stage, and a break with the 'respectable' institutions would have to follow. So when the Summer Project idea came up the coalition strategy was built into it. There were also strong practical reasons for using a coalition strategy to organise such a Project, in terms of the access this would guarantee to local premises like churches, schools and convents for housing the volunteers. The coalition was built up by George Clark from his individual contacts in the area. Most of the individuals who responded positively to his proposal saw a possible opportunity to advance their own strategies through the Summer Project.

David Mason, the Chairman of the Notting Hill Social Council and a member of the Methodist Group Ministry also had political ambitions within the Labour Party and saw in the Project signs of life and activity which he could not lose by being associated with. He took up the position of Chairman of the Organising Committee. The other two members of the Group Ministry also joined the Project Committee.

The leader of the Notting Hill Adventure Playground, Pat Smyth, agreed to come onto the Committee and took a large part in organising the play programme part of the Project. Before the Project the situation in play provision was static and localised in the Adventure Playground. The Project offered a way of expanding different forms of provision and opened up the way to the formation of the Play Association in the borough, of which Pat Smyth later became the Play Organiser.

Ilys Booker, the community worker from the North Kensington Family Study agreed to join the Committee. She had already established a reputation in professional community work for her style of 'non-directive' community work.

One of the workers at the local Citizens Advice Bureau agreed to join the Project Committee and help with the setting up of advice centres within the neighbourhood centres.

Finally the more recently established groups agreed to join the Project

Committee: the Community Workshop, the Notting Hill People's Association and the North Kensington Playspace Group.

The only other group to be involved in the Project was the Kensington Housing Trust, the housing association with close links with the Council. But despite the initial conciliatory approach of the Project to the Council, the tensions must have proved too great and after one meeting the Trust withdrew.

What were the elements with which this coalition had to juggle?

A heavy weight of moral conscience arising from Group Ministry Christianity and Workshop CND hangovers; the professionalism of a 'non-directive' community worker, of a case work oriented C.A.B. social worker and of a play leader from the Adventure Playground; the Community Workshop and the People's Association, both of which saw themselves operating in a primarily political organising way.

But all these different elements never had an equal weight within the Project. The main discussion in fact went on between Community Workshop members, with the rest either withdrawing or assenting to whatever was hammered out in the arguments. And arguments there were, because the Workshop position contained a whole set of potentially conflicting elements which ended up by forcing a split in the Workshop itself between George Clark and the rest of the group. However the pressure of both constructing and sustaining the coalition for that summer meant that the inconsistencies were not resolved and that a programme was settled for, which was far more concerned with professionalism in the running of the housing survey than with maximising the political potential at each stage. It was partly because of the Workshop's ambiguity about the kind of power base that it was trying to build up that it opted for a coalition strategy. The Workshop had rejected the strategy of building up a power base within the traditional parties, and was focussing on building up a power base within a residential community. But the only organisations it could see outside the political parties were the voluntary agencies and the churches, all manned by middle class professional people. It is interesting that the only consideration of involving Trade Unionists in the Project came a month before the Project began when Bill Richardson, the only Trade Unionist on the Organising Committee, wrote round to the local union branches asking for help and money. This letter is the only recognition in all the writing at the time of the Project that people are workers as well as tenants. The letter ended,

> "We beg the help of your organisation, not as a charity, but as an extension of the service you offer for your own members, in their streets, their homes and in their community."

But this was not followed up with attempts to contact the local Trades Council or local trade union branches. No efforts were made to build their representatives into the Organising Committee.

It was as if the very novelty of thinking and talking about community action and community projects in England defined the groups the workshop related to in terms of those charitable, liberal institutions which also talked *about* community, but were not *of* the community. The only group on the Organising Committee which was of the community was the People's Association with 2 members on the Committee. However both of them withdrew half way through because they felt unhappy about the way the Project was going, but felt unable to exert any influence over the Project's direction. One of them felt unable to articulate either his criticisms or an alternative strategy. The other argued throughout that the Project should use the energy of the volunteers to organise people and not be wasted on doing further surveys. He was embittered at the arrogance of some of the organisers of the Project in ignoring what the few local people on the committee had to say, and feels now that the organisers, in rejecting the community organising approach in the Project, were shutting themselves off from a potentially radicalising experience for themselves, opting instead for more traditional leadership roles.

The Strategy of the Project

"Something must be done to relieve the desperate plight of families living in overcrowded, inferior and highly rented accommodation."

These words from the recruiting poster represent what was perhaps the most basic element of the Project strategy to which both local people and students responded, and on which the coalition organising the Project was based. R.A. Gilmore, one of the People's Association representatives explained his decision to take part in the Project,

"It was a way of coming together to do something — I'm not quite sure what — but I had a gut feeling that something could come out of it — especially with all these students actually paying to come and work here for 4 weeks — really mind-blowing".

On all other questions of strategy the coalition was split. Some wanted a conciliatory approach to the local Council, others were more hostile; some wanted the students to be involved in the organising of community action over the 4 week period, others thought it politically irresponsible to begin organising at a time when the neighbourhood centres were only newly established and did not have the resources to sustain the wide range of issues and contacts which would have been thrown up.

One of the Workshop members on the Organising Committee, was very critical of the way in which the whole question of strategy was dealt with. He wrote an analysis of the Project[1] which made explicit these criticisms.

"Little fundamental discussion took place on this committee about the general aims and strategy of the Project. There was obviously a diversity of orientations among the members – these were not incompatible in the context of a Summer Project, but should have been talked through. At an early stage it was pointed out that there were two ways of dealing with such differences – whether we wanted to blow up the Town Hall or convert Notting Hill to Methodism, as it was humourously put. One was to talk about them so that we came to understand each other's positions, and the other was not to do so and instead concentrate on whatever common ground could be established. The Committee agreed to adopt the first method, but in practice found itself operating the second. Several times 'motivation' was tabled on the agenda; by no one's design it was never reached.

It was not a committee oriented to questions of long term strategy, partly because, while its members were not hostile to politics, they were not, with the exception of the Vice Chairman (a former LCC councillor) and perhaps the Workshop representatives, people of primarily political experience and habit."

But what this criticism failed to take into account was the volume or the pace of frenzied activity which was an integral part of the dynamic which made the Summer Project happen. This did mean a considerable amount of delegation for each part of the programme to small working groups and no machinery for people outside these groups to challenge or criticise their ideas. Also the way in which George Clark had brought the Committee together initially was by promising different things to different individuals, with none of them knowing on what basis the others had been approached. This in itself made it difficult to organise a majority to force a different point of view on the Committee to that pushed by George Clark. The pace of the whole Project was such that George Clark kept convening and reconvening new sub groups on the housing programme especially, in which he was the only link with what had gone before. So muddle and confusion were inevitable, but despite this the Project happened and was the first project of its kind involved with a large scale intervention at a community level in England.

The Three Programmes of the Summer Project

The Project had 3 major practical programmes, the first, to set up a Housing Register; the second, to set up emergency play areas on two sites; the third, to set up 3 neighbourhood centres as forums from which community action would be generated after the Project was ended.

1. The Housing Register – Community weapon or charitable bureaucracy?
In the 7 months between May and November 1967 the idea of the Housing

Register was changed completely. In May it was seen as a weapon of community struggle. By November it was seen as a specialist housing research body giving individual advice to tenants and landlords, with no relation to community struggle. Initially it was seen as being used by the neighbourhood centres as a weapon in their housing struggles but by November a whole new bureaucracy was seen as necessary and the neighbourhood centres were subordinated to a role of updating the information for the Housing Service, as the new bureaucracy was called.

It was in May 1967 that George Clark first spelled out the idea of the Housing Register as a practical record of all the houses in North Kensington which could act as a focus for community organising; for overcoming apathy by making the individual's private housing situation public; for demystifying the property market and systematising housing information. But, he stressed, "first and foremost we want to serve the interests of the people living in the area".

It was to this rough idea of a Housing Register that the Organising Committee of the Project agreed in May 1967.

Yet each of these possible uses had different practical implications in terms of how the information was to be collected and also rested on different definitions of the housing problem.

However the main argument concentrated on the first and last options, and on how they could or could not be inter-related. The initial idea of a 10% sample survey of the whole of North Kensington was abandoned in favour of a 100% survey of the 3 areas of worst housing around the neighbourhood centres, on the grounds that this would provide information to the centres with greater potential for use in community organising. But this still left a fundamental disagreement within the Project as to how the volunteers were to work in these 3 areas.

There were those who argued that the primary aim of the Housing Register should be as a focus for community organising. This would mean that there was no need for total coverage of all the households in the large areas around the centres in the month of the Project. Total coverage would be impossible because of the energy which would have to be put into building up the contact between local people and the centres, and into responding to any particular crisis which blew up over the summer.

It would mean much more concentrated contact by students working with local volunteers in selected areas around the neighbourhood centres so that continuity of contact would be ensured. It would mean a flexible interview with each tenant with time for the tenants to articulate problems as they saw them and time for the interviewer to explain about the neighbourhood centres and the kind of group actions which could be organised. An attempt could be made to locate both the issues and the key local people for future neighbourhood organisation. For a tenant to enter on the Housing Register would mean that the neighbourhood centre accepted some kind of collective responsibility for working with them to improve their conditions. It would also mean that the tenant would see himself as part of the centre's network and as a participant in any collective action which the centre organised. Though individual services could be obtained through the centres, only collective action by the centre could confront the general housing problems on which the individual problems were based. The Housing Register would only create a sense of the housing problem as a collective problem and not just an aggregate of private individual problems, if all on the Register were actively involved in the neighbourhood centres in some way.

It was argued that only if the Register were seen as a focus for community organising would the housing problem be understood as based on the conflict of interests between the property owner and the tenant. To recognise the need for people to organise collectively to increase their political leverage is to recognise that as low income individual consumers, tenants are bound to lose out and that pressure must be directed at local and national government to force them to use their powers to eliminate the exploitation which is inevitable with private landlords. If the Register were seen in this way the collection of the information by street and household would have an immediate political importance. It would be the way in which the live network of the neighbourhood centre was expanded and the problems of new members channelled back for collective discussion and action. There was talk of setting up blackboards at the end of each street with the rent levels and worst conditions in each house made public so as to make the street see its housing collectively. It was ideas like this which were intelligible and made it possible to justify the Register to doubtful tenants on the doorstep. In the Lancaster redevelopment area especially where the Council policy was not to rehouse furnished tenants, the Register had an immediate relevance in terms of locating all the furnished tenants so that they could get together and organise to force the Council to change its policy.

This strategy was strongly argued for by two members of the Organising Committee, Mike Rustin who had been greatly influenced by the American experience of community projects like that in Newark and Bill Richardson who had worked closely with Richard Hauser in Notting Hill in the Powis and Colville Residents Association in the late 1950's and early 1960's. Hauser's approach, he believed to be right:

— do a preliminary examination of the issues likely to be important in the area;
— knock on people's doors and find out what they are angry enough about to unite with others to take action;
— tell them you will call back when you have talked with more people in their street to let them know what most people want to take action on;
— get together a street meeting to report back.

Out of this way of working had come the four street associations from which were formed the Colville and Powis Residents Association. But despite the fact that George Clark had also been involved in this work for a short time he and the majority of the Organising Committee did not take the idea of involving the volunteers in this sort of process seriously. George Clark argued against it on the grounds that they were all sitting on a racial powder keg in Notting Hill and to organise a Project in this way would be tantamount to setting a match to it. So far as the majority of the Organising Committee was concerned it has already been explained that they took the view that the short term involvement of the volunteers was not compatible with their involvement in the much longer process of community organising.

So in July the Organising Committee decided after completing a pilot survey

"that we place our main emphasis on the need for adequate statistical data as a tool for effective projections and programming of housing and community facilities, for assessing the housing situation in quantitative and qualitative terms. In putting forward these as simple objectives it is recommended that we set aside consideration of the long term use of the Register".

In effect this meant that the primary aim of the Housing Programme was to conduct a survey of all units of accommodation, the conditions, ownership, management, rent and characteristics of the occupants. From this survey a public Housing Register could be compiled if the tenant wished the information to be made public. Gradually confidentiality and objectivity became the gods of the Project and were drummed into the volunteers in briefing after briefing. Volunteers who had come eager for some experience of community action arising from creative dialogue with people in the area, were groomed in the same way as Government Social Survey interviewers. Any immediacy which could have resulted from tenants eagerly agreeing to go on the Register was destroyed by a decision that for them to agree once was not good enough. They had to agree twice and every tenant had to be revisited in case they hadn't really understood what the Register was — obviously a symptom of the ambiguity of the organisers of the Housing Survey themselves more than anything else. The ambiguity must have been transmitted to the tenants. The official version of how the Register was to be explained was

"We are setting up a public Housing Register which will help to establish standards of fair rent and sort out some of the housing muddle in this area. Will you agree to go on the Register?"

This drew a half-hearted response: 60% in the Lancaster area, 45% in Golborne and 42% in Colville, agreeing to go on the Register.

What happened to cement this shift away from community organising was that individuals had been involved at the last minute in the organising of the survey, who had academic reputations to build or sustain, and were terrified of being associated with a disreputable political survey. These included a planning team from Westminster Council, a sociologist researcher from York, a lecturer from the University of Sussex and a member of the Cabinet Office. So all their energy was focused on hammering home with the volunteers the values of confidentiality, professional ethics and objectivity, all of which made the distinction between the survey and the register necessary and shifted the whole emphasis of the housing programme of the Summer Project away from community organising.

Instead a bureaucratic leviathan was set up to implement the survey. Volunteers were responsible to an administrative apparatus consisting of a Registrar, a Steering Group, Field Organisers, Team Leaders and Checkers. They were asked to undertake ten and later fifteen interviews a day. In the main they had little contact with local volunteers simply because most work was done during the day when local people were at work. There was no context for reporting back and evaluation. Interviews were to be confined to the questionnaire, and to be got through in ten or fifteen minutes. Students were to be objective and detached while completing the questionnaire, though they had to mention the local neighbourhood centre at the conclusion. There was one further concession made to the community organising objective. Each questionnaire had a blank sheet attached to it which the volunteer was to use for jotting down information of use to the neighbourhood centre in terms of potential members or follow up action needed on particular problems.

By the end of November the transformation of the potentially radical idea of the Housing Register was complete when George Clark redefined it yet again, but this time with all the emphasis on research which could be funded by charitable resources.

There is no mention of the Register acting as a focus for community organising, only of an ambiguous consumer service. There is no mention of the dependence of the Housing Register on the work of the neighbourhood centres as was intended initially. Instead the Housing Register has its own institutional form in the Housing Service which was to be a company limited by guarantee and a registered charity. In the post Project report the future programme relating to the Housing Register was seen in terms of: the analysis of the questionnaires; research into the relationship between population and urban housing using the survey information; research into landlords; the setting up of offices for the Register and the appointment of staff. The role of the neighbourhood centres was seen simply in terms of servicing this new edifice by helping to update the information on the Register. This process of institutionalisation and incorporation by the authorities followed a predictable path. In the early 1970's the Housing Service set up the Housing Action Centre in the Golborne area with a large grant from a charity and later from the Council. In January 1974 this Housing Action Centre moved in with the Council into newly built offices under the motorway to work in conjunction with the Council's Information and Aid Centre. Such is the logic of institutionalisation and incorporation of initially radical initiatives by the authorities.

But this was only possible because of the ambiguity of the Community Workshop's political position which resulted in many of its members going along with these developments for quite some time. Throughout the Project the Workshop never met as a group to clarify its view of the kind of housing programme they would like to see. It was not till 1968 that all relations were broken off with the Housing Service and George Clark was excluded from the Workshop and the neighbourhood centres. But it was perhaps partly due to pressures to exclude him felt as early as 1967 that George Clark saw the institutionalisation of his brainchild, the Housing Register, as vital, as an alternative base from which he could work if his exclusion was forced.

But all was not lost. The initial idea of the Housing Register as a weapon of community struggle did not die in the neighbourhood centres. The People's Centre decided it had to get back the information on all the houses in its area, which its members had taken part in collecting. So they went up to the Housing Service offices and took all the relevant information from the Register and built up its own files. Ever since then these street files have been used, most importantly for building up a landlord register so that landlord networks can be traced easily and quickly. The rents information was later used by the Housing Group of the People's Association in 1972 to show how fast low rent housing was being turned into high rent housing, by so-called 'improvements', to support the case for widespread compulsory purchase.

The Lancaster Centre tried to get back the information on the houses in the redevelopment area and burst into a meeting of the Housing Service to demand it, but never resorted to actually going up to the Housing Service offices and taking a copy of the information, so in the end never saw the information again. Even the information on where the furnished tenants lived was not obtained from the Housing Register and instead the Centre tried to begin its own street surveys all over again. Their failure to get the information they needed was symptomatic of many people's reaction to situations of direct personal conflict, which was what taking a copy of the information would have involved. The response of the individuals involved was to stop short of this because they were afraid of a situation full of such conflict.

So as the Housing Service became more institutionalised and more remote, so it became more irrelevant to the community struggle of the neighbourhood centres it had initially been set up to serve, and they had to fight yet another institution to win back what was theirs by right. In some ways to control the bureaucracy of the Housing Service became as difficult as confronting the Council.

2. *The Play Programme* — The strategy of the play programme was simple:

— to improve and expand the present play facilities in two of the most overcrowded areas of North Kensington in the hope that this would lead to considerable investment by the authorities in the long run;
— to establish the practice of bringing unused space into use on a permanent basis.

The need was obvious. Though less than half of the total population of Kensington and Chelsea lived in North Kensington, 70% of the Borough's children (0-15 years) lived in North Kensington.

Yet, whereas in South Kensington a child shared one-tenth acre with nine other children in North Kensington a child shared the same space with 89 other children.

The Playspace group of the Summer Project started by looking at an area of three-quarters square mile, east of Ladbroke Grove and north of Westbourne Grove, in which the best calculations indicated 4,000 children of school age and under lived. They listed the existing facilities: an adventure playground, a local authority playground, three playgroups, and two play centres run by the ILEA in the local primary schools. A close look at the area then revealed 28 potential new sites for play facilities. After negotiations of possible use that summer the list shrunk to two — one was Oxford Gardens, a building site which the Council had left vacant for two years, the other was Lonsdale Road, a designated playstreet off the Portobello Road, blocked to traffic at that end.

The Oxford Gardens site worked as well as could have been hoped with about 65 children using it each day and ten volunteers working on the site. The Playground activities focussed on building huts, aerial runways, painting and ball games. There was little involvement of neighbours or parents on the site except for plying the volunteers with cups of tea.

Lonsdale Road was more difficult in that the space had to be kept clear of parked cars if there was to be space to play. The idea was to show that a playstreet could be successfully used for creative play if there were resources available for equipment and a play leader's salary. The People's Centre, the local neighbourhood centre was closely involved in the activity throughout and continued to run play activities on Saturdays after the Project had finished.

3. *The Neighbourhood Centres* — The neighbourhood centres were set up in the hope that they could become "agencies of social change working for and with the people and organised by the people who live here" (post Project

report on the centres). It was as early as May that the Organising Committee asked the Notting Hill People's Association and the Neighbourhood Councils of the Methodist Church "to establish three centres in the Golborne, Powis and Lancaster areas — from which the work before, during and after the project can be organised." But within weeks the idea of using the Methodist Neighbourhood Councils was dropped and the level of their involvement reduced to a few individuals who became involved in the Lancaster Centre which met in their church.

The function the centres should perform were seen as providing:

- a base for the organisation of the Housing Survey;
- an advice service with lawyers and social workers to deal with the immediate individual social and legal problems thrown up by the survey;
- a forum where the people living in the neighbourhood could meet to discuss and decide on action to confront the general problems they all faced.

There was uneasiness, especially at the People's Centre about the emphasis on the use of professional social workers and lawyers since it was thought wrong to use the established procedures of the existing society in the battle for fundamental change in the institutions and structures of society at large. There was also strong resistance to the social work diagnosis of social problems, which emphasised the need to help the individual to cope better, rather than the need to change the very structure of capitalist society which produced the problems. However, all three centres ended up pursuing all three of the aims stated above to a greater or lesser extent.

By the middle of June all three centres were set up with officers and a committee. In Golborne the committee was based on the mainly Irish network which existed around the Adventure Playground. The leader of the playground had been there five years during which time the playground office had come to function as a centre for informal advice and help for young people. In Lancaster Road West, the committee included members of the Community Workshop who were working in that area over the summer, and a couple of members of the Methodist Church. Both the Golborne and Lancaster Centres were set up as part of the preparations for the Summer Project whereas in the Colville/Powis area what happened was more complex and has already been explained in the context of the development of the Notting Hill People's Association.

Over the summer each centre developed a working style of its own. In Golborne the emphasis was on running an efficient advice service and on running a market stall to publicise its existence and raise money. They held a public meeting two weeks before the project began at the adventure playground but no programme of collective action developed from this. Once the project was finished the centre continued to meet for a short time on two evenings a week, but tensions developed due to the fact that the centre was based at 60 St Ervans Road, the Community Workshop house, and the members of the Golborne Centre resented the more overt political stance of the Workshop and decided to move out, but never re-established themselves in a new base.

After the initial committee in the Lancaster area was set up by the Organising Committee a meeting to discuss the development of the centre drew in 50 people from the surrounding neighbourhood. It was decided to put energy into letting people know about the public meeting the Notting Hill Social Council was organising on the redevelopment scheme on July 12th. As a result 300 people turned up and with a barrage of angry outbursts exposed the Council's ignorance of the kind of problem faced by the community they were planning to redevelop. This gave the centre the momentum it needed to go on and build up a stock of accurate information on the Council's plans and to build up networks of contacts in the surrounding streets. Out of this came a petition from every tenant in Testerton Street demanding adequate drains and proper signposting as a playstreet. In Camelford Road there were frequent informal street discussions about what should be done about the housing, the police, the play and traffic accidents. These seemed to occur whenever members from the centre appeared in the street in the warm summer evenings, when most of the women of the street were out sitting on the steps.

The Survey area was exactly the same as the redevelopment area and the survey was slightly shortened as a concession to the fact that the houses were to be demolished in due course. However no effort was made to design the survey so that it would specifically relate to the needs of people in a redevelopment area. Once the Project ended the centre continued to open two evenings a week and each Saturday morning, and continued for years after to give individual advice and to act as a focus for action in the redevelopment area.

In the Colville/Powis area where there had been an active Notting Hill People's Association working on local issues long before the Summer Project, members of the local centre made important contributions to the Project based on their intimate knowledge of the neighbourhood. For instance, Pat McDonald, one of the initiators of the struggle in Colville Gardens, used her knowledge of the area to make sure that the nun volunteers were used to search out the recalcitrant Catholics, who were proving difficult to contact for the volunteers, to make sure they answered the questionnaire properly. Bill Richardson, the People's Centre chairman took a special interest in making the weekly meetings a really politically educative experience for the volunteers. Throughout the summer the People's Centre was a hive of activity with housing questionnaires being checked in one corner of the hall, lawyers giving advice in another and People's Centre members using the rest of the space to organise their ongoing campaigns over Powis Square and Colville Gardens.

What was learned from the experience of the neighbourhood centres during the Project?

They had acted as a base for organising the Housing Survey in all three areas, though in the main the volunteers working on the survey and the local members of the centres remained fairly distinct. It was often felt by the centre members that the Project had an existence independent of the local activists and that the Housing Survey would go on despite them. They had not been briefed and so were cut out of the interviewing. But there were direct links at each centre between members and volunteers. Each volunteer carried a blank sheet at the back of each questionnaire which was for all information which would be relevant to the Centre. These sheets were collected by the Receptionist at each centre who sorted out the follow-up action with members of the Centre. So it was a survey with a difference and the link up between volunteers and local members of the centre did exist.

Each centre had also provided an advice service of lawyers and social workers over the six week period stretching over the Project. They were all open six days a week with a full time receptionist who saw everyone who came in and linked them up with lawyers, social workers or members of the Centre. The rota of lawyers and social workers operated each night from 6.00 to 10.00 pm and Labour councillors also made it their business to attend regularly, at the Lancaster Centre especially. In every case a referral was made to a social worker or lawyer on the premises rather than to ones outside. Over the six weeks each centre had about 70 people who came for advice with housing or legal problems in the main. The relatively few social work problems brought to the centres had already been raised with another agency so the need for social workers in the centres was not established. But the lawyers were obviously tapping a very real need. The discussions around a free legal service were developed by Peter Kandler who coordinated the volunteer lawyers. This culminated in the setting up of the Neighbourhood Law Centre in 1970 based in many ways on the experience built up in the legal work done around the neighbourhood centres.

Finally it had also been shown that a centre could act as the local political forum in the neighbourhood where the central issues could be discussed and action decided upon. The People's Centre had shown the way here.

Conclusion

The Summer Project is well worth looking at in detail since it shows how early initiatives were taken in each of the major areas which this book is attempting to explore.

The mere happening of the Project, and the discussions and arguments generated around it did much to free people's minds to think in fresh ways about new kinds of political action. The first break in to Powis Square, timid though it was, opened up the idea of direct action in the area in a simple direct way.

The radical idea of the Housing Register fed into the development of a strategy in housing which the People's Association had been working out in 1-9 Colville Gardens and which saw no place for profit in housing. The determination of the People's Centre to gain possession of the Housing Register information relevant to them resulted in them building up stores of information which enabled them to gain insight into the ownership networks and into the nature of the 'enemy' which had to be fought. The play programme resulted in people thinking differently about the space around them, of the potential playstreets, and the private garden squares which could be taken over. The development of the idea of playspace together with its absence from the area resulted in all unused space being seen as ripe for take over and for opening up to the local children, with resources in the form of equipment and play leaders.

Finally, the Project shows the early stages of organisational developments in two very different directions — first, the development of the neighbourhood centres as a forum for local discussion and action and secondly, of the kind of institutions, like the Housing Service, which would end up by being incorporated by the authorities.

FOOTNOTE
1. *Community Organising in England, Notting Hill Summer Project 1967.* M Rustin Alta 1967-8. *University of Birmingham Review.*

Chapter 5

The Problems of Organisation

By the end of 1967 the Notting Hill People's Association was established with its two sister organisations, the People's Centre and the Lancaster Centre. Out of this basic framework there developed working groups on housing, street campaigns, play, for safer streets, against the police and for control of the space under the motorway. These groups were generated directly as organs of struggle by working people who wanted to gain some control over the decisions and resources which were crucial determinants of the quality of their lives.

The People's Centre. February 1967 - August 1971

From the beginning the People's Centre worked in an organic way, spawning new working groups wherever the Monday night meetings proved inadequate for the amount of organisation and action which seemed necessary on a particular front. These groups were seen as responsible for their own programme, for raising their own funds and employing their own workers, but were expected to report back to the weekly meeting of the Centre on their work. So the Centre existed in the form of a federation of semi-autonomous groups. This was to be challenged after three years by a group within the Centre who argued the need for greater centralisation of power and resources. However this challenge, though formally ratified by the weekly meeting was ineffective and resulted in the weekly meeting of the Centre as a whole being destroyed, but in the autonomous working groups continuing to control their programmes of action and their resources.

What were the groups which made up the federation of the People's Centre over the years, and what areas of activity did they cover?

Housing

The Colville Gardens Action Committee (February 1967 – end of 1968) focussed on work with the tenants of 1-9 Colville Gardens, on the fight to stop luxury conversion and the tenants' eviction.

The Notting Hill Squatters (December 1968 — mid 1969) was set up to organise squatting first in luxury flats, and then to back up more permanent squats of local people.

The St. Stephens Group (Mid 1969 — mid 1970) focussed on a redevelopment area in the adjoining borough of Westminster. The aim was to find out about the redevelopment plans and to publicise all information needed by the tenants in their fight for rehousing.

The Housing Group (mid 1970 onwards) concentrated on activity to challenge the Council's reliance on private landlords to 'improve' the area, and to disrupt the property market wherever possible. The activities described in the 'Housing Struggles' section resulted to a large extent from the work of this group.

Powis Playgroups (October 1967 onwards) started with the aim of setting up a playgroup for under-5s, especially those in overcrowded housing conditions, and opened with many of the children from Colville Gardens. The group went on to set up two other playgroups. Local women trained as playleaders, and campaigned for and won a wage for their work. Recognising the inadequacy of playgroups for parents who worked, the group set in motion the development of two all-day nursery centres, one in Colville Square and the other under Westway the elevated motorway.

The Powis Square ad hoc Committee (mid 1968 — 1969) took over the responsibility for getting the Council to equip and resource Powis Square for play, once the fences had been torn down and the Council was forced to buy.

The Notting Hill Youth Project (1969 — 1971) organised play activities for children over five. This included the employment of playleaders for the sites in Colville which were part of the Play Programmes each summer, the pioneering of Easter holiday play schemes, work with teenage groups, the opening of an after-school group in September 1969 for 5-10 year olds, the setting up of a youth club in 1969 and the running of it for a year and a half, every night of the week. It was to unite all these separate activities that the Youth Project was set up in October 1969. The house at 90 Talbot Road, W.11 was obtained by the Youth Project from Westminster Council as a base for play activities in 1970. In mid 1971 the Youth Project lost this house and as a result of the confusion in the People's Centre as a whole the Youth Project stopped meeting.

Playspace (1972 onwards) was formed by many of those who had been involved in the Youth Project who wanted to continue youth activities in the area. In addition to running play schemes Playspace have put a great deal of work into developing the two garden squares, from closed, private squares, into public play areas, and in pressuring the Council to resource them adequately.

Traffic

The Mothers Traffic Group (mid 1969 – mid 1970) drew up a set of proposals for the transformation of the traffic system in the area, to reduce the speed and flow of traffic with one-way streets and road blocks. This was backed up by a concerted campaign of direct action and resulted in a one-way system being introduced and a very dangerous road being paved over by the middle of 1970.

West London Claimants Union (early 1970 – end of 1972) was set up as part of the National Federation of Claimants Unions and also as a working group of the People's Centre. It started opening two afternoons a week to help people with their Social Security claims, but then in September 1970 it started up an office in the premises of the Lancaster Centre every afternoon for four hours. It worked on national campaigns for the winter heating allowance and against the cohabitation rule. It also linked up with local strikers to help them fight for their Social Security money together and launched campaigns of collective representation in the local Social Security offices.

The Police Group (mid 1970 – early 1972) was organised as a result of several trials involving people from the Centre and their friends. It was thought necessary to work on a collective defence since they were obviously charged as a group. The group was involved with the trial resulting from the demonstration against police harassment of black businesses like the Mangrove restaurant in August 1970; in the trial of the Powis Square 8 arrested at a November 5th bonfire party in Powis Square in 1970; and in the trial resulting from the police siege of the Metro Youth Club in May 1971. Together these trials showed the police that they could no longer get away with their consistent harassment of black clubs and meeting places or community festivities. The magistrates rapped the police firmly on the knuckles and urged them to treat the community more sensitively in the future. This resulted in a new 'Community relations' type policeman being appointed in the area and old heavier types being transferred to other areas.

Once the Police Group ceased to meet the North Kensington Law Centre continued to act as a focus for collective defences in trials involving local people.

Over the years the weekly meetings of the People's Centre went on (1967 – 1971) there were several attempts to tighten up the organisation of the Centre. This was inevitable in an organisation which had been set up with no formal constitution and an open but unenforced membership. The weekly meetings in All Saints Church Hall were open to all-comers and anyone could speak for as long as they liked or rather as long as the rest of the meeting would let them hold the floor without interruption. It was rare for the Chairman to control the discussion or even the order of speakers. On the rare occasions when a vote occurred everyone present ended up voting whether a formal member or not. The lack of formal institutional controls on meetings meant that the Centre was wide open to groups or individuals moving into the Centre and trying to dominate the proceedings. Despite this there was an amazing tolerance and interest in all kinds of views on the left expressed. No-one was ever physically forced out of a meeting though at times suspect police spies were made to feel so uncomfortable that they left! Meetings would go on for hours, from 8pm through to 1.30am quite often.

It was at times when the exhaustion produced by meetings did not seem to be offset by the productiveness of the meetings themselves that efforts were made to tighten up the way the meetings were run. In September 1968 there was general concern that the meetings were not as democratic as they could be and that it was very difficult for newcomers to the meetings to get a word in. The minutes for the Centre meeting of September 30th 1968 report that it was agreed to experiment for three months by holding more democratic meetings, that there should be greater discipline at meetings, with one person speaking at a time, more control from the chair, and meetings should begin and end at 8pm and 10.30pm prompt.

In Feburary 1969 another attempt was made to increase the democracy of the Centre by a decision that the main offices should rotate amongst as many people as possible and that there should be quarterly elections as a safeguard against individuals or groups building up entrenched positions of control in the Centre.

But in an organisation as open as the People's Centre formal safeguards like rotating offices could never ensure that groups did not try to use the People's Centre for whatever plans or ideas they wanted to work on, and lots of groups tried, with varying degrees of success, depending to a large extent on the amount of work in the area they were prepared to put in between meetings to back up their speeches at the weekly meetings. It was in response to criticisms of the lack of discipline and structure of the People's Centre that Bill Richardson, a founder member and the then Chairman of the Centre, made this statement in his report at the end of 1968:

> "Some of our members will be reporting specific events and campaigns, successes and failures, and others of a tidy organisational turn of mind will be stressing the latter, labouring the apparent lack of order in our affairs. I want to rationalise that lack of order, quite seriously and evaluate the success of our community work upon the degree of anti-community effect we create.
>
> "If we are serious about the kind of changes we wish and work toward

in Notting Hill, then we must treat seriously the view that the community as it now stands, with its structured politics, and control, its graft, slums and rundown services, with its volume of sheer human misery, its immoral Council and on its other side apathy among people *is not disorganised* . . . Call it organised apathy or organised non participation if you will — but life goes on in an organised form, albeit in quiet desperation.

"It is our job to attack those prevailing patterns if we are ever to advance new ones, and that is why I suggest before Community, we must deliberately set about Anti-Community-Disorganisation.

"Therefore the lack of structure within our own organisation and the conflict of views at our own meetings should not cause us too much concern — this freedom is absolutely vital if we are to create new forms of influence and struggle.

"The important issue for me from the past year has been our debate and our rubbing off on each other and the abrasive agent we have become in the community. The coming year I hope will see us rubbing raw the latent hostilities of people to a point of overt expression."

By the end of 1970 as working groups proliferated to such a degree that one or other group of the Centre was meeting each night of the week, the need for clarifying the relationship between the working groups and the Centre was felt. At the meeting of November 23rd 1970 the Structure of the People's Centre as a federation of semi-autonomous groups was formalised. The minutes for the meeting stated:

"After wide-ranging discussions over the past few weeks the 70 odd people at the People's Centre last Monday decided to break down into working groups so that each person would concentrate on the work which he felt to be most important.

Five working groups were recognised: Housing, Playgroups, Education and Youth, Claimants Union, and Police. Each group is planning its own meetings, and the work to be done and is to have one person to report back regularly to the Monday night People's Centre meeting."

Within two weeks it was decided to give more coherence to the weekly People's Centre meetings by having a central Chairman's committee made up of the Chairman of each subgroup, to draw up plans for joint action for the centre as a whole.

However, at the next week's meeting it was discovered that the crucial factor of finance had been left out of all this restructuring, and a finance committee was created to be made up of one person from each working group and the Treasurer. This group was to coordinate the funding of all the groups, and the Centre as a whole. On looking at the finances many of those at the meeting realised for the first time that one of the groups, the Powis Playgroups, had managed to raise a grant of nearly £3,000 pa for three years to pay the wages of the women working in the playgroups. All the other groups had virtually no resources. This immediately set in motion

PEOPLE'S CENTRE STRUCTURE

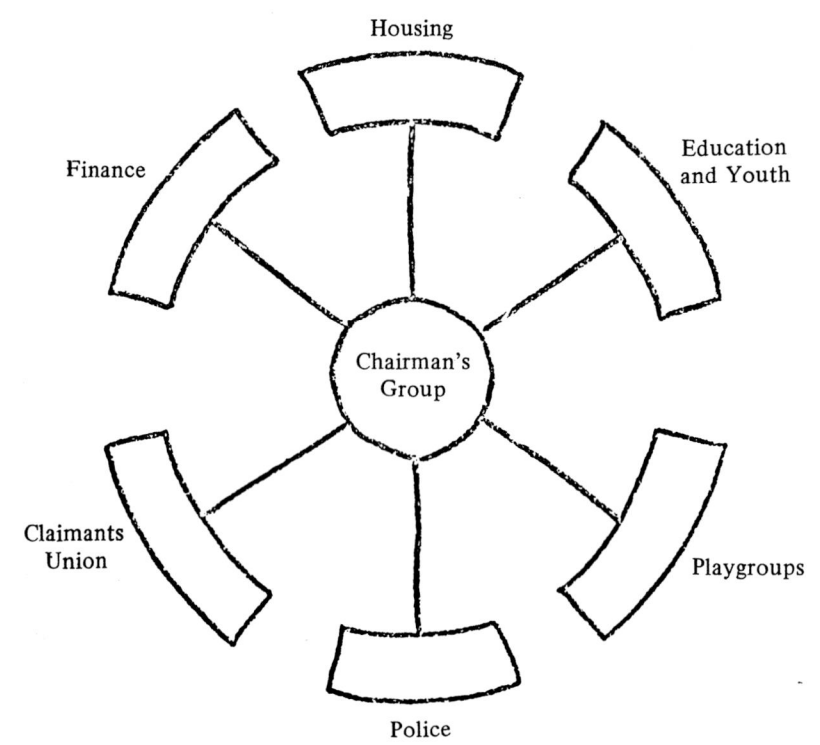

- Housing
- Education and Youth
- Playgroups
- Police
- Claimants Union
- Finance
- Chairman's Group

a desperate scramble for centralised control of all the working groups, and their finances so that the Playgroups money could be used for whatever the central body of the People's Centre, the Monday night meeting, thought most vital. For the first time in the history of the Centre resolutions were put to the vote, and two main resolutions passed which aimed at destroying the autonomy of the working groups. The first on 21.12.70 stated that all subgroups should be answerable to the People's Centre, and the second on 4.1.71 stated that all the funds in the People's Centre should be pooled into a central fund which would be centrally controlled. Both resolutions were passed by a majority of those who happened to be at the meeting. It was also decided to move the physical base of the Centre into 90 Talbot Road, the house the Youth Project had got from Westminster Council for play activities. From this time on the weekly meetings became more and more exclusive, partly because the meetings were in a house and not a public hall and partly because a group within the Centre established themselves in a controlling position in the house and the vetting of those who passed through the front door began. Those who saw themselves as the revolutionary elite set themselves up as a People's Tribunal to conduct show trials of the working groups of the Centre. First it was the turn of the Playgroups. The women firmly resisted all attempts to intervene in the control of the playgroup which they had set up, funded and trained themselves to run. They were the workers and felt they should control how the money they had raised for their wages should be spent, especially when they were working for an equivalent of £12.50 for a full week's work.

One by one the programme of each working group was examined by the Monday night tribunal and one by one, each was found wanting, so that by the summer of 1971, the working groups on housing, playgroups and the Claimants Union still existed but their active members did not go to the Monday night meetings, and the purified rump who remained in occupation of 90 Talbot Road busied themselves with running a soup kitchen and organising the Carnival for that summer.

What was the motivation behind this drive for exclusivity?

Back in November 1970 one of the main personalities still in occupation of 90 Talbot Road after the purges had declared to a People's Centre meeting that he would go on returning to the meetings and shouting at them till the Centre broke up since it was better that the Centre should not exist than that it should exist in the form it did. One of the main objects of attack was the influence of the Community Workshop in the Centre, because they were seen as white middle class entrepreneurs from outside the area, with resources and time which no-one else had. In addition to all this some of their members were thought to spend too much time on organisations like the Amenity Trust and the Play Association which involved them in talking to councillors. However the discussions in the Centre as to the rational differences between the two groups within the People's Centre were very rare and so it is very difficult to clarify the differences of position.

One member of the People's Centre who was Treasurer throughout the scramble for centralisation of the funds saw developments in the People's Centre as the working out of what he called "the Harlem Complex" — the belief of the West Indian group within the Centre that it was necessary to build a black power base within the Colville/Tavistock area. The mistake they made was to focus on too small an area where all classes and cultures of people lived. This meant that their deliberate policy of exclusivity became a weakness rather than a strength, since it rejected many people of the area with 'legitimate' rather than 'social conscience' interests, and all other left groups found themselves on the 'bourgeois' side even when those involved were themselves industrial workers.

This reasoning tied up with the view of another member of the Centre that the attack on the Centre was the result of the growing emphasis among black people from the late 1960s onwards on the importance of reinforcing black identity. For black people like those involved in the purges who had lived in England for over 30 years, mainly in a white world, this produced a certain confusion of identity, which the growth of the People's Centre accentuated. It was not an all black group, but it did have growing influence in the area and to this extent it was a threat to the idea of the need to reinforce black identity. Instead it reinforced a kind of locality based working-class identity and as such it had to be smashed.

But the Centre did not split on clear black/white lines. A white member of the People's Centre who acted as prosecuting counsel in most of the purges of groups from the Centre and who finally found himself excluded by the West Indian group, saw the whole process as "brainstorming — a struggle for power between elite groups with no clear political arguments at the base of it all."

So it is really difficult to present a clear set of reasons for the attacks on and the disintegration of the People's Centre as a political forum.

However, despite the attacks, the confusion and the bitterness, the three working groups which still existed, the Housing Group, the Playgroups, and the Claimants Union all set up their offices on the ground floor of 60 St. Ervans Road, the Community Workshop premises, and kept in touch with each other by frequent chats around the house rather than formal meetings.

In March 1972 there was an attempt to rebuild a local political forum, like the People's Centre had been. Members of the Claimants Union, the Housing Group and a local paper, *Frenz,* called together a meeting of all those active in political groups in the area. It was generally recognised that the destruction of the People's Centre as an open political forum in the area had created a void in the political life of the area which it was worth trying to fill again. The letter calling all groups to the meeting ended up:

> "In isolation, we can too easily lose our energy and initiative and that's what 'they' want — together, we can start to turn Notting Hill into a liberated zone."

Two meetings were held and about 50 or 60 people turned up to each, but there was not enough fusion of interest among those at the meeting to generate the energy to sustain a new political institution and, at the third meeting, virtually no-one turned up.

The Housing Group, and the Powis Playgroups went on working, the West London Claimants Union ceased as an organisation in 1972 and in the same year Playspace was formed to continue the work with young people and children in the area. By the end of 1973 it was these three groups, the Housing Group, Powis Playgroups, and Playspace which saw themselves as part of the Notting Hill People's Association and as continuing the struggles which had been started by the Association in 1967.

The Lancaster Neighbourhood Centre

The area covered by the Lancaster Road (West) Redevelopment scheme in which the Centre was based, had a long standing white working class population, with a high number of controlled tenancies. (In 1967 the Housing Survey showed that 20% of all tenancies were furnished in the Lancaster area in contrast to over 40% in the Colville area.) This meant that the area was far less open to young activists or what might be called the "metropolitan intelligentsia" moving in.

This inevitably had an effect on the way the Lancaster Centre developed after the initial steps had been taken to set it up for the Summer Project in 1967. Quite early on stalwarts of the local Labour Party moved into prominent positions in the Centre, one of whom concentrated almost entirely on setting up a reliable filing system for the legal advice service run by the Centre. The Labour Party members contributed a style to the centre which was slow, steady and reliable in terms of running an advice service but which was fairly insensitive to the ebbs and flows of community activity going on around them.

Like the People's Centre, the Lancaster Centre spawned a number of working groups but unlike those of the People's Centre, the Lancaster working groups were focussed on an individual street for a short time and their attempt to challenge those aspects of the redevelopment process which they thought needed changing.

Street groups developed in Ruston Close, Camelford Road, Fowell Street and Walmer Road and tenants associations developed in two blocks of Council flats: Nottingwood House and Talbot Grove House. The struggles in Camelford Road, to speed up rehousing, and in Walmer Road, to force the GLC to recognise the need to rehouse people living beside Westway, will be explained in more detail in the section which focusses on struggles which span both centres. In addition to these street groups there were the twice weekly meetings of the Centre as a whole, where matters of general concern could be raised. However, these meetings focussed to a large extent on the efficient servicing of the legal advice sessions.

Partly because of the great emphasis placed by the Centre on providing a smoothly running legal advice service and up to date information on the redevelopment for the neighbourhood, the Lancaster Centre was far less a forum for political argument than the People's Centre.

The Centre was involved in several campaigns on issues resulting from the redevelopment scheme, first on getting basic repairs done in houses due for eventual demolition, and then on fighting for swifter rehousing for all the tenants as general living conditions in the area deteriorated.

Whereas most of the action in 1968 was focussed on the issue of repairs, in 1969 the emphasis shifted to rehousing.

It was early in January 1969 that Maggie O'Shannon decided to squat in an empty house in Camelford Road in order to drive home the demand of the street for early rehousing. This served as a focus for organisation in the redevelopment area attracting support and energy from the East End Squatters and the People's Centre as well as the Lancaster Centre.

The way organisation and action developed in Camelford Road illustrates well the pattern of the Centre's organisational development. While the Centre continued its slow, steady groundwork in the area: publicising information in the area with street exhibitions, knocking on doors to find out who was threatened by the redevelopment with eviction and no rehousing — the initiative for direct action in the area came from the street committees. Maggie O'Shannon was quite confident in taking the decision to squat with her friends from the street, and turning to the Lancaster Centre, the People's Centre and the Notting Hill Squatters for practical back-up support. As a result of the action in Camelford Road three tenants from the street, including Maggie, took up positions in the Centre for some months in 1969.

However, as happens time and time again in a redevelopment area, this kind of support is no sooner built up than it is lost when people move out of the neighbourhood as they are rehoused. After rehousing, some families did revisit the Centre from time to time. Many of the tenants from Camelford Road got themselves rehoused together in an estate in the next borough of Hammersmith. This sometimes resulted in their new neighbours bringing their problems to the Centre on their recommendation, but the rehousing of activists outside the area was in the main a real loss to the organisational strength of the Centre.

For the first three years the Lancaster Centre was based in the Lancaster Road Church Hall and opened two evenings a week. However in April 1970 the Centre got a short life house from the Council as a full time base for the Centre, open five days a week as well as the two evenings. During the day when the rest of the Centre members were at work, the Centre was manned by the Centre's community worker who lived in the house.

However, other groups also started using the house and this led to unforseen problems. The West London Claimants Union set up office there and early in 1971 a Youth Club was opened by a group from the People's Centre. The mixture of youth club and offices was not a success and by June 1971 the building was virtually in ruins due to fires, break-ins, and smashed windows. The Claimants Union had to move out, and the Lancaster Centre as such ceased to exist, partly because of the damage done to the building and partly because the area was becoming increasingly depopulated. Individuals from the Centre kept up links with the new council tenants associations, however there ceased to be a full time worker and the free legal service the Lancaster Centre had pioneered continued in a much expanded form as the North Kensington Neighbourhood Law Centre.

The pattern of the development of the Centre was for one issue or a street's problems to be focussed on in turn, and once a partial victory was won, the people who had been involved dropped back to await rehousing, while the focus shifted to another group or street. Partly because the process of redevelopment was tearing the community apart and because the Centre came on the scene too late to challenge the redevelopment plan itself, this pattern was inevitable. That is why there are no groups spawned by the Lancaster Centre still alive today. Most of the streets where the street exhibitions and meetings were held are now under the bulldozer, and the people all gone. The immediacy of the problem of rehousing meant that there was no long term interest in the area in organising groups around issues like playgroups, or resistance to the police. The emphasis was much more on individual and street rehousing and repair problems. This Centre faced the dilemma of how to combine the giving of individual advice with the organisation of collective action, even more acutely than the People's Centre due to the heavy demand there was for individual advice due to the redevelopment scheme.

In the Centre Report of May 1969 the Chairman wrote:

> "Of the 200 or more people whose cases have been taken up by the Advice Service, very very few have thought to engage themselves actively in the affairs of the Centre once their own particular problem has been resolved."

However the issue of rehousing which people in Camelford Road and Walmer Road faced both individually and collectively did produce strong collective action.

The way in which the full time workers and the Centre members chose to work was also an important factor in limiting the outbursts of collective action. Throughout the life of the Centre there was a great emphasis on maintaining the highest possible standards in the advice service and little effort was made to collectivise individual problems as much as possible. For instance from the start of the Centre the issue of furnished tenants being excluded from the right to rehousing was always recognised as an important issue but this was never tackled in a collective way, by building up an organisation of furnished tenants to fight the issue themselves. Instead the Centre relied on the occasional petition and fighting rearguard action against evictions in the Rent Tribunal. It could be said that the collective action in the redevelopment area happened despite the Centre and not because of it.

Links between the two Centres

Although both the Lancaster Centre and the People's Centre had distinct and very different patterns of development, they did sustain links with each other. Members of one centre were in touch with the actions the other Centre was involved in, and gave mutual support when it was needed for demonstrations, squatting, or public meetings.

However it was not until a meeting of both centres in December 1967 that these links were formalised and both centres agreed to see themselves as two parts of an overall Notting Hill People's Association, with the four original aims of the People's Association when it was formed in January 1967.

It was agreed that each centre would retain its autonomy. At a later stage it was agreed an attempt would be made to institutionalise the People's Association as the overall organisation with a committee elected from all the members of both centres. However this never happened. Several clear views emerged from this first joint meeting. It was felt that the centres should extend the scope of the political action they took to include an attack on low wages and high prices, but it was felt that the centres should consolidate their organisation first. This aim of extending the political action of the centres was seen as necessary if the centres were to develop a more total perspective of the political position of the centres. It was agreed that both centres needed a physical base in their areas like the house at 60 St. Ervans Road and also they both needed to have their own full time workers. However the necessary finances were never available.

Both centres agreed to meet again in January 1968 to discuss in more detail their programme of action, their organisational structure, and the services they provided.

However the most practical way in which the centres did keep in touch with each other's activities was through the weekly newsheet of the Notting Hill People's Association started in January 1969. The decision to start the newsheet, *People's News* was made at a joint meeting of the centres in December 1968. It was agreed that representatives of the People's Centre, the Powis Playgroups, the 1-9 Colville Gardens Action Committee, the Lancaster Centre, and the Powis Square committee would come together to put out *People's News* for an eight week trial run. From January 1969 through to the middle of 1973 *People's News* came out weekly, with special issues on housing, claimants and play issues whenever they were needed by a working group. Every Sunday night people would get together and pool the actions of the week, write and type out the stories ready for printing and distribution first thing Monday morning. Between 300 and 500 issues were printed each week and distributed in bundles of half a dozen or so, to members of all the different working groups in both centres for them to sell in their street or to their contacts. Street selling was also carried out as a back-up to any street exhibition or demonstration.

People's News was invaluable as a way of keeping people in touch even when they missed the regular centre or working group meetings, and it provided an immediate and simple way of introducing people new to the centres to the kind of activities which were going on. Not only did it cover activities of the People's Association groups, but also explained what the Council was up to, it leaked confidential information and made public all kinds of facts which it was important for people to know if they were to have a chance to challenge those things which were not in their interests. *Peoples's News* produced libel suits and fear and angry tirades from individuals whose trickery was exposed in it, but it was read avidly and passed around. People would buy it and scan its two sides immediately to get an immediate idea of what were the issues of the week. It was simple enough to produce and quick enough to read never to become too much of an end itself, but to remain much more as a reflection or an impression of all the events of the week which were seen as important from the People's Association's perspective.

People's News cost 1p and throughout its life never made a loss. It even managed to make enough money from the weekly sales to subsidise the special issues, so that they could then be sold below cost.

However *People's News* could never have developed so easily and rapidly without the Notting Hill Press.

Notting Hill Press

The Press was set up by two members of the People's Centre in consultation with all the local groups in October 1968. From that time on the Press has made good quality cheap printing accessible to all the working groups of the People's Association and to all other local groups (barring right wing groups that is). Not only has this helped communication between groups, but it also increased the confidence of groups in their ability to present their challenges to and attacks on the authorities in a clear and forceful way.

The Press was set up by Beryl Foster and Linda Gane who had given up their nurses training and learned to print on an offset litho machine on a short training course. They found free premises in a basement of a Toc H hostel in the area, and bought the basic equipment: the offset litho machine and a platemaker and formed a company limited by guarantee.

The directors of the Press were representatives nominated by the Lancaster Centre, the People's Centre and the Notting Hill Community Workshop. Other groups were contacted, including black groups, but they did not want to take on the commitment involved. The machines were brought by Beryl and Linda with borrowed money and then given away to each of the groups represented on the Board of Directors, these groups in turn leasing them back to the Notting Hill Press at a peppercorn rent. This meant that if the Press later encountered financial difficulties (as it did) it would have no assets to be seized and the Press could continue to service the groups in the area under a different name and with different workers.

Beryl and Linda worked for nothing till a reputation and custom was built up and until the loans were paid off. Charges were then fixed to cover overheads, paper and printing costs including wages for the two workers at £10 a week, but no profits. In this way the printing costs for local groups were kept as low as possible. In addition to providing a low cost printing service, the Press workers were involved in most local struggles and activities, and the Press functioned as a local coffee house where everyone dropped in both to get their printing done and to meet and discuss. Through their involvement in local activities, the Press workers were able to encourage local groups to use the Press and to show them how to prepare the artwork. In this way many local groups came to see printed material as something they could control and use to counter the mass of printed material normally controlled by the authorities. It is because of the importance of the Press in facilitating communications between the centres, other groups and the authorities, that some of the practical details of how the Press was established have been explained.

Links between the People's Association and other groups

For long periods in the life of both centres of the People's Association there were members of both the Labour Party and Communist Party involved. The Labour Party members never tried to push a Labour Party strategy as such and took part in the activities in the main because they saw it as a more relevant or at least equally relevant sort of work to the routine electioneering which went on within the local Party. One member who was involved in the People's Centre tried to argue that the local Labour Party was the political wing of the People's Association but this never won much support from the rest of the Centre.

Members of the Communist Party were involved in the People's Centre because they recognised its value as a broad forum for all left wing people, and saw the work done in the centre as one, very valid level of class struggle, in addition to the parliamentary and industrial level.

The Fulham branch of the International Socialists made a number of forays into the People's Centre but made little impact, and did very little work with the Centre between meetings. The Paddington branch only showed interest in mid 1973 after the night of the lock-in, May 8th, when they were holding a branch meeting a hundred yards from All Saints Church Hall.* They noticed a lot of police about but continued with their meeting oblivious of the political event going on but a stone's throw away. It was in the aftermath of the lock-in, when an attempt was made to call together all left wing groups in the area to challenge the Council's refusal to shift their housing policy, that IS members started coming to a few meetings in North Kensington. However, their emphasis on industrial work led them to see many of the activists, who did not work full-time for a wage, as marginals and irrelevant to the real struggle for socialism.

---

*See Ch.8 for explanation of the 'lock-in'.

Mutual support links between the centres and other working class groupings were limited to a large extent by the absence of a strong network of trade union branches in North Kensington, which was a function of the virtual absence of any industry in the area. The main type of workers in the area were in services of one kind or another. The Trades Council covering the area met in Hammersmith where most of its members come from and work, and where most of its activities are focussed. However despite all these limitations, links were built, though they were tenuous and sporadic.

At the beginning of the squatting in Notting Hill in January 1969 a message of support was received by the Notting Hill Squatters from the Cricklewood Branch of the Amalgamated Engineering Union. They had passed a resolution that "this Branch congratulates the Notting Hill Squatters on their efforts to find and make homes in property that has long been empty. We call on the membership to support such actions and request the Executive Committee to raise with AEU MP's the question of pursuing an Act so that rates be paid on empty property."

In April 1969 a systematic effort was made by one of the active trade unionists in the Notting Hill Squatters to involve all other local trade unionists in the housing march in May. The letter asked each branch for its members to turn up on the march with their banners and to give financial support, and ended up with the declaration:

> "Our fight is for a decent home for every family. We see this as a parallel struggle to that of Trade Union recognition, better pay and conditions."

There was little union response except for the National Union of Railwaymen whose members were represented on the march and read out a statement of support from their branch.

The first instance of mutual support between the People's Centre and the dustmen was in October 1969 when the Centre organised a petition in support of their wage claim. In November 1970 this link was reinforced by a march in support of the dustmen's claim and the lower paid generally, organised by the People's Centre, the Claimants Union, the Lancaster Centre and the Communist Party. "People's News" carried regular reports in support of the dustmen's struggle for more pay in contrast to the other local papers which consistently attacked the dustmen and tried to stir up opinion against them. When the Housing Group of the People's Association was involved in the squat of Merle Major in May 1971, in an attempt to force the Council to get tough on bad landlords and take over their houses, the dustmen, alone among trade unionists, offered real support and volunteered to man the barricades if the Council attempted an eviction.

When the postmen went on strike in January 1971, the centre page spread of a *People's News* special was offered to them to explain their position. They took up the offer and links were sustained from that time on, mainly by the Claimants Union who helped single postmen claim emergency payments from Social Security collectively, and also by Powis Playgroups who took the children of striking postmen free.

A strong link was established between the Housing Group of the People's Association and the building workers in September 1972, when the building workers went on strike. After stopping work on all the major new building sites the building workers were keen to stop work on the private speculative rehabilitation schemes. They approached the Housing Group for lists of suitable properties where work should be stopped. Once furnished with lists of properties the building workers' intervention proved effective, and private speculative conversion schemes which the Housing Group had been keen to put a stop to, ground to a halt till the building workers' dispute was settled.

In March 1973 when the hospital workers went on strike a Notting Hill Support Group was formed, with the aim of raising funds for the strike fund and in drawing in extra support for the pickets.

So, few as they were, there were occasions when the community/industry/public services barriers were breached and working people recognised they shared common interests and both needed and gave mutual support.

Chapter 6

Planning, Play and Motorway Space

The struggles which involved both centres of the Notting Hill People's Association were aimed at forcing the local authorities to carry out their planning policies in a socially responsible way, and at forcing them to have policies and spend money in areas which they had never thought about, like play schemes and the development of the space under the motorway.

Whereas the two planning struggles, in Camelford and Walmer Road, reached a climax which resolved the issue in 1969 and 1970, the struggles over play and the motorway space went steadily on over the whole period from 1966 to the early 1970s. In both cases the Council was forced to respond and so-called independent, charitable organisations were set up: the Play Association in 1970 and the North Kensington Amenity Trust in 1971, within which the struggle has been continued for more resources and more local control.

Struggles Against Bad Planning

The people of two streets, Camelford Road and Walmer Road, challenged the way the Council was implementing its planning decisions without any concern or understanding as to the effect they were having on the lives of the people involved. The aim of both streets' struggles was to force the Council to carry out its rehousing and motorway building schemes in a more publicly accountable and socially responsible way.

Camelford Road

The first of these was focussed on Camelford Road, a street in the Lancaster Road West redevelopment area.

It was at a public meeting on the redevelopment scheme, in July 1967, that the people of Camelford Road first made their anger felt. Their anger was focussed on the remoteness of the plans from the needs of people like them. For example there was to be one nursery in the scheme for 50 children. There were over that number of children in their street alone. Members of the Lancaster Centre went down and talked with them the next day. However it was not till the spring of 1968 that half a dozen members of the Centre went down to Camelford Road again with the aim that a campaign should be waged to involve the whole street in a protest against the dreadful conditions its tenants were forced to endure.

The first street meeting was held in mid-July 1968 and at this a street committee of five was elected, and the priorities of the street were decided: rehousing for all in the worst conditions before the official date of 1973. It was decided to hold another street meeting, but this time with tables, and typewriters in the street so that a start could be made in drawing up the list of all in need of priority rehousing, and of all the repairs which had to be done.

The street committee had agreed on a plan of sending a letter of complaint from each tenant in Camelford Road to the Town Hall, listing the repairs outstanding and the urgency of rehousing, and demanding action by the Council as soon as possible. This was backed up by a centre page spread in the local newspaper featuring the conditions in Camelford Road. Council investigations followed and some repairs were carried out as a result of Council pressure on landlords, though no mention was made of speeding up the rehousing.

Early in January 1969 the Council held a public meeting to explain the redevelopment scheme to the people of the area. In advance of the meeting the news had been leaked through *People's News* that the rehousing of people in Camelford Road had been put off until 1975 as a result of the street having been shifted from Phase 3 to Phase 5 of the redevelopment scheme. Spurred by this news as well as by her own appalling housing conditions, one of the tenants of Camelford Road, Maggie O'Shannon, decided to squat with her family in No.7 Camelford Road — the best house in the street and empty for nearly a year.

Maggie describes the factors which led to her decision to squat — firstly her housing conditions:

> "The lavatory from the flat above flushed straight into the kitchen. There was sometimes three inches of sewage in the place. The house produced £20 a week rent, but there were no repairs done. The agent said he couldn't do any without a letter from the landlord and he lived in the south of France. Why should he bother? If we didn't pay the rent the next tenant would ... "

Maggie was right. Soon after she moved out to squat she discovered her old basement had been let to a West Indian woman and four children with no repairs done at almost double the rent. She goes on to explain how, over the months at the beginning of 1968, people from the Centre started coming into the street and talking with the tenants.

"I began to ask myself, why should I live like this? The Council was no help at all. The Chairman of the Housing Committee is a woman called Shelagh Roberts, a working class Tory. She has our lives in her hands. We're pleading with her to help us, to give our children somewhere to live. In August 1968 I noticed that the house across the way was empty and had been a long time. I said to myself, I'll squat in it.

"The real decider came when I asked Miss Shelagh Roberts when I could move out of my basement and she said it would not be for at least another five years. I then approached the People's Association and asked them if they would help me move into No.7.

"For three weeks we prepared — we had to get stocks of coal and food in, arrange for electricity from another house, water, guards and the rest of it. Everyone in the neighbourhood knew, but nobody told. I moved in at 8am one morning in January and by 8.05 all my things were across and the house barricaded."

Maggie did not know who owned the house when she moved in but by a piece of political luck it turned out to belong to the Greater London Council, the very authority which had the responsibility for rehousing the street. She had picked a perfect pawn in the bargaining game. Within a week she was joined by another woman and her family, Bridie Matthews, and together they put out a Squatters Charter on January 24th 1969 to make their demands clear to the authorities:

"We see our act as the first step in a fight for better conditions for all the people of Camelford Road and the Lancaster Road (West) Redevelopment area. If we are allowed to remain in No.7 we are prepared to be the last families to be re-housed from Camelford Road."

The Charter went on to demand permanent tenancies for both their families and the immediate delivery of full information on the phasing of the redevelopment and the time of rehousing, to every tenant in the area, including a guarantee that everyone who wished would be rehoused in North Kensington.

Huge white letters were painted on the street outside the house 'This is Maggie's and Bridie's house. Defend it.' Frequent street meetings were held with Maggie addressing the crowd on the street through a loud hailer from the top window of her new home. She ended one of her speeches with the following words:

"When they do come to evict us, they'll have as big a fight as we do to get a Council house — and you know how hard that is."

Many of the tenants from Camelford Road joined with Maggie and Bridie in a visit to the Kensington Council meeting at the end of January. They felt it was important that the Council should be made to feel what it was like to live in Camelford Road. They collected choice pickings from the rot of Camelford Road:

- a jar of rain water which had fallen in 15 minutes through the ceiling of a bedroom;
- a large piece of paper from a kitchen ceiling sodden with overflow from the toilet above;
- wallpaper which had fallen off a bedroom wall because of damp.

All these, well labelled, were banged down onto the highly polished tables where the Councillors sat. This alone, together with Maggie's speech, was enough for the order to clear the Chamber to be given and the Mayor, mace and Councillors began to beat a hasty retreat. On the way out the largest parcel of all, a stinking parcel of old rubbish which had been left by the Council outside a basement flat where five children had recently moved in was presented to the porter labelled "For the Mayor" and the group left the Town Hall shouting, "We'll be back".

As she was being hustled out, Maggie retorted: "What do you mean, leave. These are the people you should ask to leave" she continued, pointing to the crowd of Councillors rapidly withdrawing from the Chamber because one of the citizens of the Royal Borough had raised her voice in a Council meeting and had actually presented material evidence of the rotting conditions of parts of the Royal Borough.

Early in February the first official response was made by the Chairman of the GLC Housing Committee:

> "The property is owned by the GLC but held by the ILEA. It has been represented as unfit for human habitation by the Royal Borough and is included in a confirmed CPO made by the Borough. It is expected that the site will be required by the ILEA for the rebuilding of a primary school . . . in the meantime the premises must be cleared as soon as possible . . . "

However on March 5th Maggie had a GLC rent book shoved through the letter box, for the rent of the whole house, together with a statement from the GLC that they could stay in No.7 which though technically unfit was better than their previous homes.

Maggie's response to this was firm:

> "The struggle was for Camelford Road. This statement just sorts out the squatters and makes no mention of the road. Neither Mrs Matthews nor I would be happy with getting a tenancy here and forgetting the rest of the street."

A few days after getting the rent book Maggie and Bridie were out organising another street meeting in Camelford Road about how to mount pressure for the whole of the street to be rehoused within the year by the GLC. It was agreed to draw up a petition signed by every tenant in the street as a first step.

However by March 23rd the fight had been won. The GLC announced that rehousing would begin in Camelford Road and the adjacent streets in a few months, but would probably take a year to complete. No distinction was to be made about the rehousing of furnished or unfurnished tenants. On the 1st June the first three families moved out, and by the end of 1970 only one family was left. The O'Sullivans, a family with 12 children, seemed to have been forgotten. Maggie and Bridie rushed back to the area and gave a seven day ultimatum to the authorities. If the family was not rehoused by then they would be forced to consider direct action again. The O'Sullivans were rehoused within the week.

So, effective action was taken by the people of Camelford Road to force the authorities to speed up their rehousing and that of the people in the neighbouring streets by five years. However in forcing this the people inevitably destroyed their own organising network and were scattered to Council housing estates throughout London. Small groups of tenants did manage to get rehoused together but a friendship rather than an organising network was sustained.

Walmer Road

In Walmer Road the struggle was to force the council to recognise the need for the rehousing of the people living in the houses in Walmer Road and three adjoining streets which faced onto Westway the elevated motorway section of the Western Avenue Extension. This meant constant traffic noise and the glare of headlights all night.

On July 19th 1970 the local Council, the Royal Borough of Kensington and Chelsea, had shown their recognition of the need for a limited amount of rehousing in a press statement they issued, urging the Greater London Council, who had built the motorway, to compulsory purchase all the houses which faced the motorway in another street, Acklam Road and just eight of the houses in Walmer Road. Before this in January 1970 the Kensington Council had approved the setting aside of £200,000 so that they could buy and demolish Acklam Road if the GLC refused. In response to local pressure from the people of Acklam Road and the Council, the GLC announced on July 14th 1970 that they would rehouse the tenants from Acklam Road and from just eight of the houses in Walmer Road, ignoring the other houses in Walmer Road and in the three adjoining streets. So while the tenants of Acklam Road were planning a street party to celebrate the victory, the tenants in Walmer Road were angrily planning disruptive direct action. They had started off by organising a petition to the GLC in mid-July, signed by all who were demanding rehousing in three months. However this was obviously not enough to establish their case with the authorities. After four street meetings in two weeks the decision was taken to disrupt the opening of Westway on July 28th.

A convoy of lorries, vans and cars full of 100 children and adults surprised the security forces controlling access to the motorway in the morning of the official opening, by driving *up* the exit slip roads onto the new motorway. Bewildered policemen just raised their hands in horror as they watched the motley parade gaining access so easily to the precious motorway. On the convoy drove along the new road, towards the place of the ribbon cutting ceremony. Once the white ribbon came into sight, the vehicles stopped and disgorged the angry demonstrators who surged towards the white ribbon just as the official party was arriving and presented a petition demanding an immediate meeting to discuss their rehousing. George Clark, who had been invited to the official opening reception representing the tenants of Acklam Road, tried to welcome the demonstration as his followers. But the people from Walmer Road would have none of that, since only the day before the tenants from Acklam Road had refused to help them in their struggle, once their own fight for rehousing was won. Amidst angry shouting the ribbon was cut, but the people of Walmer Road had not finished. After the representative of the Minister of Transport had made polite noises about visiting Walmer Road in the near future to see what conditions were like, the Walmer Road tenants issued an ultimatum to the authorities that unless a meeting to discuss the future of Walmer Road was fixed up by August 7th — in four days time — plans to disrupt the traffic on Westway would proceed. In the absence of any official response, the second demonstration took place on August 9th on the motorway while traffic was running. Over 60 people got out of cars onto the hard shoulder of the motorway and filed back slowly carrying banners and shouting for the rehousing of Walmer Road. They lined up on the shoulder of the motorway above their homes while a meeting was organised in the street below.

After 20 minutes police arrived in force and the demonstrators were slowly escorted right along the motorway to the nearest exit after which they marched back to Walmer Road to join the street meeting, chanting and shouting. Four people were arrested for obstruction but the Magistrate in court the next day imposed token fines of £1 and expressed sympathy for the cause of the demonstration. However while the people were being arrested and the demonstration was going on, down the road in Acklam Road George Clark was staging a pray-in thanksgiving for the rehousing of Acklam Road!

Acklam Road had again been asked to join in the demonstration but again they decided against it, under the guidance of George Clark. At a street meeting in Walmer Road after the demonstration accusations of treachery were made against George Clark. After using the publicity gained from tne Walmer Road tenants demonstration on July 28th to successfully argue for urgency in Acklam Road, he denounced the plans for a second demonstration to the press as "bloody minded", "jumping on the bandwagon" and "for the wrong cause and with the wrong objective". The feeling of betrayal was expressed at the street meeting when one tenant propped a placard on his car saying "Only one man could live in this hell-hole – George Clark, the devil himself".

Throughout August both the GLC and Kensington Council refused the Walmer Road tenants' request for a meeting. After three weeks of being ignored the tenants decided it was time to force a meeting and to go down to County Hall en masse. *People's News* reports:

> "The corridors of power trembled a little last Friday when a deputation of 25 tenants from the Walmer Road area called at County Hall. They walked up to the teak-panelled executive suite on the first floor and asked for a word with the Director General. A polite but firm refusal to be ushered back the way they had come brought the Chief Security Officer offering his every assistance."[1]

The tenants stood their ground till they were offered a meeting with a member of the GLC Housing Committee, and out of this a meeting was fixed up with the Chairman of the Housing Committee for September 4th.

At the meeting on September 4th, the Housing Chairman told the 30 tenants who came to the meeting that all the houses in Walmer Road and the adjoining streets were already the subject of a compulsory purchase procedure started by the GLC. Rehousing was promised within 12 months if landlords agreed to sell before the CPO came into force. So they had won the first round. What remained was to speed up the rehousing as much as possible, by pressuring landlords to sell in order to avoid having to do the repairs themselves.

By December 1971 the CPO was confirmed and most of the people living in Walmer Road and the adjoining three streets rehoused. The issue of the people's need for rehousing was fought and established but just as in Camelford Road, the winning of earlier rehousing meant the destruction of street organisation, so in Walmer Road the winning of the right to rehousing meant the end of street organisation there too. This raises very fundamental questions about the potential of redevelopment areas as a base for class organisation.

The Struggle to Play

From 1967 through to 1970, the People's Association fought a battle to force the Council to recognise the need for properly resourced play provision in the area. Every kind of weaponry was used: illegal break-ins to private garden squares, the organising and manning of play sites, and the building up of a coalition of organisations in the area committed to expanding play provision. The Council's response was to set up the Play Association in 1970, a theoretically independent, charitable organisation from which it tried, unsuccessfully to exclude all the groups which had been involved in play organising in the area up to that time. Just as the housing struggles forced money from the Council's coffers, so did the struggles in play. Whereas the Council had got away with £5 for play in 1967, it was spending over £26,000 a year out of its own money by 1973.

Before 1967 the only voluntary organisation providing play facilities in the area was the Notting Hill Adventure Playground. This had been founded in 1960 in response to the race riots, on the initiative of Lady Allen of Hurtwood and a group of public spirited local residents. Charitable money was raised for the construction of purpose-built indoor and outdoor facilties.

Summer Play Programmes

It was in April 1967 that the Summer Project Planning Committee started meeting and one of the members, Ilys Booker, was determined that play should be an important part of the Project. She was working as the community worker with the North Kensington Family Study, and was convinced that something could be done about increasing play provision. A list of all available sites was drawn up and the possibilities of play sites for use that summer were narrowed down to Lonsdale Road playstreet and a building site in Oxford Gardens. Two paid playleaders were appointed to each site together with a team of volunteers. The play programme of the 1967 Summer Project set the pattern for the play programmes in all the following years. Play sites were picked by local groups, volunteers drafted in from both inside and outside the area and the money raised wherever possible.

In 1968 far more sites were run, in three play streets, two garden squares and in six bays under the elevated motorway.

"By 1968 the pattern of the organisation of play provision in North Kensington was fairly clear to see. Much effort, idealism and planning was put into the temporary summer schemes with the aim of inducing the immediately local people to take over their particular play facility, continue running it, if possible expanding it to permanence."[2]

Every year the number of locally controlled play sites increased and the network of people involved in running play schemes expanded. However, in the Colville area especially, where the People's Centre was based, the running of the play sites was bound up with the struggles on every other front — housing, traffic, the police.

In 1969 the play programme expanded to even more sites and paid leaders and the total budget doubled from £2,500 in 1968 to £5,000.

"By 1969 the play programme had extended itself to the limits of viability for an organisation built around temporary play provision. It was still very much part of a political movement based on local self-management through direct action, but many of the aims of this movement were becoming buried in the undergrowth of practical, pressing day-to-day tasks of running play facilities."[3]

By this time the running of summer play programmes by an ad hoc voluntary body with no permanent staff or guaranteed resources, had served its purpose. The programmes had shown the Council and the people of the area what the possibilities of play were if the resources were made available. The local groups had also proved they were able to take on the responsibility of running sites and selecting play leaders, if the resources were provided.

The Politics of Play

It was because play was seen as just one of the battle fronts of struggle in the area that people found the energy for the taxing and often routine responsibilities involved with running play sites. An important element which had sustained these play activities was the ideological impetus from events like the seizure of Powis Square. It is worth looking at the events around Powis Square over the years to get an idea of the interaction of play and other struggles.

Powis Square was a privately owned garden square in the centre of the Colville area. It had been locked up for years and the weeds were over three foot high. In the early 1960s it had been up for sale, and the estate agent's advertisement read:

> "Powis Square Ornamental Gardens. Privately owned Garden Square free from all rights of entry, possibly the only one in Central London. Half an acre at present derelict. Unique opportunity for sports club. No building allowed beyond changing rooms."

As early as 1961 the Colville and Powis Residents Association had called for Powis Square to be opened up to the public. In response the owner offered its use for rent of £500 a year which the Association set about raising. However the owner promptly raised the rent to £2,000 a year and the Association gave up.

In 1964 the Young Communists had organised a petition signed by more than 300 people asking the Council to buy the square. The Town Clerk's response was that he thought it would be unsuitable for use as a public open space. New private owners bought the square and the policy of exclusive neglect continued.

In 1967 when the Summer Project Committee had been clearing the use of Lonsdale Road play street with the local police, the Chief Superintendent had advised using Powis Square instead of the inadequate space of the play street. However independently of this helpful suggestion the People's Centre decided to put pressure on the Council to buy the square so that it could be opened up to the public. The petition, the picketing of the owners house and the symbolic play-in one rainy Saturday morning, have all been described as part of the early history of the People's Association. The Council response was clear — they deferred any decision about buying the square till January 1969 "in the light of the need for nationwide economies."

By the time the 1968 play programme was in progress Powis Square was already the focus of the People's Centre activity again. At a public meeting called by the Centre in May, the idea of more direct action on Powis Square was put forward. A new group had come into the Centre, the Vietnam Solidarity Campaign, and they were convinced that all conventional channels had been tried by the Centre and that more direct action was needed. So while other members of the Centre picketed and lobbied the Council over the buying of Powis Square, the VSC spent the week advertising what they called "a free party in Powis Square" on Saturday May 25th. That same morning a child was hurt in a road accident in Colville Gardens, a vigil was organised in the street and the bells of All Saints Church tolled to mark the accident. The vigil turned into an angry march of children and adults circling around the closed garden squares. It was as this was going on that the VSC came on the scene and marched on the square supported by a pantomime donkey and a gorilla! As they advanced they were met by a large body of police, angry scuffles followed and eight arrests were made. The party was not held in the square but tragic emphasis was added to the whole day's events when another child was knocked down two days later. A week later 600 mothers and children marched from North Kensington to the Town Hall chanting 'Open the Squares'.

Then on Saturday June 15th the VSC came back for another attack. They held a public meeting outside the locked gates, and called on all residents to join with them in opening the square for the people. Then they moved forwards, past the immobile policemen, and forcibly pulled down the fences which surrounded the square. In a few minutes the square was filled with jubilant demonstrators and children, though many parents held back more hesitantly. During the next few days the square was filled with people at all times of day and night. Opponents of the opening exercised their dogs. The People's Association issued a statement disassociating themselves from the methods used by the VSC without the active support and involvement of local residents. However at the next meeting of the People's Centre, the Powis Square Committee was set up to concentrate on working out the best way in which the square should be laid out and used, and to continue to pressure the Council to buy. This committee organised the clearing up of rubbish on the square and started organising painting and games for the children.

Then barely three weeks after the fences were torn down, on July 9th the Council announced that,

"agreement had been reached with the owners. Preparations are in hand to convert the square into a playspace for children."

At a victory celebration in the square bunting fluttered above a large banner proclaiming:

"At last the square belongs to the people. The Council have learned a simple lesson from the local people and children. The Council is the servant of the Community."

However this was in many ways just the beginning of a long struggle to force the Council to provide enough money for the square to be properly resourced with playleaders, equipment and proper maintenance — a struggle which was still going on into 1974.

The Council made obvious their instinctive response to becoming the owners of an open space in North Kensington. Within three weeks of announcing they had bought the square they sent the steamrollers in to make the square conform to what they understood by a playground — a rectangle of tarmac with 12 foot fencing surrounding it! But this was not what the square had been opened for. The steamrollers were turned back and the Chairman of the Public Amenities Committee was forced to appear on Powis Square in her pink feathered hat to meet the Powis Square Committee and to make her understand that people had not fought for the opening up of the square only to be pushed aside. They had ideas on how the square should be laid out, and were preparing plans which they would put to the Council. Having been forced to agree to this the Chairman withdrew, having fixed a date for a meeting with the Committee in two days time. At this meeting the Council agreed to abandon their tarmac and 12 foot fencing plans and to consider the detailed plan of the Powis Square Committee when it was ready, after the square had been used for the school holidays.

At a second meeting in November the Council agreed to spend £3,800 on five foot fencing around the square, a small area of coloured paving stones, and the building of a slide on the mound in the centre of the square. They agreed in principle to the need for a playleader and a play hut but said that would have to wait till the next financial year. The to-and-fro over plans for the layout of the square has gone on ever since, the Council stalling whenever the question of doing anything imaginative or costly was raised. After spending £6,272 on buying the square and £2,754 on the initial fencing and seats, the Council has got away with just over £100 a year up to 1970. Salaries for full-time playleaders and equipment have been paid for each year by the Play Association, which also raised a grant of over £10,000 from a local charity to build a play hut on the square. This grant was passed over to Playspace, the local play organisation. They raised an additional £4,000 and organised the building of the hut with a local builders cooperative set up to do the job. The hut was completed in the spring of 1975.

It would seem that whereas the violent action of the VSC compelled the Council to capitulate and buy the square, forcing a rapid shift in the situation, the task of generating adequate financing of the square by the Council has been a much more protracted up-hill struggle.

However, throughout the long struggle over Powis Square, the square itself has provided a public forum for all kinds of community events – for carnivals, for bonfire parties, for housing rallies, puppet shows and concerts, and so has always been seen and used as much more than a play area. The interaction between play and politics was not confined to Powis Square. Both the squares of Colville Gardens and Colville Square had to be fought for, and Colville Square was also won as a permanent public play area. Also in Moorhouse Road, another People's Centre site, the site itself was used as a forum for showing films and having meetings about the St. Stephens redevelopment area which surrounded it.

The Building up of a Play Coalition

The third prong of the play offensive consisted of the building up of a play coalition. A tentative start was made with the Play Programme committee of the Summer Project at the beginning of the summer of 1967, which did together the leader of the Adventure Playground, members of the North Kensington Playspace Group, working for the use of motorway land, and Ilys Booker, the community worker from the North Kensington Family Study.

However by the end of the summer it was felt that this group should be strengthened and given some permanence to ensure continuity. The decision was taken to set up a new subcommittee of the Notting Hill Social Council, a recognised charity, and to call it the Leisure and Amenities Committee. This committee agreed to coordinate a summer playscheme in 1968 and to give some continuity to the pressure for permanent and varied facilities for play. It also saw itself as coordinating schemes put forward by local groups, recruiting volunteers and raising funds to support these schemes. This committee was set up as a respectable front for the play programmes, guaranteeing charitable status to groups which worked through it – groups like the People's Centre, which never wanted to claim such status and would hardly have been recognised as charitable.

However by 1969 as already explained, the summer play programme had expanded to the limits of viability for an organisation built around temporary play provision, with no permanent staff or guaranteed resources. The alternatives were clear. The committee could reduce the scale of the play activities they organised, which was impossible since it was generally recognised that even the 1969 level of play provision was totally inadequate. The summer schemes needed to be expanded to all year schemes, and even more sites were still needed not less. The other possibility was for a permanent play administration to be set up to service and expand the play network. The Leisure and Amenities Committee recognised these alternatives and met to discuss a paper in December 1969 which stated that either the Committee should cease to meet or else it should take its job far more seriously. It should become more of a representative body drawing members from all the local groups involved in play, and should have a full time worker to generate activities. But to suggest a permanent play administration raised the questions of who was to pay for it and who was to control it.

So far the cost of the play programmes had been financed from charities, the Inner London Education Authority, and the Kensington Council.

The total income increased from £5 in 1967 to £2,500 in 1968 and £5,000 in 1969.

The possibility of charitable money was decreasing. As one of the charity experts on the Social Council said, "Notting Hill is suffering from a backlash because we have had so much money for so long from the charities." ILEA could be approached for an expansion of play leaders salaries but could not reasonably be expected to pay the cost of a permanent administration. This left the Borough Council, who had already embarked on preparing a new strategy of response to what they saw as the threat of play being organised by politically motivated popular groups.

"The real opposition is not between alternative rational means of organising play provision, but between the different ideologies, moralities, ambitions, strategies and tactical styles of the two Kensington communities, as they are played out in that charitable buffer zone which has for so long protected the rich and cheated the poor. Now a situation had arisen where the buffer zone had been occupied and used as a strike base by the agents of the poorer community. This constituted a real threat to the power and security of the otherwise impregnable Council establishment. Their hitherto successful strategy of control by neglect no longer worked, and only some kind of direct counter-action could now control the plague of anarchy and revolution which they imagined to be sweeping over the north of the borough."[4]

This is the interpretation of Bob Marsden who has written a history of the Play Association, but he admits the difficulty of plumbing the depths of the Council's mind. He explains that by the end of 1969,

"The working party which recommended the setting up of the Play Association had already completed most of its labours. Its proceedings were confidential and are not available to the researcher, which invites the inference that it contained politically sensitive material, in particular the real rationale for the organisational form which it laid down for the new Play Association in the draft constitution (November 4th 1969). This ensured that
1. the Council, through the statutory identity of the Borough Treasurer and the Town Clerk with the Association's Treasurer and Secretary, could both monitor and to some extent control all financial transactions within the Assocation.
2. the determining policy was in the hands of the Council's members or its agents i.e. 'good' charity buffer zone people.
3. existing 'bad' i.e. people's movement controlled groups, were excluded from founder membership."

The Council rationalised the very limited consultation in terms of the urgent need for immediate action, and argued that every play organisation in the Borough could not be on the Management Council as this would produce an unwieldy body. It was obviously far easier to select only the trusted middle-of-the-road, non-political groups, like the Adventure Playground for consultation and for positions on the Management Council. The Notting Hill Social Council was also invited to nominate a representative to the working party to set up the Play Association but when they let the Council know that their nominee would be John O'Malley, the Chairman of the Leisure and Amenities Committee, the Council withdrew the invitation since he would be unacceptable!

The inaugural meeting of the Play Association took place on January 28th 1970 and the minutes give an image of what Bob Marsden describes as a "sincere, enlightened, efficient, responsible, democratic, charitable, much-needed body determined to better the lot of the Borough's children . . . " But this image of earnest endeavour is strangely at odds with the coverage given in *People's News*.

> "The Kensington and Chelsea Play Association will be launched this Wednesday in the midst of bad feeling from Notting Hill. Although the new association will be open to all interested in its aims, it will in fact be run by a management committee of 20 with only two people elected from its membership. The other places will be filled by five councillors, two representatives from the Adventure Playground and representatives from a dozen other groups. Groups missed out of the organisation from the outset include the People's Centre, Interaction and the Motorway Development Trust, even though they have played a major part in the development of play facilities over the last years. The suggested constitution rules out these groups being admitted to the management committee at a later stage. Letters protesting at the manner of the Association's formation have been written to the Council by a number of local organisations."[5]

At the inaugural meeting the Council was forced to include the deliberately excluded groups on the Management Council and the proposal was accepted that the People's Centre, Interaction and the Motorway Development Trust be added to the Management Council. *People's News* summed up the rest of the meeting, focussing on the issue which was to dog the Play Association for the years to come:

> "An ominous note was struck in Sir Malby Crofton's speech when he suggested that it was no bad thing to work with the community particularly if it saved the ratepayers a bit of money. Kensington's contribution to play is now £7,500, Camden's over £100,000. Any new play organisation will be stymied if the funds are not forthcoming to build up a proper system of permanent play provision throughout the area."[6]

The Play Association in 1974

By early 1974 the Play Association had been in existence for four years and had expanded the network of play provision pioneered by the Summer Play Programmes since 1967. Two new permanent adventure playgrounds had been set up in North Kensington, one under the motorway at Acklam Road and the other further north at Emslie Horniman's Pleasance in Kensal. As for the temporary schemes, seven summer schemes were run in North Kensington of which two were extended into six month schemes, and over the Easter holidays there were four projects in the area. A Sports Organiser and a preschool playgroups organiser were added to the existing full time staff of Administrator, Play Promoter, Assistant Administrator and mini-van driver.

All this, together with the play schemes in Chelsea, cost a total of around £40,000 of which just over £26,000 came from the Borough Council in 1973, and just over £8,000 each from ILEA and charities. Income totalled around £45,000. This was certainly an increase on the £5 spent on play by the Council in 1967. However still in 1974 money was the basic constraint.

When the Play Association was initially set up it looked as if the Council was going to try and constrain the operation of the Play Association by limiting the access of potentially demanding, radical local groups. But once the Council was made to yield to pressure to include these groups at the first meeting, the balance of control of the Management Council of the Play Association has progressively shifted more and more in favour of local groups, till in 1974 there were 19 representatives of local groups, two member representatives and five coopted members as against five Council representatives.

This has revealed what is in fact the basic constraint on the operations of the Play Association — money. Since the charitable sources are limited, the Play Association has to rely primarily on Borough Council financing, so despite the Association's independent, charitable status, it remains under Council budgetary control. This meant that once the Council put a block on any real expansion of the budget in 1974 the work of the Play Association was automatically restricted to the continuation of existing schemes with no further expansion at all. Consolidation and quality of provision became the focus of discussion.

In this context the Play Promoter, the main employee of the Play Association, has chosen to operate as a buffer between the Council and the local groups rather than as a political organiser to mobilise pressure to release the additional funds to make play promotion a real possibility. Local groups attempted to challenge the Council blockage of play expansion with a rally outside the Town Hall in April 1974 — but this was the first locally based political action in play since the marches for playspace and the activity to open Powis Square in the late 1960s.

The Struggle to Control the Motorway Space

In February 1971, the Council set up the North Kensington Amenity Trust, a charitable organisation, to run the space underneath the elevated Westway motorway, for the benefit of the local community.

In 1966, the houses along the route of Westway were demolished leaving a wasteland 2½ miles long and covering 23 acres, cutting through North Kensington. There were no firm plans to use the ground level space beneath the motorway for anything except possibly car parks and warehouses. The setting up of the Amenity Trust was the Kensington Council's response to over four years of sustained pressure from the North Kensington Playspace Group, renamed the Motorway Development Trust in November 1968.

This group was involved in three types of activity of which the most time-consuming was sustained lobbying. This involved confronting the responsible authorities with ideas for the use of the space which they had never considered, and with better prepared plans than those of the official planners. This lobbying was combined with the organisation of play schemes to demonstrate the potential of the space under the motorway, first in the summer of 1966 on the Acklam Road playground and then from 1968 onwards in Summer Play Programmes using different sections of the motorway space. Backing up both these was a coalition of local groups which was built up and kept informed, so that when public pressure was necessary as an additional lever for the lobbying, it was forthcoming.

In the summer of 1966, one of the activities of the London Free School was to start an adventure playground on the site cleared for the building of the Westway motorway in Acklam Road. Steps were built down from the road to give children access and rough structures and swings were knocked together. After the summer a group, the North Kensington Playspace Group, was formed and continued to meet with the aim of consolidating the playground. Over the winter they got an architect to draw up plans for a permanent playground in Acklam Road and these plans were used as the initial weapon in confronting the authorities with the idea of using the space under the motorway. In January 1967, the plans were sent to the GLC who were responsible for the building of the road and also to the local Council.

However by January the North Kensington Playspace Group had expanded its horizons as a result of members arguing that it was not enough just to look at the Acklam Road land under the motorway. Since the motorway was to cut right through North Kensington all the 23 acres beneath it should be considered by the group. It was agreed, and the group went ahead immediately to raise the question of what use was planned for the motorway space with the authorities.

From the start Adam Ritchie and John O'Malley, the Chairman and Secretary of the group did the bulk of the lobbying. They developed an effective double act, one combining charm and simple directness, while the other really enjoyed hard bargaining. The early meetings were with the permanent officials of the GLC and the GLC representatives from Kensington and

Chelsea, but gradually more people were involved, including the GLC Councillors on the Highways Committee and the consultant engineers responsible for building the motorway. By February, it was clear that no one was certain about the use planned for the motorway space. While the Chairman of the GLC Highways Committee had a vague idea that the space was to be used for recreation, the engineers building it, believed the plans were to use it for warehousing and a car park. The maps in the GLC offices supported the engineers' view since they showed the motorway space coloured in red and labelled car parking. In July 1967, the North Kensington Playspace Group approached the local Council and the Chairman of the Kensington Planning Committee, the Town Clerk and the Planning Officer met with the Group. The Council was sympathetic to the Group's ideas and agreed to inform the GLC of their interest in working out a scheme to use the land for the community.

It was early in 1968 that things began to gain momentum. Continuous probings revealed that the GLC's claim to have planning permission to build a car park under the motorway was a lie. No decision had ever been taken. Yet despite this they had gone ahead to instruct the engineers to prepare the space for a car park with screen walls and small gaps for cars to enter. Once this was exposed work was held up on the motorway for six weeks. An important defence of the GLC had been stripped away so making them more vulnerable and open to other ideas for the use of the space. The Playspace Group followed this up in March 1968 by applying for outline planning permission themselves, for their scheme on the motorway space. Their scheme was for the land to be used for a wide range of amenities and services for the local community: general recreational space, community space, extension of living space and community service space. Having applied for planning permission, the Group seriously considered surcharging the GLC for starting to build car parks without planning permission.

Very soon after this the first joint meeting of both GLC and Kensington officials and Councillors with the Playspace Group was held. The Playspace Group came well prepared to the meeting. Not only had they conducted a survey back in June 1967 of all the needs of the groups in North Kensington for space under the motorway; they had also used the architectural skills of one of their members to bring all these different facilities together on a map so as to give some idea of the very real potential of the site as an integrated scheme. Drawings of what the scheme might look like together with a possible lay-out for the whole 2½ miles had been put together in the form of a well-designed brochure which was rushed to this meeting hot off the press. The brochure described the possibilities:

"The space should be designed to relate and integrate these activities: an adventure playground near a supermarket, so mothers can shop while their children play in safety out of reach of traffic, seats with fixed concrete chess tables near a pre-school playgroup, an exhibition wall of children's school paintings near an old age pensioners' club a Citizen's Advice Bureau near a Post Office, a self-service laundry near a mothers' club. These things must relate to each other as the whole scheme relates to the surrounding environment."

An impressive list of sponsors and supporters of the scheme was at the end of the brochure together with ideas for the way in which the users of the facilities could be involved in the control of the site through an independent non-profit development corporation. Dazzled by the clarity of the whole idea, the joint meeting agreed to set up a Joint Working Party involving the GLC, Kensington Council and the Playspace Group. There were to be two levels of meetings at member and officer level, with only the two members of the Playspace Group having the privilege of attending both meetings, being neither Council members nor officers. The aim of the Joint Working Party was to set out,

"to produce detailed planning proposals for developing the motorway site for recreational, social, educational and related community purposes."

The idea of the North Kensington Playspace Group was now officially accepted and an organisation launched to bring the scheme into being.

A press release was put out by the GLC in which the Kensington representative on the GLC declared enthusiastically,

"I am very pleased that, through the initiative of local voluntary effort, there is now every prospect that this section of the motorway may set the pattern for the imaginative use of the land around the elevated sections of our great new motorway network."

So within just over a year both Kensington Council and the GLC had been forced to shift their position over the motorway space and take up active involvement in working out an alternative scheme. This was the end of the first phase of intensive lobbying. The principle of using the motorway land for community uses was established and accepted, and an organisational framework was set up to develop the plans.

The second phase consisted of attending the three sets of Joint Working Party meetings from April through to November 1968, and in trying to force them to contact all organisations so that no group needing space would be excluded from the plans. The target date set for finalising plans for the use of the motorway land according to the Council was 1969, so that leases could be let in mid-1970. It seemed as if everything was moving fast.

However the atmosphere of momentum felt early in 1968 was short-lived. After the third meeting of the Joint Working Party in November, no more were called. The Playspace Group, sensing that the Council was dragging its feet, decided it was necessary to take steps to build up an organisation, a development trust, to run the motorway space. It was with this aim in mind, in November 1968, that the Playspace Group renamed themselves the Motorway Development Trust. They saw themselves as the temporary trustees of a critically important idea which needed to be developed if the motorway scheme was ever to become a reality.

They started by looking into possible constitutional forms, and then, in January 1969, a paper was produced on the kind or organisation which would be necessary. A non-profit corporation was suggested open to local users and members. The case was also made for the need for paid officers to administer, raise funds and to perform a community development function in the scheme. The Council was resistant to these ideas. In February 1969 the Town Clerk wrote to the Motorway Development Trust,

> "I am still not convinced that it would be necessary to have a director and full-time staff. Nor could I accept the view that my colleagues are inexperienced in large scale community development."

But despite this initial resistance the case for an organisation to run the scheme instead of just relying on the Council officers was established and in April, when the Joint Working Party was formally disbanded, a Steering Group was set up to prepare a constitution for this organisation. The Steering Group was made up of five members of the Council and two of the MDT, with an independent chairman.

It was in the arguments over the constitution of the new organisation that the determination of the Council to control the body was made clear. The Council wanted the best of both worlds. They wanted an independent charitable organisation to run the site so that charitable funds could be used instead of the ratepayers' money. But they did not want the new organisation to be too independent or else it would threaten the Council's authority in local government.

The first and only meeting of the Steering Group was in October 1969. The Council had prepared a draft constitution which stated that Council officers would take up the jobs of chief executive and finance officer of the organisation. The Management Committee would be made up of eight Councillors and four representatives of local organisations together with an independent chairman. The MDT representatives bargained hard to fight these points and shifts were won both at this meeting and over the months which followed. This resulted in the total number of the Trust Management Committee being increased to 15, including an independent chairman. Six would be Kensington and Chelsea Council members and one would be the Council's representative on the ILEA. The remaining seven would be representatives of voluntary groups in the area. Seven long established groups were to be approached for nominations, all groups "which one could envisage existing in 100 years time" as Crofton the Leader of the Council put it. These shifts were announced in a Council press release in May 1970 and were a result of bad publicity generated by the MDT in the press, and by important local charities threatening that no money would be forthcoming if the Trust was not independent of Council control. This was by no means the end of the argument over the constitution. The charities were still not happy about the power of veto the draft constitution gave the Council over all expenditure, the stipulation that the Town Clerk and the Borough Treasurer should be the Secretary and Treasurer of the Trust, about Kensington Council selection of the ILEA representative, or about the way in which the selection of seven representatives of local organisations was to be carried out. No meetings of the Steering Group were called to resolve or modify these points. Instead the Council operated in secret, and made those modifications it felt forced to.

Meanwhile the MDT tried to open up the whole affair as much as possible. In April 1970 they decided to explore the possibility of holding elections among all the local groups to select the seven local representatives. Thirty groups were invited to a meeting at the end of April and a second meeting was held in May. Around 20 groups sent delegates to both meetings. It was agreed that an open election should be organised to select representatives instead of the Council's plan to hand-pick 'responsible' organisations. However four of these organisations refused to go along with this strategy and agreed with the Council to be founder members. The four were the Headteachers, the Play Association, the North Kensington Community Centre and the Rowe Housing Trust. This left three positions free. The election was held in November 1970 and Adam Ritchie and John O'Malley from the MDT and Pat Smyth from the Golborne Neighbourhood Council were elected elected as the three representatives. However even by the end of 1970 the constitution was still not finalised.

Towards the end of 1970 the mood of local organisations was bitter, *People's News* echoes this mood well:

"Betrayal

Two and a half years ago the Borough Council, together with the GLC, the ILEA and the local MDT were party to a decision to develop the motorway space as a joint scheme involving the North Kensington community and the authorities. Since then the leaders of the Kensington Council have worked to keep control and to keep local people out of the decisions. The last joint meeting took place a year ago and since then all discussions have been directed by the Council's own Policy and Coordinating Committee. Although much has been done in North Kensington to get the space used by and for the people, the Council's present approach could kill the scheme at birth."[7]

By the time the North Kensington Amenity Trust was launched in the first week of February 1971 this feeling of bitterness and suspicion continued. *People's News* tells of

"The Birth of the Amenity Trust

Last Friday the North Kensington Amenity Trust was launched with a blast of hypocrisy surprising even for the Royal Borough. After refusing to invite many local organisations — including the MDT, who have co-ordinated the Motorway ideas for over four years — to the press conference and feast. to mark the setting up of the Trust, Sir Malby Crofton claimed that one of the objects was to build a bridge of practical cooperation between the Council and community groups in North Kensington.

"The Motorway scheme could cost £2½ million and depends on its financial success, and so on the goodwill and cash of Councils, industry and charity. Even after years of pressure it looks likely that the people nearby will miss out on this opportunity as well, and be given what their masters think is good for them."[8]

Alongside the lobbying and the building up of pressure for an independent organisation to run the space, the MDT was involved in running schemes under the motorway from 1966 onwards. As the North Kensington Playspace Group they had helped with the Acklam Road playground before the motorway was even built. From 1968 onwards the MDT took the initiative in organising summer play schemes using the motorway space, in the St Marks Road bays in 1968, in Acklam Road bays in 1969, and up Bramley Road in 1970. Help was given to the Acklam Road Adventure Playground to set up a permanent playground from July 1970 onwards. The negotiations conducted by the MDT in 1968, which resulted in the GLC agreeing to allow six bays to be used for the summer play scheme, were forced through by the MDT and this was an important breakthrough at that particular time. The Joint Working Party had just started meeting and different ideas of possible uses were being discussed. The play scheme in 1968 provided a real demonstration of what part of the reality of the overall scheme might be, and concretised the decision by the authorities to accept the principle of the idea of using the motorway space for community facilities.

The third part of the work of the MDT was the translation of all their back-room lobbying to the local groups so that popular pressure could make itself felt. The goals were too distant and the time scale too protracted for any larger, more popular group to have patience with the long drawn out negotiations. So the MDT performed the role of the middle man, conveying the gist of the positions reached in their negotiations whenever they thought it necessary.

Before drawing up their initial scheme to illustrate the possibilities of the motorway space, the North Kensington Playspace Group had produced a report in 1967, the *Chapman Report* which was based on the responses of all the local groups to the possibility of using land under the motorway. The land use scheme they then produced relied heavily on this report for indications of local needs. So from the start the North Kensington Playspace

Group did take the local people and the local organisations as their reference group.

In the weeks before the March 1968 meeting, when the authorities decided to take up the idea of using the space for community facilities, the Playspace Group had encouraged local people and groups to write in to the GLC and local Council opposing the car park plan and supporting the motorway scheme of the Playspace Group, and many groups responded. In December 1968 the MDT organised a public meeting to which representatives of the GLC and local Council were invited to speak, to explain the stage which the scheme had reached.

Representatives of both the GLC and the Kensington Council turned up and spoke at the public meeting, which after brief speeches opened up into a long discussion session with the audience crowding around a huge map of the whole site marking with stickers uses which they would like to be included.

Local opinion was again mobilised in November 1969 to oppose the plan to place a bus garage under the motorway bringing noise, dirt and fumes to an already congested and overcrowded part of North Kensington. All kinds of groups and individuals wrote in to the authorities in angry opposition, and a public meeting was planned. However the bus garage plan was dropped the day the public meeting was due to be held!

Despite accusations against the main activists in the MDT of elitist compromising, by those who claimed that all the negotiations were unnecessary, since the space would be taken over when it was needed, the MDT did manage to sustain a consensus between a very wide range of local groups over a long period of time. All the groups in the area were kept informed of developments whether by public meetings, by *People's News* specials, or circulars asking for supportive action.

The Motorway space in 1974

By October 1974, when the Amenity Trust gave its third annual report, there certainly had been some development in the use of the motorway space for local community use, rather than for car parks as originally planned.

The first developments to be completed in terms of bricks and mortar were those schemes initiated by the Borough Council. The Council had got Urban Aid to finance the building of an Information and Aid Centre providing local offices for their social services department, and for voluntary advice groups, including the Housing Action Centre, the Citizens Advice Bureau, and the Voluntary Workers Bureau. This took up three bays under the motorway with a fourth being used as exhibition space. The Centre was completed and opened in 1974. Just the other side of Ladbroke Grove from the Information and Aid Centre, an old people's Luncheon Club and Meals on Wheels Centre was built by the Council. This was also completed by 1974. The third Council development was a new laundry, on which building started in 1974. This was west of Ladbroke Grove and was built to replace the old wash house which was due for demolition within the Lancaster Road (West) redevelopment scheme.

In Acklam Road there was a group of developments in which the Amenity Trust was involved. Building work had started on a community hall in Acklam Road paid for by an Urban Aid grant obtained by the GLC. The hall was due to be completed in June 1975. Another bay in Acklam Road had been turned into hard surface all-weather pitches, with floodlighting for evening use. This was paid for by a charity. An Adventure Playground had been established by a local group of people in July 1970, before the Amenity Trust was set up, and this continued to function in five bays in Acklam Road as a permanent playground with a hut and full time play leaders. The only other development in Acklam Road in which the Amenity Trust was involved was a terrace of eight houses facing the motorway, from which the residents had been rehoused, because the noise of the motorway made living conditions unbearable. The Amenity Trust was given responsibility for these houses and converted them into offices. Twenty seven rooms were let to 16 local organisations at low rents.

On the other side of Portobello Road from Acklam Road, two bays had been turned into a theatre and a group was working on plans to develop the space as a full time permanent local theatre. The theatre faced onto a space which had been left after houses had been demolished to make way for the motorway. The Amenity Trust took over responsibility for this space along with the space under the motorway, and grassed it over, landscaped it with mounds, planted shrubs and built seats and tables out of railway sleepers. This space became known as Portobello Green.

Further west still, under the huge roundabout at Bramley Road, the Amenity Trust had organised a sports project to demonstrate the possibilities of using the space for a sports complex, but these plans were in abeyance for quite a time due to the occupation of the site by gypsies, while the Council refused to give them a site.

Further west still under the huge roundabout at Bramley Road the Amenity Trust had organised a sports project to demonstrate the possibilities of using the space for a sports complex, but these plans were in abeyance for quite a time due to the occupation of the site by gypsies, while the Council refused to give them a site.

So the motorway space was being developed gradually, making real many of the early ideas of the Motorway Development Trust back in the late 1960s. However, it was only too clear the the Council had a firm grip of the Amenity Trust provided they had a compliant Chairman. This gave the Council a 8:7 majority on the Management Committee of this supposed independent charitable organisation. The Council's determination to preserve its strong position on the Management Committee provoked a series of constitutional rows within the organisation in which the representatives of local groups tried to alter the constitution to give the Trust greater independence from Council domination. In 1974 the struggle was still going on.

One effect of Council control was that the Amenity Trust schemes progressed in a piecemeal way, with no scheme for comprehensive financing of an integrated plan from public funds. Instead those groups with money, like the Council, could forge ahead and develop the space, leaving the unresourced local groups with no real possibility of using the space for anything which required the construction of permanent buildings. Back in the late 1960s the Motorway Development Trust had got a qualified quantity surveyor to cost the integrated development of the whole 2½ miles of motorway space and the figure produced was £2¼ million. The Amenity Trust itself went to the same experts a few years later and got a very similar quote. But despite this the Trust went ahead on a piecemeal basis. A starting grant of £25,000 was given by the Borough Council and the leader of the Council Sir Malby Crofton declared:

> "From now on the Trust will have to make its own way in the world. It is on its own to develop its ideas in its own way. I am sure that some of the leading charitable foundations will recognise this as a unique experiment."[9]

One charity, the City Parochial Foundation, did respond with an annual grant to the Trust of £10,000. A couple of other charities gave much smaller annual grants. Urban Aid was obtained by the Borough Council, the GLC and the Westway Nursery Association for the individual schemes mentioned. However, this left the majority of the bays undeveloped with a long list of interested groups with no resources to develop their projects. The Borough Council must have realised they had miscalculated to some extent the amount of charitable money to be tapped and in 1974 announced that, for three years from April 1975, they would pay the Trust £22,000 a year to cover administrative expenses, including the salaries of the staff. But this still left no resources for the development of the remaining bays.

Another effect of Council control has been the closed unaccountable way in which the Amenity Trust has worked. Only one public meeting has ever been called about the work of the Trust in general and that was in July 1972. Also there has been very little publicly available written information on the work of the Trust other than the annual reports. This has meant that local access to the Trust has been restricted to the seven individuals elected to the Management Committee by the groups who are members of the Trust.

As with the full time workers of the Play Association, the staff of the Amenity Trust have failed to take up a political organising role to mobilise pressure for a larger share of local authority resources to be available for local groups to develop their ideas of how to use the motorway space. Instead the staff have to a large extent accepted the Council's domination and their definition of what is possible so that they perform a buffer function between local groups and the Council. So the Trust has become yet another institution with which local people have to do battle.

FOOTNOTES

1. *People's News*, Vol.2, No.32, 24 August 1970.
2. Bob Marsden, *Play Association History*, Draft paper (unpublished).
3. Bob Marsden.
4. Bob Marsden.
5. *People's News*, Vol.2, No.4, January 26th 1970.
6. *People's News*, Vol.2, No.5, February 2nd 1970.
7. *People's News*, Vol.2, No.38, October 12th, 1970.
8. *People's News*, Vol3, No.6, February 8th 1971.
9. *Municipal Review*, March 1974, p.74.

Chapter 7

Housing Struggles Against Private Capital

The area of North Kensington can be seen as a battleground — between the profit hungry property converters, who sold to the highest bidder, and the non-profit housing trusts, who made an attempt to allocate their housing on the basis of need. The scars of the battle were obvious throughout the area: the eviction of the present residents, spiralling house prices and luxury conversions into mews cottages and expensive town houses.

For this battleground to be a reality to all the people in the area, the People's Centre recognised the need to declare battle in all kinds of public ways, to organise demonstrations at which people could show their allegiance and to do battle in as many different ways as possible. The aim was to destroy confidence in property investment in the area, so that private landlords would pull out, prices would drop, and the Notting Hill Housing Trust, as the most active non-profit buyer in the area, could buy. If the private market showed signs of slackening the Council might even be forced to consider the role it should play in housing. Another strategy was pursued at the same time, to put pressure directly on the Council to try and force them to use their powers to take over houses and improve them themselves. This could help with the first strategy since the basis of confidence in property — that there will be no official interference in the private market — would be destroyed.

Over the years every kind of idea was tried to make the housing battle a visible and public one. The hard core of the People's Centre and the People's Association Housing Group which grew out of it, followed the local property scene in the closest possible detail to find out where tenants were being pressured and where the pace of the market was hotting up. The landlord register compiled from the Housing Register in 1967, was used to trace networks of property ownership, so that different tenants of the same landlord could be brought together. A real attempt was made to strip away the anonymity of property owners, to discover the real people hiding behind a facade of company names. This often meant lengthy company searches but often yielded dividends in terms of locating the home address of owners so that their peace would no longer be undisturbed. But all this was the background work which had to be done to provide a focus for other forms of more public action.

1-9 Colville Gardens – *The Struggle Goes on*

The story of the struggle of the tenants of 1-9 Colville Gardens has been told up to the time in October 1967 when the Council refused to compulsory purchase the block, and the nine houses were sold to another private property company. They took over where the bankrupt Bowen Davies had left off in the process of using the block to maximise profits. However, whereas Davies had pursued a strategy of cramming as many tenants as possible into the block, the new company was faced with the rent income being stabilised as a result of the tenants applying to the rent tribunal. The only answer if profits were to be boosted was to change the use of the block to cater for a higher income section of the market. If the block was emptied and converted into luxury flats to be sold on long leases or let at high rents, they stood a good chance of avoiding all legislative controls.

But the company did not show their hand for nearly a year, and it took nearly this long to track down who the new company was. Sustained investigations finally located them in the Bahamas. Their name was Trade and General Investments (Bahamas) Ltd. and their office in Nassau, Bahamas. However after following leads all the way to the Bahamas their agent Oscar Mintz was discovered just a bus ride away from Colville Gardens, in St Johns Wood.

The first the tenants heard from the new company was in July 1968 when nearly half of them received notice to quit "in view of the proposed reconstruction". The solicitor who sent the notices said that no hardship was intended to the tenants and that it was just a "necessary formality". He went on that the tenants "are all protected by something or other", meaning presumably the Rent Acts. But he had his orders to get the tenants out and so offers of anything between £700 and £3500 started to be put to individual tenants. Meanwhile Trade and General applied to the Council for planning permission to convert the nine houses into: 12 three-bedroomed flats, 45 two-bedroomed flats and 39 bedsitters.

The Council meeting considering the planning permission was picketed with placards like "People's lives before profit". But the Council response to the planning application came over loud and clear:

> "We understand that the town planning application would provide a first class conversion of the property which is much in need of improvement . . . Any question of the Council using a CPO at this stage was out of the question since it would have been a question of the Council compulsorily purchasing a property in order to prevent the owners from improving it."
> (*The Guardian*, August 7th 1968.)

The Council gave planning permission for a slightly modified plan reducing the total number of flats from 96 to 94 and increasing the number of 3-roomed flats by two "to ensure the provision within the development of a reasonable minimum of family accommodation"!

But Trade and General wanted planning permission not to carry out the plans, but just to increase the value of 1-9 as an investment which they intended to sell for the highest price they could get. Efforts to clear the block of tenants was part of the same strategy.

Meanwhile the People's Association was going ahead with its plans to obstruct the new owner's eviction plans. The 22 tenants who had received notice to quit in July went back to the Rent Tribunal for security. The hearing was fixed for September. All the cases were argued together on the grounds that they were all in fact unfurnished and not furnished tenancies since the value of the furniture and services did not make up a "substantial portion of the annual rent" — as the law required. Bruce Douglas-Mann, a local solicitor and Labour Councillor had hit on this idea as a way of using the words of the Rent Act to question whether a so-called "furnished" flat was in fact furnished. A test case had been fought with one of the tenants in Colville Gardens, Alex Jeffers, and he had won and had been declared an unfurnished tenant by the County Court. The result was that all 22 cases were adjourned for three months while the tenants applied to the County Court for a declaration that they were unfurnished. Once the three months were up in December it was back to the Tribunal again and again an adjournment was obtained for another three months since the County Court cases for reclassification had still not been heard.

But while this legal strategy was being worked out and while Trade and General sat on their planning permission, the living conditions in the nine houses deteriorated. No basic repair or maintenance work was done and life became more and more unbearable for the tenants. Gradually tenants left, some with the feeling that anywhere would be better than Colville Gardens, some who had just had enough after seven or eight years in cramped decaying rooms with uncertainty and the threat of eviction hanging over their heads. In January 1969 the People's Association wrote to the leader of the Council, Sir Malby Crofton, as the miserable conditions in the buildings showed no signs of ever being improved by Trade and General:

> "Our suggestion was and is that the Council should CPO these properties . . . such a step more than any other single action would show the speculators that they need not look to North Kensington for the quick pickings of the future."

The next thing they knew towards the end of February 1969 was that Colville Gardens was sold again, to Cledro Developments for £120,000. Trade and General had made a tidy £55,000 — nearly 85% profit over the 16 months they had owned the property with virtually no outgoings to set against it!

The only advantage of the new owners was that they were a lot more visible and contactable than distant Trade and General. Their Director, Robert Gubbay was a former surveyor for Paddington Council and lived on the outskirts of London. A meeting was fixed with Gubbay at the end of February. He started with the hard line — he intended to clear the block and none of the present tenants would be able to live in the houses once they were converted because it would be too expensive. But the People's Association told him clearly that all the tenants had to be rehoused since they were all getting reclassified as unfurnished tenants. In the face of this, Gubbay agreed to withdraw the notices to quit while rehousing possibilities were discussed and declared his intention of rehousing the remaining 27 tenants in alternative unfurnished accommodation at rents fixed by the rent officer. Minor repairs would be done as a precondition for the tenants beginning to pay off their rent arrears. Gubbay's conscience had been pricked. To the press he came out with statements like these:

> "I truly sympathise with them (the tenants). Some of them are living in terrible conditions and on seeing them it is hard to believe that we live in a country which boasts social services." (*Kensington Post* February 28th 1969).

Within a few weeks the builders had moved in and were starting work on the conversions and Gubbay had bought his first house in the area for rehousing the tenants from Colville Gardens. It looked as if Gubbay was going to move fast but it was not to be. It was not until the end of September that the first tenants were rehoused. Houses had been bought for ten of the remaining tenants. But right up to this time the living conditions in the houses got progressively worse as the builders knocked about the adjoining flats.

In one basement where one tenant, Bill Blachford, had lived for 23 years, the ceiling collapsed as the workmen tore down the flats above. Bill was tired and resigned and did not bother to complain any more.

> "Since I have been here the property has changed hands several times but I have never met the landlord. There has never been anyone to complain to. I have had to bale water from the flat on many occasions and for nearly three years I have had no lighting. Burglars have broken in during the middle of the night and my windows have been smashed. When I am in bed at night I hear many strange things but now I don't take any notice of them. I have had to put up with a lot but I suppose I have become used to it."

The Health Inspectors had visited in September 1968 and ordered repairs but nothing was done. Instead of enforcing basic repairs the Council concentrated on helping with the conversion work which Gubbay was involved in.

In October they offered him over £38,000 as an initial improvement grant. This was just two years after the Council had declared it to be impossible to lend the £7,000 over the District Valuer's price to the Trust to allow them to buy the nine houses. This was not the end of the Council's largesse to the owners of 1-9.

When Gubbay sold the block to the Crown Agents in 1970 they continued the conversions and got more improvement grants making a grand total of £111,000. By the end of 1969 the newly converted flats were already let, at rents between £12.60 and £18.90 a week. Only two of the original tenants moved into the new flats, one a longstanding controlled tenant and the other, the tenant who had won the test case to get reclassified as unfurnished.

Crown Agents of Overseas Territories completed the conversion to smart middle class apartments and renamed the block "Trident House". Within two years the buying and selling began again in earnest. In 1972 Crown Agents sold to a Mr Hart; Mr Hart sold immediately to Prisdaly Investments Ltd. and Prisdaly resold to Elkington's (PIF) Ltd. for a sum of £800,000 just 100 times the sum paid by Bowen Davies in 1953. This rapid series of sales resulted in yet more speculative profit for all those involved. Having completed this deal Elkington's set about a few changes. They renamed the block again, as "Pinehurst Court" this time and in October told all the new tenants that their fixed term agreements would not be renewed but that they could buy a flat if they liked. More improvements were planned; the garden was landscaped with cherubs and statues to adorn the rolling lawns.

The wheel had come full circle — the higher income tenants who had displaced the low income families were now faced with a plan to displace them with even higher income tenants or flat buyers. They organised a public meeting and formed themselves into a tenants association and considered using the reclassification trick, on the advice of the same solicitor who had advised the former tenants. There was no other legal way of fighting since the landlord had used the trick of fixed term agreements which means that no notice to quit is necessary to end the tenancy once the fixed term of three or six months is up. No more security can be got from going to the rent tribunal. But there was no element of common interest strong enough to bind the new tenants together. Many of them could and wanted to buy the leases offered at £8,000 upwards. Those who did not had the money to pay the kind of rents being charged elsewhere. Very few had any children and a move was no great disruption, so the tenants association disintegrated and the flats were sold off.

But what happened to the 72 original tenants who did stick together and organise?

In May 1972 an effort was made to trace them all using the contacts of tenants who were still involved in the People's Association. Of the 72 tenants 54 were traced:

5 households	(8 adults, 16 kids) were rehoused by non-profit owners, Council or trust, direct.
11 households	(16 adults, 13 kids) were rehoused by owners in private accommodation as a result of People's Association pressure, and ended up as trust tenants since the owner sold the houses to the trust.
2 households	(4 adults, 6 kids) were made homeless and went into Council temporary accommodation and were eventually rehoused by the Council.
36 households	(62 adults, 46 kids) moved to other private accommodation. Of these six households (11 adults, 14 kids) were later rehoused by the trust.
2 households	(4 adults, 2 kids) bought their own home.

This leaves 28 households (47 adults, 30 kids) still in private accommodation. Of these 11 still lived in North Kensington; the rest had moved to other areas of London like Kilburn, Willesden and North Paddington.

These figures just show that, even when all the tenants know their rights, there is no legal way tenants can ultimately resist market pressures if the Council refuses to use its powers to take a block out of the private market. Once the Council decided not to act at this basic level in May 1967 all that was left to do was to bargain with the owners to rehouse the tenants using legal tricks like reclassification. But the bargaining was not over staying in the block in decent conditions — it was about being rehoused and not just evicted. The future of the block as an investment was no longer being threatened.

Conclusion — An Important Failure

The struggle to get 1-9 Colville Gardens out of private profit making hands failed, but this was an important failure in all kinds of ways.

It represented for many tenants a first step towards a more conscious self-determination and a growing resistance to the dictates of those with wealth and power over the lives of others. Whereas groups like the Labour Party had argued for years the need for wider use of compulsory purchase to eliminate private profit in housing, the People's Association had shown ways in which this battle could be taken up in real terms outside the walls of the Council debating chamber. The battle certainly had to be fought with the odds clearly against the tenants with whatever weapons were to hand, but the significance lay in the People's Association's preparedness to take up the fight which others deemed to be lost.

The experience of the struggle in 1-9 provided all who were involved in it with an insight into the workings of the private housing market. Housing was just another sort of investment — finance capital yielding profits to the owners in the same way as stocks and shares yield profits to their owners. The tenants of the house are taken together with the space they occupy (when they cannot be got rid of before sale) and are seen as units of investment to be bought and sold and speculated in to maximise profit. Colville Gardens showed how you can fill a block with the most insecure, desperate people, milk it for a few years and then evict them all in exchange for another type of speculative investment unit — the high income individuals eager to pay thousands of £s for a tiny luxury flat.

Though the demand to the Council made over Colville Gardens was to take all properties owned by one particular property company — Davies Investments — out of the private market, the logic of the argument was clear. The way was laid wide open for the demand which was later made by the People's Association, that all private landlords should be eliminated from the area and all houses taken into non-profit ownership.

Squatting

It was at the beginning of December 1969 that organised squatting started in the East End of London with one day token occupations of properties — first in "The Hollies", a luxury block of flats, on December 1st, and then in an empty vicarage on December 21st. The message was simple — there were 470,000 empty properties in England and Wales in 1966 and these should be used to house the homeless. There were 18,689 homeless people in England and Wales in 1968.

Just before Christmas in Notting Hill the Notting Hill Squatters (a sub-group of the Notting Hill People's Association) formed, took over an empty luxury flat in Arundel Court and occupied it for a day. The aim was to use the squatting idea as a tactic in picking out the targets of the property battle in the area. The mere existence of an empty luxury flat priced at over £8,000 not half a mile away from decaying, overcrowded homes was a threat to every low income person in the area and an indication of a wave which would sweep the area if left unchecked.

Early in January 1969 the Notting Hill Squatters took another property — this time an empty luxury town house in Clarendon Road priced at £17,450. It had been empty for two years and had been opened up as a show house by the agents. Being a show house, take-over was easy. The door was open so the squatters could enter and lock the door behind them, making sure that the agent's representative who's job it had been to show people around the house was outside and not inside the house. They stayed in for the day using the action to get publicity for their arguments. But the squatters were seen as no real threat by the owners. It was token squatting and people knew they would not stay long. The agent responsible for the show house said:

> "There is a certain sympathy with the squatters. As long as they don't do any harm or annoy people there is no reason to remove them."

One touch of irony was that the show house had just been bought by a man who worked for Shelter. He happened to visit while the squat was on and was overcome with embarrassment and vanished as quickly as he could with a casual word in a squatter's ear about keeping the place as clean as possible.

The first and only attempt of the Notting Hill Squatters to squat homeless families into a privately owned luxury converted house was made in March 1969. It was felt that since the house had been empty nine years already that the landlord was in no hurry to let it. It was an old terraced house at 43 Artesian Road which had been converted into self-contained flats but the final jobs had been left uncompleted. So toilets were plumbed in and floorboards put back and two homeless families moved in, supported by Notting Hill Squatters. One family had already moved five times in the two months since Christmas and was in a homeless hostel — the other had been evicted the day before after having gone back to the rent tribunal five times for more time. They had lived in a single room with two adults and five children for over five years.

Letters were sent to the owners — Ostacchini Enterprises Ltd., and to Westminster City Council informing them of the situation and asking the owners to give a rent book to both families and accept them as tenants. A guard was mounted on the house all day and night and everyone waited. Nothing happened for two weeks then all of a sudden one lunch time the owner appeared with a hatchet, a crowbar, his wife and a policeman and smashed down his own front door with the policeman standing by. He had chosen a moment when only the children, one father and a single squatter 'guard' were there. There was just time to phone the contact list before the door caved in but everyone took too long to arrive.

Even had there been dozens of people there to defend the house the families had said they did not want any violence so it is doubtful what would have been done in the face of the hatchet — except to argue that the owner was breaking the 1381 Forcible Entry Act — however, this was written out large and clear on the front door in case he had not read it but he hatchetted right through it.

The squat and publicity around it had one good effect — a flat was found for one of the families. The other went back to the hostel where they had lived before

The experience put a damper on the idea of squatting in the area for quite a time.

It was not until May 1971 that squatting was used again as a tactic in the battle against private landlords.

Merle Major, a tenant of 62 St Ervan's Road and a West Indian mother of six decided she had had enough of private landlords and was going to squat in a Council flat to make the Council face her housing problem once and for all.

Since March 1968 when she moved into No.62 she had experienced almost every Council department and their fumbling inaction. Her problem was quite clear. She had taken the two rooms at the top of this house because she was desperate after being evicted by another landlord. She had five children at the time, the back room leaked so much they all had to sleep in the front room despite the gaping hole in the wall by the window. The Children's Department response had been to take all her children into care eight years' ago, because of the bad housing conditions in which they were living. However, they never did anything about the bad housing. They did not even make sure Merle was on the housing list. The Public Health Department had been visiting the house since 1964 when Reilly the landlord bought it, but never succeeded in forcing the necessary repairs. The family in the basement was left without a roof on their kitchen for 18 months. The whole house had dangerous wiring which caused fires on more than one occasion.

Before Merle moved in the other tenants had started to fight back. In October 1967, the basement tenants, the Wrights, won an important test case to get themselves reclassified from furnished to unfurnished tenants so gaining greater security. They then got their rent cut by the Rent Officer from £4.50 to £1.50.

Another tenant on the first floor — Ann Worsfold — had followed their lead. She became an unfurnished tenant and got her rent cut from £6 to £2.37½.

Merle had taken her two rooms at the ridiculous figure of £8.50. The rent tribunal cut this to £7.50 but as long as she was a furnished tenant she was insecure. In May 1969 Reilly gave her notice to quit which she successfully fought by getting reclassified as unfurnished. The Court also awarded her damages for the bad living conditions and imposed a 28 day repair order on Reilly. Her rent was then cut by the Rent Officer to £2.37½. Reilly appealed only to have it cut further to £2. So, together the tenants had made a big hole in Reilly's rent income cutting it from its original total of £19 a week for the three floors to £6.25 a week. Reilly did not take this assault on his income lightly. In 1967 he had tried his hand at illegal evictions throwing all Ann Worsfold's possessions on the street while she was out. The Council was pressed to prosecute resulting in a fine of £25 for Reilly, which obviously did not deter him.

In May 1970 he was at it again. Merle and Ann had both gone shopping together one Tuesday afternoon. Ten minutes later they came back to find the front door boarded up, a furniture van waiting and keys nailed to the door with a note telling them that they had moved to Wandsworth to a house they had never heard of! An angry crowd gathered together with horse, cart and battering ram to force in the boarded up door. But negotiations started instead and four hours of police/solicitor bargaining with Reilly eventually resulted in the tenants going back in only to find furniture thrown downstairs, clothing stuffed into boxes and many doors off their hinges.

But the street was angry. Eighty five residents of St. Ervan's Road immediately signed a petition demanding the Council take 62 off Reilly's hands. The People's Centre and the Golborne Social Rights Committee organised a march in June to the Town Hall, led by Merle and Ann demanding (amongst other things) that the Council should take over No. 62. The Council response? They accepted that the management was bad and the conditions filthy but could do nothing because of the uncertain future of the area.

But Reilly had not finished.

Later in June he took off the front door and locked it in the basement, leaving the tenants to break into the basement and rehang the door. Then, after a few months had elapsed, in February 1971 he and his brother attacked Merle one Sunday morning, brought up stinking rubbish from the basement and threw it all over her kitchen. The night before he had cut the electricity off. In March the ground floor tenant found a microphone under her bed connected to the basement, and Reilly sitting on a chair in the middle of her room in the dark. A week later she was locked out. On both these occasions the Law Centre acted with great speed to obtain injunctions against Reilly — one to stop him going into Merle's flat or interfering with her in any way, the other to make him allow Maureen, the ground floor tenant back in her flat. These injunctions were served on Reilly within 24 hours of the Court granting them, by a People's Association member — in contrast to the Council who had taken nine months to serve a summons on Reilly for his illegal eviction in May 1970. In April 1971 Reilly was fined £200 and £60 costs for harrassing, assaulting and illegally evicting Merle, thanks to Law Centre and People's Association energy in speeding up the legal machinery.

This was the background against which Merle decided to squat. She had tried all the legal remedies open to her. However much she got Reilly fined, however much she got the rent cut, however often she called in the Health Inspectors, she still did not have enough room to have all her children back home, with repairs still undone, and she still had to live with an ever present Reilly. There was just no knowing what he would do next.

So, she asked the People's Association Housing Group to find her an empty Council flat and she would squat. 11 Powis Square, a newly converted Council basement was found and in May 1971 Merle moved in with three of her children she had got back from the Children's Department and another child nearly a year old. Merle informed the Council what her demands were:

— a decent home for herself and all her family
— the compulsory purchase of 62 St. Ervan's Road.

Once in, Merle proceeded to organise a People's Rally the coming Sunday afternoon. She involved a steel band, and people with guitars, mouth-organs and tambourines. She wrote songs and built an effigy of Peter Reilly for the occasion. Starting out from 62 St. Ervan's Road which she described in detail as the 'house of horrors' she led a swaying, dancing, procession around the streets chanting rhythmically "Get involved, get involved, Power to the People, get involved". Once in Powis Square the steel band struck up and Merle then climbed up on a ledge and told the 500 people in the square her story. After a massive show of hands in support of the squat, and pledges to come and support her if eviction attempts were made, Merle stepped down and set fire to her effigy of Peter Reilly. Then there was more music and Merle sang the song she had written:

Fire in the Hole
Merle's Song

There's fire, fire in the hole
Let the people explosion of human emotion
You know there is fire, fire in the hole
Let the people explosion, all over this land.

You may be able to kill somebody dead,
You may be able to bust their head,
But you can't kill emotion
You can't kill human emotion

Man, woman, man take the people's hand
Open up your big food bin
Let the people in.
To have your corpse all running like that
While the people are homeless
It's a sin
Let my brothers and sisters come on in
You fool – going to blow over,
Going to bust your building down
Going to tear your building down to the ground.

The people are the wheels that run your car,
The people of the Borough pay for your car,
The people do everythin', everythin',
The people brought you your strength
They fight your war.
The poor men ain't fighting no wars no more
Unless its for their own salvation
To help their own dedication.

Remember when you were fighting for your independence
You said that you were right, right day and night,
Dying don't mean nothing, dying is living
And living is dying just across the river
And nobody's scared of dying no more.
Its better to be dead than to live on and be scared
Its better to be dead than to live on and be scared
Fire, fire in the hole.

Within two weeks of her squatting the Council responded to Merle's demands. The Housing Chairman called for special reports from his officers on 62 St. Ervan's Road and said the Council was prepared to go all the way to using a CPO if it was needed. Council negotiations brought an offer of a six roomed house for Merle from the Kensington Housing Trust initially for a period of six months — since the house was due for demolition. At the end of eight weeks squatting Merle decided to accept the offer, to get all her children back and get her strength up for another fight in six months time if necessary. But the demolition was delayed and Merle got a transfer at the end of a year to a newer Trust property.

In July the Council announced its decision to put a CPO on 62 St. Ervan's Road — the first time ever that the Council had used their powers against a landlord because of his harassment and bad management. But their heart wasn't in it and they produced a very insubstantial case to the Ministry for the CPO. Meanwhile Reilly got to work with a paintbrush, put in a few sticks of furniture and relet the floors at £13 a week. He got single short-stay tenants from West End agencies who left rather than put up a fight. In October 1971 the new tenants moved in but within only a few weeks they were reduced to sleepless wrecks by Reilly and his brother's constant presence in the house, moving stealthily about till 3 or 4 am, banging, knocking, footsteps stopping outside the door. The girls downstairs took to sleeping with friends and came back with mattresses to find their water heater smashed with a meat hook hanging beside it and a crucifix with a skull and crossbones on it outside their door. They confronted Reilly's brother who admitted he'd been through the room but that it was common practice. Five of the six tenants were too scared to do anything but move out, making way for the next wave of tenants.

All this was going on after the CPO had been put on the house and while the Minister was considering it. When the Inspector came to visit, Reilly showed him round and all the tenants were out. Ignoring the long history of harassment and bad conditions the Inspector was taken in by the touch of Reilly's paintbrush. He turned down the CPO saying that the internal and external conditions of the ground and first floors were satisfactory and that there were plans for the whole area to be CPO'd shortly by the GLC and there was no grounds for taking 62 out of turn!

True enough the GLC did put a CPO on the area in 1973 but this still left Reilly with far more years of grace than he deserved.

But despite the delaying action of the Ministry, Merle's decision to squat forced the Council to take two actions which years of legal actions, Health Inspectors and Social Worker's visits had not achieved: to put a CPO on 62 and to find Merle a six-roomed house to live in. This was an experience of power and political effectiveness which was entirely new to Merle who had for years been on the receiving end in relation to authorities, whether receiving Social Security or having her children taken into care. It had a lasting effect in terms of the way she saw herself in relation to the authorities. She had a new confidence and assertiveness of her needs and demands and a real awareness that the authorities — be they Social Security, the Housing Trust, or the Council are there to be your servants and not to dictate your needs.

Merle used this new confidence to make the Trust move her to a more permanent larger flat, where she was no longer plagued by leaking roofs, mice and crumbling walls. As for the Social Services, Merle has made it clear to them that she is going to look after all her six children from that time on, and the whole family has lived together ever since.

As well as providing an important political experience for Merle, the whole event provided a focus for the work of the Housing Group in the Colville area for the two months the squat lasted. It meant that all day, every day, members of the Housing Group combined guard duty at the squat with continuous discussion on the street about the issues raised by the squat — ownership of property, compulsory purchase, and what had to be done if the speculators were to be stopped in the area.

In terms of the housing battle ground, the demand for the CPO of 62 related to a property outside the Colville area where the battle between speculators and non-profit ownership was most intense, but to force the Council to use a CPO on this one house increased the possibility of them being forced to use their powers of CPO in the Colville area too. As over 1-9 Colville Gardens, the main demand of the People's Association was that a particular property should be taken out of private hands because it was badly run and not just because it was privately owned. It was still to take some time till the position of the group shifted towards a more total stand against all private property in the area.

The squatting which followed Merle's squat in Powis Square fell into two rather different kinds of waves. The Housing Group of the People's Association went on to use squatting as a tactic, in the battle against the speculators, as a way of highlighting the targets to be won — the houses most threatened at any one time by speculator take-over. But they deliberately did not encourage or look for homeless families to squat in these houses since it was felt that it was wrong for families who had not been part of the on-going battle in the area to be put in what was in fact the firing line. The second wave was of homeless people who did squat wherever they could, off their own initiatve, who wanted no publicity and usually opted for Notting Hill Housing Trust property as the safest bet since they hoped they could rely on the Trust not using strong arm men and hired thugs, which was always the risk with private landlords. The Trust could be relied upon to go through the Courts. It was at the beginning of 1972 that this wave of uncoordinated squats started.

However the focus here will be on the way squatting was used as a weapon in the battle against the speculators together with the tactic of auction-busting.

Auction-Busting

The idea of auction-busting was first hit on in October 1969. The People's Association had heard that the Council had plans afoot to sell off 35 of the houses requisitioned during the war, at public auction. The Council had got permission to do this in 1966 from the Labour Minister of Housing on the grounds that the proceeds of these sales would "enable them to purchase other more suitable houses, more easily convertible into self-contained units". (Letter to People's Association, October 2 1969 from Anthony Greenwood.)

The Council gave all sorts of reasons for wanting to sell the houses. They argued that they were too expensive for the tenants to curtain, carpet and heat and the rates were too high so putting them out of the reach of families in need of rehousing. But these were not the real reasons. The houses were all full of tenants already, many of whom had lived there for 20 years and were perfectly happy. The real reason the Council wanted to get rid of them was that they could not run them at a profit. They were in fact, running them at a loss of over £10,000 p.a. and this really hurt them, as the true representatives of the property owning classes that they were. So with 4,000 on the waiting list and with no intention of buying more suitable property elsewhere with the proceeds, they put two of the houses up for public auction on October 2 1969 in Chelsea Old Town Hall.

The brochure for the auction set out the details of the two houses: 14 Lexham Gardens, W8 and 18 Sydney Street, SW3. Though the Council had argued to the Minister that it was difficult to convert the houses into self-contained flats, the brochure actually advertised 14 Lexham Gardens as "suitable for conversion to flats, flatlets or hotel". It went on "it is understood from the local planning authority that planning permission for a hotel would be favourably considered". Nothing like using your own power to grant planning permission in an attempt to inflate the price of a house you are selling!

Members of the People's Association and the Notting Hill Squatters decided the Council's auction should not go unnoticed so some of them planned to attend.

An article in *People's News** tells what happened:

"KENSINGTON HOMES PRICELESS
"A well filled auction pushed the price of Council owned property to unheard of levels last Thursday. Two houses at 14 Lexham Gardens and 18 Sydney Street were on offer, both recently cleared of Council tenants. Bidding for 14 Lexham Gardens passed £20,000 (the reserve price for the rotting house) at a spanking pace and went on to pass £30,000 and

---

People's News Oct. 6th 1969 No.37

£40,000 to cries of 'You're being taken for a ride'; 'the whole thing is a farce' and 'get the police', from more staid property dealers. With no sign of flagging in the bidding, the auctioneer withdrew the property at £55,000; after one bid of £½ million for Sydney Street he tried to close the auction.

"When asked why he stopped the auction by the local press the auctioneer said: 'When the auctioneer thinks he is being taken for a colossal ride he can stop the auction and this is what I am doing.' He went on 'I have never had this trouble before. I have spent three months getting this auction set up and now it is all wasted'."

The real property dealers had watched in amazement as calm, well-dressed people around them bid higher and higher to levels nearly three times the reserve price. But their amazement turned to anger as they realised a desirable property was slipping through their fingers and their valuable time was being wasted. They attacked the high bidders for their crazy bids only to get the response "We had only just started when the auction was stopped. Space for families in Kensington is priceless. I would have gone beyond £1 million to get Lexham Gardens for family use."

But some of the genuine bidders were otherwise affected and were shocked into sympathy with the whole event. One man told the local press that as a result of the action he was no longer interested in buying the Lexham Gardens house.

"The squatters are fighting for a very good cause and this will make a lot of people think twice about buying these houses."

But this was not the end of the day. *People's News* recaptures the spirit of the day:

"Just as the auction stopped a large group of 12 mothers and 30 children descended on the Town Hall and flooded into the auction room and took over all the chairs. Banners and posters were strewn everywhere demanding that all houses should be used for families in need, and not for luxury hotels.

"The children started up a chant of 'We shall overcome'. After a quarter of an hour the party left the financiers cowering in the auction room looking as if they had never seen real mothers and children before. All then set off in a procession down Sydney Street, still singing and sticking posters up on all available surfaces. On arriving at 18 Sydney Street they found the door open and took over the whole house, to show that it was fit for family accommodation. Oddly enough when a similar occupation was attempted at Lexham Gardens the house was found to be full of policemen who refused to allow the families to 'inspect' the property.

"All went well in Sydney Street and a party was held on the top floor wth music and chocolate cake. After an hour's residence the families departed out the back garden."

The auction bust and squat succeeded in expressing in a very direct, vivid and public way the opposition of people in North Kensington to the Council's policy of selling off houses. It provided a way in which families who were shortly to become homeless could confront directly the property dealers at the auction. Two worlds which are normally kept distant and remote from each other, met face to face and the property dealers were visibly embarrassed. The confusion and the ludicrous bidding at the auction contributed towards the disruption of confidence and calm in the property market and the Council was forced to withdraw from using auctions for several years.

The Council was upset but not upset enough to change its policy. Shelagh Roberts, the Housing Chairman, said after the auction-bust:

"This is highly regrettable and an indication that law and order is being rapidly eroded." (*Kensingington Post*, October 9, 1969.)

She went on

"It is highly regrettable that there are certain anarchists in our community who are seeking to take the law into their own hands. We cannot allow a group of irresponsible people to dictate policy to the duly elected representatives of the residents of the Borough." (*Kensington News*, October 10, 1969.)

However within a month 14 Lexham Gardens was sold by sealed bids instead of public auction and by September 1972 the Council was intensifying its efforts to sell off one tenth of the total housing stock of the Council — 500 of the 5,500 Council properties with 30% discounts in the price for sales to sitting tenants. The 500 properties selected were not individual requisitioned properties like the original 35, but purpose built Council flats!

It was not until March 1971 that the auction-bust tactic was tried again — this time with no squat as the house was fully occupied and the tenants played a full part in the auction-bust.

It is worth quoting the *People's News* report in full to recapture the scene at the auction:

"£35,000 BID FOR 25 POWIS SQUARE TURNED DOWN
"If you want to see what the people of Notting Hill are up against in their fight for a decent home, go to an auction.
 "Last Thursday, 25 Powis Square was up for auction. Some tenants and about a dozen people from the People's Association went along to the London Auction Mart down by Blackfriars Station. 25 Powis Square was lot 32 so there was plenty of time to watch this crowd of thuggish characters and old women at work, cheered by their ringmaster, the jolly auctioneer.

 "As each house came up, the auctioneer gave helpful bits of advice like: 'These are all furnished tenants. You'll have no problem in getting rid of them', 'This tenant owes rent so it will be easy to get rid of him', 'These rents are registered at the Rent Office but they're due to be re-asssessed next year and there's a chance that by then the government will have changed the Rent Act to take them out of control altogether'. Lot 32, 25 Powis Square, was finally reached. The auctioneer said what a fine house it was and how easy it would be to get most of the tenants out — but he was interrupted by a voice from the back: 'I am a tenant of this house and would like to draw your attention to the defects of this house. This "beautiful columned portico" described in the brochure is an extremely flimsy structure and the wiring is in a perilous condition. As for the tenants we all intend to fight together to get decent treatment from any new owner.' By this time the other bidders could contain their indignation no longer: 'How dare he!' 'What cheek for a tenant to speak at an auction.' 'We'll see he suffers for this'. And then the bidding started. It began at £17,000 and quickly rose to £21,000. Only two or three buyers were interested at first but soon members of the People's Association started bidding too. They raised their newspapers and cocked their forefingers like the rest of them. And how the price went up. From £21,000 upwards they were on their own, bidding against each other. £25,000 was reached. The auctioneer threw in a cheery 'I've known a house in Lansdowne Road — not far from Powis Square — go for £50,000, so we may have a long way to go'.

"But the other bidders thought otherwise. They know how they rigged the prices, and they soon caught on that the rules of their price rigging games were being broken. They were being challenged by others playing a different game of bidding the price up indefinitely so that the house would have to be withdrawn. Meanwhile private buyers might be frightened off, the price might fall and a non-profit body like the Notting Hill Housing Trust who bid £20,000 but could go no higher, or the tenants themselves could buy it. Higher and higher the bids went; and angrier the other bidders got — 'They're playing games' one shouted; 'How childish' cried another. But our cheery ringmaster continued to take the bids. £35,000 was reached. Suspicion forced him to pause. He cautioned the bidders: 'You are fully aware I hope, that you must leave 10% of what you bid before this auction or be arrested.' He went on to the last bidder: 'I have reason to believe you are not worth £35,000'. There were consultations with the solicitors selling the house. Two or three angry bidders rushed up to the front to say that they were worth what they had bid. A private agreement was reached and the auctioneer banged down the hammer, saying he was selling the house for £21,000 and was taking no more bids. Needless to say the Notting Hill Housing Trust is not the new owner. We have since checked that it is more than they could afford."

But this was not the end of the story. In May 1972 it came up for auction again. *People's News* tells what happened:

"25 POWIS SQUARE SQUAT

"On Monday last, 25 Powis Square was occupied by militant squatters because the house was due to be sold by public auction on the following Thursday. The Notting Hill Housing Trust didn't look as if they stood a chance of buying, when the asking price was £36,000. So it seemed like another house ripe to be taken over by speculators, who would throw out the tenants and convert into luxury flats for rich outsiders.

"Going Going – not gone

"25 Powis Square has frequently changed hands at ever spiralling prices. In March 1971 it came up for auction and was sold for £21,000 by private agreement, after bids by the People's Association had forced the price up to £35,000 and it was withdrawn from the auction. Ironic that the price which the auctioneer thought was ludicrous in 1971 should be the kind of price which the Housing Trust thought reasonable to pay in 1972. Only a few months later it was sold again for £24,000 this time; the top floor tenant was paid to get out, leaving a vacant flat which was converted into a 'luxury penthouse apartment'! (the flat occupied by the squatters).

"The house came up for auction for the very last time this Thursday. The plush room in the Cumberland Hotel was full of the usual types of speculators – smart young lads, thick-set thugs and old ladies. Two o'clock arrived but the auction did not begin. Mr Collins the auctioneer, apologised for the delay which he said was caused by the presence in the audience of some 'people called squatters – undesirable elements that should be eliminated from our society'. He also held up a document which had been handed out by two young ladies to all in the audience, headed 'Supplementary Particulars – 25 Powis Square', and told everyone to disregard it since it was a pack of lies. But everyone in the audience had taken the document quite seriously and had been perusing it for the previous 20 minutes. It obviously contained information very relevant to the speculators. The auctioneer then ordered all the squatters to leave the room and said that the police would be waiting for them outside. But no one moved and no one could find any squatters.

"The next thing to happen was for the agent for the Notting Hill Housing Trust to rush up to the auctioneer at the front with the owner of 25. Negotiations went on for a few minutes then the auctioneer announced that 25 Powis Square had been sold to the Housing Trust. A great cheer went up from the audience. Rumour has it that the Trust paid between £32,000 and £35,000 for the house – a mere £14,000 or so more than they would have paid had they bought it last year!"

The 'Supplementary Particulars' document referred to was printed on the headed notepaper of the estate agent selling the house and looked just like the rest of the auction information. But on closer reading the difference became clearer!

The document described the situation of the property in Powis Square as a "noisy, unstable, multi-racial, high crime area, where political demonstrations, affrays and rioting are frequent occurrences." It then went on to itemise the defects of the property: the faulty wiring, damp, outstanding

Health Orders for repairs and the structurally unsound portico. It ended with a note referring to the occupants of the house: "The unfurnished regulated tenants and the squatters have resisted all forms of harassment, intimidation and substantial cash inducements to vacate their flats. This house has been and *will continue to be* a focal point for the escalating militant community hostility towards the activities of property speculators in the area."

The final sale to the Trust was a clear victory. At the first auction, the only threat to a new owner was the tenant's intention to fight and resist any eviction. Buyers expect a bit of trouble from odd tenants and so it had little effect in putting off buyers despite the chaotic bidding in the auction itself. However it would seem that the professional looking information handed round as 'supplementary particulars' gave an impression of organisation and strength in the area which was effective in putting off prospective buyers.

Until 1969 the most clear territorial battle between the speculators and the Notting Hill Housing Trust was fought in Colville Gardens and Colville Square. Both sides won their victories. On the side of the speculators:

1967 1-9 Colville Gardens sold for luxury conversions
1969 11-12 Colville Square sold for luxury conversions to Sheraton Securities Ltd. The Council said the price was too high and refused a loan to Notting Hill Housing Trust.

On the side of the Trust:

Oct.1969 18-26 Colville Square bought by the Trust for £71,000
Dec.1969 Six more Colville Square houses bought by the Trust.

There had been a significant Council policy change in 1969 which greatly increased the financial aid they gave to the Trust to enable them to buy in the Colville area. (This will be explained in a later section.)

These developments, together with squatting and auction busting were important in posing clearly the two possible futures of every house in the area. While 1-9 Colville Gardens had gone to the speculators, most of the next square, Colville Square, had been saved for non-profit ownership and the tenants were safe and had guaranteed rehousing.

During 1971 it was the turn of Powis Square. Half the houses were already Council owned. But what was important was that in almost all the remaining privately owned houses tenants took up the battle and fought to get their houses bought by the Trust.

Chapter 8

The Fight to change Council Housing Policy

The struggle of 1-9 Colville Gardens, the squatting, the auction busting and the resistance of tenants in their homes throughout the area, were part of the build up of pressure on the Council to change its housing policy. All these struggles strengthened the case for non-profit housing as an important step towards solving the area's housing problems.

But there were several occasions when the conflict between the people of the area and the Council came out into the open and the Council was put on trial and forced to explain its housing policies or lack of them. The first occasion was in May 1969 when the Notting Hill Housing Survey came out — the product of the survey done during the Summer Project in 1967; the second was in 1972/3 when the Council carried out the Colville Study. Just as it was important to strip away the anonymity of the property speculators who owned the homes of the area, so it was important to do the same to the Council who allowed and encouraged the speculators to flourish in the area.

The Notting Hill Housing Survey 1969

On May 5th 1969 the Interim Report of the Housing Survey carried out two years earlier in 1967, was published. It was a well produced, official-looking document crammed with facts and figures about the housing in the three survey areas of Golborne, Colville and Lancaster.

It focussed on two main aspects of the housing: rents and overcrowding. With regard to rents it showed what tenants got for their money. Since 77.9% of all accommodation in the survey area was privately rented, 5.4% local authority owned and 8% owner-occupied, the pattern of rents and conditions in the private sector exerted an overriding influence on the overall pattern.

By tabulating rents with different variables the survey reached the following conclusions:

— the more rent you paid the less value for money you got in terms of space, furnished tenants coming off worst and controlled tenants best;

- the higher the rent the more basic amenities you got (baths, toilets);
- the relative newcomers to the area (those at their present address for under five years) pay higher rents than the longer term resident;
- West Indians pay, on average, higher rents than white people.

A "Value for money" analysis supported these findings and also showed:
- furnished tenants get worse value than unfurnished;
- uncontrolled tenants get worse value than controlled;
- tenants of private landlords get worse value than Council or trust tenants.

The Report went on to show how the overwhelming bulk of overcrowding is in the privately rented sector. Families in general and West Indians and Irish in particular bear the brunt of the overcrowding.

- Families account for over 86 per cent of all statutorily overcrowded households.
- 44% of all children under 21 living at home are in statutorily overcrowded conditions (though they are only 23 per cent of the total population).
- West Indian households account for nearly 35 per cent of those statutorily overcrowded (though only 16 per cent total population), Irish households for 21.4 per cent (though 13.8 per cent of total population) and UK households for 26.5 per cent (51.9 per cent total population).

This all added up to a total of 16.6 per cent of all households statutorily overcrowded and 33.1 per cent living at over 1.5 persons a room, in the survey area. This 33.1 per cent compared with 2.4 per cent in Greater London and 1.6 per cent in Great Britain as a whole. The report challenged the accuracy of the Council's figures for statutory overcrowding, claiming it had found in the survey area alone three times the number of cases the Council had found in the whole of the Borough.

The Report concluded that "the people we have surveyed have no chance of competing successfully in the housing market for accommodation of a reasonable standard" because there was no room for low cost redevelopment, because of the high purchasing power of other people in the Borough and because of the popularity of the adjoining residential areas. It went on to say that "housing is the responsibility of the Borough and it is clear that more could be done" but then concluded that "it is a problem far greater than can be tackled by the resources even of a wealthy borough like Kensington and Chelsea . . . Greater London and Government intervention is clearly called for".

Compulsory rent registration and more security for furnished tenants were recommended changes in the law. At the press conference on the Report, David Mason, the Chairman of the Summer Project, declared, "This report must raise the question as to whether the private landlord has outlived his usefulness in areas like Notting Hill".

But this, together with all the conclusions of the Report were far too hesitant and weak for a large group of people who had taken part in the Summer Project and had been involved in the housing struggles in the area over the two years since the project. They united behind a counter-document entitled *A First Response* which tried to do what the Report failed to do — to identify the causes and spell out solutions to the housing crisis which it had described.

Whereas the report stressed the need for GLC and Government intervention, the *First Response* laid the prime responsibility for the bad housing conditions on the Borough Council and showed how its policies over the years had been a "wholly ineffective response to century old problems". The reliance on housing associations and endless inspection programmes — the Council's main housing policy at the time — could do nothing to stop speculative market pressures eroding the stock of low income housing, or to add to the housing stock.

> "The Borough Council have created the misery of Notting Hill by a century of inactivity; by the refusal to buy up property through compulsory purchase; by the poverty of their building programme; by the tacit support for speculators and racketeers. The need now is for action to change it."

A long-term solution was seen as depending on Council building and converting more accommodation at rents within the reach of local working people. Central government finance would be needed to back this up. Immediate steps should be taken to achieve this by compulsory purchase of all properties in bad repair and all property threatened with conversion to luxury developments and planning permission for luxury developments refused.

However, the *First Response* was not the only public reaction to the Report. The same day the report came out a public meeting was held to put the findings to the people of the area in Lancaster Road Church. A 300 strong audience packed the church including dozens of local people who had taken part in direct action in housing themselves and were impatient for more action.

Maggie O'Shannon who had recently led her street in their fight for rehousing by squatting gave an angry impassioned speech: "I don't know what you English people are made of. Everything they want to slap on you, you just stand there and take it. You should squat, resist and stand up for yourselves".

Another speaker invoked the spirit of Bogside and pointed to what they had achieved there as an example of the power of civil disobedience to shake those in power.

Sensing the anger and the impatience of the audience, George Clark started talking about direct action too, but not immediately. He warned the Borough Council:

"If you ignore the message of this Report then from 1st January 1970 you will see a campaign of civil disobedience the like of which this country has never seen before. But let us try the constructive way first".

Back came the shouts of "Now! Now! Why wait till then?"

People in the area had already taken direct action and could not understand why there should suddenly be an eight-month moratorium in the housing battle. George Clark went on to make vain efforts to dissipate the anger by talking about the mass rent registration drive to be launched in June as a first step to "mobilising the community for further struggle". But this did not hold water. He had said at the press conference that morning that 80% of all furnished tenants applying to the Rent Tribunal left within a year. With such a high proportion of furnished tenants in the area and while the law on security of tenure remained unchanged, a mass campaign along these lines would only be urging tenants to speed up their own eviction.

People were not satisfied with this and went on with organising their own activities. A march through the area was planned in two weeks' time by the Notting Hill People's Association and the Notting Hill Squatters. The aim was to involve as many local people as possible in protesting at the wretched housing conditions which they experienced and the Report described, and to make clear the demands on the Council for immediate action. The demands of the march were:

— compulsory purchase to end private landlords and make good homes at low rents;
— no more luxury flats;
— control by tenants over their own homes;
— a crash plan for home building.

Five hundred people joined the march, which took three hours walking through almost every street in the area, stopping at each place where a battle had been fought. It started at Colville Gardens with speeches and street theatre, went to 43 Artesian Road, St. Stephens Gardens hostel for the homeless; Camelford Road and many other local landmarks.

The publicity for the march had been stickers saying "Squat, Colville Gardens, May 17" which produced panic padlock buying by Gubbay, the owner of Colville Gardens. The publicity also attracted the police. Three coach loads followed the march the length of the route. Their confused reactions reached comic proportions at times. *People's News* tells how, in Camelford Road:

"Forty police swarmed out of their green buses, and lined up outside Numbers 9, 11 and 13 Camelford Road to protect them from potential squatters. They did not seem to know that each of these houses is well filled with families some of whom went on the march. However, the police had their orders and stood firm despite the laughter of passing marchers and the reaction of a small boy who ran his hands along the row of policemen's knees, just as if they were rather thick railings. Lucky dogs didn't take the same view".[1]

But there were no plans to occupy any houses that day. Instead the marchers concentrated on distributing to everyone in the streets the 1,000 copies of a *People's News* special issue on housing — it included a popular version of the Survey results and also large sections on housing struggles people had fought and were fighting in the area. The council was provoked by the publication of the survey into calling a press conference in June to explain its response to the survey and to announce some shifts in policy. The significance of these shifts will be evaluated once all the actions taken to put pressure on the Council have been considered.

The Colville Tavistock Study 1972-3

Not to be outdone by the publication of the Housing Survey in 1969, the Council announced in October, 1971, that they were appointing a Mr Clinch, the former Director of Technical Services, to be Director of Redevelopment and to carry out a study of the Colville/Tavistock area. £45,000 was voted for a year-long study. The local press hailed the announcement with headlines like "Colville, Brave New World". A Council press release in January, 1972, stated that "People in Colville and Tavistock are to be asked by the Council to take part in planning a new future for their area..."

But as soon as the first announcement of the Study was made, the suspicions of the People's Association Housing Group were roused. The issue of *People's News*[2] for that week explains why. Entitled "Fiddler on the roofs", it read:

> "An expensive trick is about to be played on North Kensington. This Monday, October 25th Mr. Clinch has taken up his duties as Director of Redevelopment... But surely most information about Colville/Tavistock is already in the Council's hands. Public Health Inspectors have called on every house to make sure there are basic facilities provided. In 1967 it was surveyed by the Notting Hill Summer Project. By 1969 the Council's Town Planning office had a detailed assessment of properties fit to rehabilitate and those to be pulled down. Indeed detailed redevelopment proposals have already been examined at the Town Hall... Now it looks as if the decisions are being shelved for at least another year while the deposed Borough Engineer tries his hand at the same old problem.
>
> Housing problems in Colville are far too serious to be monkeyed around with like this by the Council. If the Council really intend to do nothing for the area they should say so and people will know what they have to fight.
>
> To drag on with expensive follies like Mr Clinch and his merry men is a savage joke at our expense".

It was felt that what was needed was not yet another survey but a fundamental change in Council policy to establish much greater public control of housing so that some guarantee could be given to the people of the area that the houses would be improved for them.

The Council's decision to carry out the Colville Study set in train a whole series of angry actions led by the Housing Group of the Notting Hill People's Association, which stretched from the beginning of 1972 through to the middle of 1973.

The Non-Cooperation Campaign

In December 1971 Clinch sent letters to known members of local organisations to "secure their cooperation". He asked them to share their insights into living conditions and community activities with him and went on to declare that "Any plans should be firmly based on the housing and social needs of residents in the area and designed to dislocate their lives as little as possible". It was agreed by the Housing Group to meet these approaches with a wall of silence and to encourage others to do the same.

Clinch sensed the hostility and resorted to appealing to social workers and clergymen at the Notting Hill Social Council in February, 1972.

> "I will seize every opportunity to break down the hostility of the people to the Council . . . My job is a difficult one because the Council is distrusted. The people are tired to death of surveys and hungry for action. It is only with the help of social workers like you that I can succeed in getting the cooperation of the people."

He went on:

> "I have no ambition to draw up a blueprint for high standard redevelopment but rather to ensure a contented community. Total redevelopment can be extremely cruel since it results in communities being torn up by their roots. In Colville this would mean that the true Colville, the human Colville would be lost forever. We must ensure that the present population has a real chance to remain. The aim of the Report is to give people who want to stay in the area the opportunity to do so."

So he had got a clear message through the wall of silence — that many people would not cooperate with the Study unless there were guarantees that they could stay in the area and the improvements would be for them.

But the words of Clinch were not enough — he was just a paid employee of the Council, not a policy maker, and he knew it. He said at that same meeting

> "I would be very frustrated if the doors were shut in my face. I don't believe my task is to hoodwink the people but I can't give any guarantees to the people that the Council will do what we recommend. It will just be a consultative report".

And truer words were never spoken as it turned out at the end of the day.

So an angry call went out from the Housing Group and leaflets were delivered to everyone in the area urging them not to cooperate unless four basic demands were met to ensure that people had a real chance of staying in the area in decent conditions. The demands were that:

1. A written promise be given by the Council to all in Colville now that when their house is improved they will have the choice of permanent rehousing *or* staying in the improved home with regulated rents.
2. The Council give every landlord notice that:
    a. they have six months to send in improvement plans;
    b. planning permission will only be given for improvement geared to the needs of the present tenants;
    c. grants will only be given on condition that regulated rents are fixed for the improved flats, and on condition that the Council nominate new tenants if the present ones do not want to remain.
3. The Council use compulsory purchase powers to buy up every house where:
    a. no improvement plans are submitted in six months;
    b. there has been harassment by the landlord.
4. The Council make the money available to do all this.

At this stage the Housing Group was thinking in terms of improvements being done by private landlords subject to specific controls. As the economic facts of improvement became clearer, this came to be seen as unrealistic and the demands became more extreme.

The non-cooperation campaign found ready support in an area which was tired of surveys. Within the first week a hundred new members of the Housing Group were signed up. The survey team reported a very poor response to the survey team's requests for people to fix appointments for interviews and by March the decision was taken to cut the survey from 100 per cent to 25 per cent of all houses in the area.

In April a "Declaration of Non-Cooperation" was presented to the Study Steering Group by the Housing Group signed by 23 groups in the area supporting the Housing Group's demands. The response of Councillor Methuen, the Chairman of the Group, was predictable: "It's stupid for the Council to give undertakings in advance of what we will do after the study", and that he saw cooperation not as a favour to be granted by the people to the Council's initiative, but expected it as a natural response.

However, Clinch reported to the same meeting of the Steering Group, "The survey is having tremendous difficulty due to the high level of organised opposition in the area". The response of the survey team was to recommend the freezing of improvement grants in the area as a step to satisfying the Housing Group's demands. The Notting Hill Housing Trust, who were jointly involved with the Council in organising the study, supported this view, together with the wider use of CPO's.

However, the Council representatives on the Group would not budge. Methuen declared:

> "I am an improvement grants man. I believe in a mixed community so that more money will flow into the area and the shops will do better. But if the bad effects of giving improvement grants outweigh the good ones then we would have to reconsider the policy . . . but we would require very considerable chapter and verse of the hardship involved by the improvement grants scheme before advising it should be discontinued".

Yet he could rest assured that the Colville Study would not provide him with any evidence since it was not asking any questions to show the processes at work in the area; it concentrated on a once off view of how things were at one moment in time. But the Housing Group was working on the evidence.

Having resisted any major shifts in their improvement grants policy, the Steering Group agreed that it was necessary to give some guarantees of good faith to the hostile and suspicious people of the area, and suggested "some relatively inexpensive improvements which could be carried out immediately like the imaginative reconstruction of the closed space in Talbot Road" — an environmental scheme already in the pipeline and so not involving any additional finance. But it was not that easy to fool the people.

"Losing Out"

In May the Housing Group produced *Losing Out,* a report on the way the process of improvement was forcing out the low income people of the area. It took the Group a month to produce at virtually no cost in contrast to the Colville Study taking a year and £45,000.

What the Housing Group did was to take a 10 per cent sample of all the privately owned houses in the Colville/Tavistock area and compare the rent levels and types of flats with those in 1967, using the information from the Summer Project Survey. The study focused on privately rented housing since it made up 80 per cent of houses in Colville. They found that 40 per cent of all privately rented houses in the area surveyed had changed from "low rent" to "high rent" accommodation in the five-year period.

Whereas in 1967 the average rent of flats was £4.50, in 1972 the average rent of flats in converted houses was £14.50, though the size of the units in converted houses was only two-thirds of the size they were before.

The 1967 GLC Housing Occupancy Survey was cited, showing that half the households of Colville had less than £20 per week income. So the large rent increases and the decrease in size of the newly converted units provided a formidable barrier to the local people in need of housing, many of whom were families. Improvement grants had obviously been important in speeding up this process of conversion since in almost every case conversions had taken place since 1969 when the restrictions on their use were lifted and the size of the maximum grant was increased. (More detailed evidence of where grants had been used was refused by the Council, despite Methuen's request for hard evidence of the effect of the use of improvement grants!) A calculation of the rents a private landlord would have to charge even if he received an improvement grant, in order to cover costs and a 15 per cent profit margin produced a rent of £9.50 a floor exclusive of rates. (This was based on 1969 prices so that it would be more comparable with the income figures available.)

Experience of what had happened where grants had been used in 1-9 Colville Gardens and 11 and 12 Colville Square was examined to show that in both cases over 60 per cent of the households were forced out into other private accommodation despite organised resistance both legal and political. "Out of 68 households displaced in these two developments that were traced, 73 adults and 49 children had to find accommodation in a private market which ultimately is unable and unwilling to house them."

The report concluded that if left unchecked by Council intervention, this process would speed up and intensify so that all "low rent" privately rented housing in Colville/Tavistock would have disappeared well before 1980. In the light of this, any stated commitment to the local people was seen as "empty and specious" unless certain conditions were met. In addition to the written guarantee to everyone in the area that they could stay in the area after improvements and the Council making the finance available to improve the area for the people, *Losing Out* added a third condition, "the elimination of private landlords from Colville/Tavistock who, as the evidence shows, are not capable of providing sound low rent accommodation".

Copies of *Losing Out* were circulated to all involved in the Study, who claimed to be so eager for participation, consultation and feed-back, but no official response to its findings was ever made.

The First Community Forum

Then in June came the Community Forum, the Council's first formal attempt at participation. In January the Council press statement had declared,

> "Throughout the survey the team . . . will be in continual consultation with the people living in the area . . . the Colville/Tavistock area is primarily the concern of the people who live there and their views are vital".

Despite all this they had waited seven months since the study began to hold a public meeting. Yet having called the meeting the agenda was geared to avoiding any discussion of the most controversial issue of housing. There was no mention of *Losing Out* as an item for discussion, though it was the only written response to the study by people in the area. Environmental improvement was the only issue the Council thought important enough to discuss. A film of tree planting and street closures in a northern town were shown and Clinch made a speech about the "cosmetic" improvements which should be carried out while the survey went ahead. But the housing discussion was forced on the platform and for an hour the Councillors were battered by attack from the floor. Though the Housing Group had decided to boycott the Forum as a group, as a continuation of their non-cooperation campaign, it was agreed a few members should go to find out what happened and to push the Housing Group views in whatever ways they thought best. Under pressure Muller the Housing Chairman, came out with, "Some people might think compulsory purchase was the answer, but I am not one of these - I believe in private landlords". In response to a demand for a change in policy and greater intervention he said, "We must remain consistent". Methuen when pressed on what would happen once the study was finished promised, "The Council has both the means and the will to implement the results of the Colville/Tavistock survey". But this was countered by Muller who was forced to admit that one use to which the survey would be put would be to help the Council to decide how many of the present residents were essential workers, implying the rest could be left to whatever the property speculators had in store for them.

So the inconsistencies in the Council's position were forced into the open — on one hand promising to carry out the proposals of the study whatever they were, and on the other, saying that any policy change would be inconsistent for them and they knew what policies they believed in.

So far as public consultation went, the first Community Forum was a failure. There were about 50 people there, of whom 40 were workers for social agencies in the area, and only the other 10 local residents. One of the Housing Group ended the meeting by proposing that there should be no more Community Forums till the Council had decided what new policies they were willing to consider to provide guarantees for people in the area, since only this would end the doubletalk. It was agreed that this should be on the agenda of the next forum.

The Housing Group's Action Meeting

In July 1972 the Housing Group showed what public meetings in the area could really be like. They called an Action Meeting with the two aims of saying "no" to the Colville Study and making the area a "no-go" area for speculation.

The local press report (*Kensington Post* 28.7.72) entitled "Crisis meeting declare Colville and Tavistock a no-go area to 'sharks' ", read,

"More than 300 people, young and old, militants and not-so-militant who responded to the call from the People's Association Housing Group to 'act now' met in All Saints Church Hall. The Housing Group succeeded where the Borough Council and the Trust have failed — they got the people of Colville to tell them what they wanted for the area . . . action in line with the Housing Group demands . . . Individuals, single people, old age pensioners, mothers and young couples gave first hand experiences of pressures, inducements and harassment . . . The momentum of their resentment and determination to fight for their homes overwhelmed the meeting".

The Housing Group was amazed by the strength and unity of the meeting: "We have never had a meeting before where people have displayed so much unity. We expected to have to persuade them to join us, but they were already with us." But this had not happened by chance. For weeks before the meeting the Housing Group established a full time presence on the streets, distributing thousands of *People's News* special issues, explaining the background to the battle in housing, all about the Colville Study, about the victories won so far and what still needed to be done.

Out of the meeting came plans for action: for a full scale attack on the Council and Colville Study at the next community forum; for a network of street organisers meeting weekly to keep abreast of all property developments and struggles against them; for a wall newspaper at the end of each street to publicise what was going on; for a permanent squatting group and for a people's property agency to step up the pressure on the Council to CPO individual houses.

The meeting had an immediate impact on the local property world. The next day Arthur Lawrence, a local estate agent, gave a long hysterical interview to the *Kensington Post*. He announced he was planning a meeting of property owners and estate agents and was going to ask them to offer a reward of up to £1,000 for information leading to the arrest of people organising disruption of the property market. He claimed property owners were subject to a lot of pressure: his windows had been plastered with posters and smashed, auctions had been disrupted, owners threatened, and he himself had had 500 bogus telephone calls about particular properties he was selling. He went on to warn the militants that the police were on the look out for them since his meeting with a top police officer.

People's News declared,

"So it's open war. The people are going on the offensive against the speculators and the speculators are regrouping their forces and trying to use rewards and the police to trap the people who are fighting for their right to a decent home".

Crofton, the leader of the Council, also gave an interview to the *Kensington Post* after the public meeting. He said that he was well aware of tenants' fears that they will be forced out of the area, "But the Council will not shift, we are not going to be put off by agitation".

Last Community Forum – First Lock-in

The second Community Forum was planned for the 2nd August 1972. The Housing Group mass meeting had agreed that this should not be ignored. They had not cooperated with the Colville Study so far, but now they would force their cooperation on the Council and see whether they were still so eager to talk of consultation and participation. Hundreds of leaflets were distributed throughout the area inviting everyone to the Community Forum, in contrast to the virtual absence of any Council publicity. The leaflet read, "The Council are coming to a so-called Community Forum. We must now make them listen to what we want for a change". People were asked to meet in Powis Square and march to the Forum together. The hut chosen for the Forum was so small that the first 80 or so people to arrive packed it out and the rest had to stand outside looking in through the open windows. Everyone made a point of being early and there was barely room for the Council officials. The chairs had been rearranged in what was felt to be a more democratic circular formation and the platform was taken over for more seating space. From the moment the Council officials entered and had to walk down the central gangway watched by dozens of angry eyes, and saw their seats on the platform already occupied, the hostility of the audience must have been obvious.

Eaton, the Housing Chairman, tried to win over the audience by making a special announcement on the subject of improvement grants. The Council had decided to shift their policy on giving improvement grants. Though they would still be given to owner occupiers and where they would benefit the present tenants the Council wanted to prevent them going to speculators. So they were going to send a questionnaire to all applicants for grants who were not owner occupiers asking questions to see if they were speculators or not! Inspectors would visit and talk to the tenants if they were still there. If the owner gave the answers the Council wanted to hear, the grant would be given with no condition at all, and would not be taken back even if the owner went ahead and evicted all the tenants.

Instead of placating the audience it made them angrier. The Chairman moved on to the first item on the agenda – the terms of reference of the Colville Study. The Council announced all options were open for consideration and the Study could recommend whatever policies it saw to be necessary. At this point the Housing Group introduced their own alternative agenda, just to test how open the Council was to policies it didn't like. The "independent" Chairman, Rev. Peter Clake, refused to accept the alternative agenda and tried to close the meeting. Whereupon,

"'All the 'dignitaries' made a rush for the door — only to find the doors locked and people blocking their paths. One by one they were confronted and tackled by people from the audience. One of the more agile notables, John Coward, jumped through the window — dispersing the onlookers who had been peering through the windows. His goodbye from the meeting was a threat that he'd end up in Brixton if he called the police. Clinch and Methuen anxiously tried to unbolt the door behind the audience but it wouldn't budge. Seeing there was no possible escape for them, they had to return to their seats and listen to what the people wanted."

From then onwards the "People's Agenda" was discussed. This included resolutions that the Council must give a written guarantee to every resident that they will be able to stay in the area in improved homes at low rents; that private landlords be eliminated from the area since they have proved themselves incapable of providing decent homes at low rents, and that the Council must start the compulsory purchase of every badly managed house immediately. All these resolutions were passed unanimously, except for the Chairmen of the Housing and Planning Committees, who voted against every resolution.

"Clinch was the one who really let the side down when he was forced to admit that the level of rents charged by private landlords would be way beyond the average income of people in Colville. How startled Methuen and his cronies looked — but there wasn't much they could do. Their blue eyed boy Clinch had really disappointed them: perhaps they'll have to train him better in future! After forcing them to swallow the bitter pill of 'Public Participation', the people finally released them well after 10.20 p.m. The Chairman was 'reminded' to announce the date of the next meeting, which is, October 24th."[4]

One point this report omits is that during the proceedings a second public promise was made by Methuen that when the recommendations of the Study are made "they will be honoured by the Council".

But this was the last of the Council's attempts to consult the people. The Steering Group decided to cancel all future Community Forums. In September Clinch wrote to all participants:

"Unfortunately the Community Forum has not been a great success. The last meeting was largely 'taken over' by a highly organised group which has actively opposed the survey from the beginning. They have sincere and very strong views which should be expressed and must be carefully considered, but it is quite wrong to allow them to dominate proceedings as though they were able to speak for all the people of the neighbourhood ... There is an alternative to periodic meetings of the Forum — by circulating papers for study at home and discussion informally among yourselves: any criticism could be sent here in writing."

Participants were asked if this method of consultation would be acceptable. The Housing Group responded immediately:

"Any pretence that a circulation of papers among the select few on the mailing list is a kind of 'community forum' is fraudulent. Since so few people in this area are used to communicating in writing, this would cut even more people out of any discussion . . . In the light of this we feel that the Steering Committee should continue to hold a Community Forum on October 24th . . . However, the whole study team should take the responsibility of publicising the forum this time instead of leaving it to us. The Housing Group has made its position perfectly clear at the last forum and has nothing more to say. People from the area have backed up the Housing Group demands, both at our own public meeting when 300 people attended and at the last forum. It is the job of further forums to report back on the Council's response to our demands."

But on October 16th the Council put out a press release announcing, "Members of the Colville/Tavistock Community Forum have elected not to hold any more meetings before the publication of the consultative report."

Clinch's report out

In February 1973 the housing section of the Study appeared in draft and the Housing Group got down to analysing it and publicising it. The report explained in detail how improvements by private landlords were forcing low income people out of the area. A typical four-storey house in the area costing £15,000 was taken as a basis for calculating what the cost rents would be for different types of owners after improvement. This showed that the average cost rent for each of three converted flats would be: £25 for a private landlord, who would include a profit element in his cost rent, in contrast to nearly £13 if the owner was a housing trust or the Council. The Report looked at these rent levels in the context of the income levels of the present population and stated that even for the 11 per cent heads of households with an income over £40 a week a rent of £25 would be virtually impossible. So the conclusion is reached that private improvement "must result in a complete change in the social structure of the neighbourhood . . . it would rob Colville/Tavistock of its traditional role in the community, providing houses for unskilled and semi-skilled manual workers". The policy advocated for the area was for the Council "to use such powers as it has to secure that wherever possible, terraces pass into the ownership of the Council or a housing trust for treatment as a whole".

However, the Report said the Council had no legal powers to compulsory purchase whole terraces and that new legislation was needed. Meanwhile, the Council should compulsory purchase the 450 houses in the area which were multi-occupied, unconverted, and not in the proposed Tavistock redevelopment area. So the Report had argued much of the Housing Group's case. What remained to be done was to show that the Council had the legal powers for widespread compulsory purchase. Within the week the work on the legal powers of the Council was completed and proved that the Council did have power to take over whole streets in the area by control orders and CPOs. *People's News*[5] explains:

"Mr Clinch says in his housing report that the Council has not got the legal powers to compulsory purchase whole streets for improvement by the Council — though this would be the ideal solution he thinks.

"We've got good news for him — the legal powers are there. The People's Association Housing Group sent his report to a top barrister, Stephen Sedley, last week to get his opinion on the Council's powers. The Housing Group put the argument to him that the Council has powers to put a control order on every house in Colville/Tavistock which: (i) has not already been done up with improvement grants; (ii) is not owned by the Council or trust.

"This would immediately take all the houses out of the control of the landlords for five years, and should be used as a way of freezing the property while a CPO was applied for. (There are special powers in the 1969 Housing Act for using control orders in this way, following it up with a CPO within 28 days.) The grounds for using control orders would be: (i) that the houses are in multiple occupation; (ii) that there are health orders outstanding on lots of the houses; (iii) that the safety of all the tenants is threatened by the economic factors of private improvements (minimum rents of £25 a week as Clinch shows); (iv) that the welfare of all the tenants is threatened by the general bad conditions. As soon as the control orders are put on major conversion work should be started. Even if the CPO is not confirmed the cost of the work would be a charge on the house and would depress the price nicely.

"The Housing Group argued that the council had powers to CPO for rehabilitation under the 1957 and 1969 Housing Acts and 1958 Town and Country Planning Act.

"Stephen Sedley has written back to the Housing Group:

'It seems to me that the use of control orders under the 1964 act as an urgent short term measure, coupled with the use of CPOs under the 1957 act, is a proper and more effective remedy for what is evidently a crisis situation' — than the selective CPO Clinch suggests."

Seven Demands

So having cleared the legal obstructions out of the way, only the political objections of the Council remained. So the Housing Group drew up a list of seven demands based on widespread use of control orders and CPOs for which they rallied support.

The seven demands were:

The Council must:

1. Buy every house in Colville/Tavistock by compulsory purchase, except those already owned by the Council or reputable housing trusts.

2. Put control orders on all the above houses since the "health, safety or welfare" of the tenants is at stake whilst CPOs are going through.
3. Start improvements on all these houses as soon as possible after the control orders are served.
4. Withhold all discretionary improvement grants in Colville/Tavistock.
5. Decide that no houses converted by the council be sold, but tenants cooperatives should be encouraged.
6. Undertake to retain or rehouse all residents who wish to remain in the Colville/Tavistock area, and to this end draw up a Register of Housing Requirements for all residents who
   a. wish to stay in the area;
   b. wish to move away.
7. Set up the machinery to take all these actions.

Between February and May the Housing Group worked as part of a coalition built up by the Notting Hill Social Council of all the different local agencies in the area like the churches, the social workers and the Notting Hill Housing Trust. Out of this came agreement with all their seven demands. The only exception was a decision to exclude houses from CPO where the owner occupied over half the house. The backing of the coalition meant that the Council was faced by a united front of all the "respectable" agencies, whose opinions they normally respected (even a member of the local Conservative Party), plus the Housing Group which they otherwise referred to as "extremists" and "militants". The coalition did their bit towards publicising the Study by distributing free 5,000 copies of a four-page supplement on the Study produced by the *Kensington Post*.

Meanwhile the Housing Group went ahead with its own plans to get the ideas raised by the Study around to people in the area. Thousands of broadsheets were distributed explaining what the Colville Study report said and how the Council had all the powers it needed to improve the area for the present tenants. Hundreds of duplicated letters were distributed to and signed by local people asking the Council to put a control order and CPO on their house, and supporting the Housing Group demands for the area.

For two weeks during April the Council mounted an exhibition on the Colville Study proposals but it was not in a very public spot. The Housing Group decided to put up an alternative exhibition in the open, out in front of All Saints Church. For two weeks before the Council's meeting the Housing Group manned the exhibition all day, continually explaining to everyone who passed by, the issues at stake.

In May a public meeting was held by the Housing Group to explain the seven demands and to see if they were supported by people in the area. This was just a week before the Council's public consultation meeting and the aim was to see if it was possible to agree on a common position with which people could confront the Council at their meeting. Between 200-300 people attended and the overwhelming feeling was that the seven demands of the Housing Group should be pressed on the Council as representing the interests of the people in the area.

As soon as the meeting had finished, about 50 people went off to inform Methuen, the Chairman of the Colville Study Steering Group, of the views of the meeting. They arrived on his doorstep at 11.30 p.m. and carried on a debate with his wife and the police from four squad cars and one black maria which had also happened to arrive. After an hour when it was thought Methuen himself had probably been warned not to show his face by returning home, it was agreed to depart and leave Mrs. Methuen to tell her husband all about his angry nocturnal visitors.

One important admission the visit may have helped to produce was that Methuen, when contacted by the press the next day, announced a shift in the Colville Study debate. He declared,

> "Our legal department has now confirmed that we have the necessary powers. All that could stand in the way of the 'ideal' approach in our report (i.e. widespread CPO) is the Minister's willingness to agree".

So by the time the day of the final consultation meeting was reached, there was united support in the area for the seven demands of the Housing Group. The Council had admitted they had the legal powers to carry out the solution recommended by the Study of widespread compulsory purchase and the Council had declared it had "both the means and the will to implement a programme for the improvement of the area stemming from the Study".

Council "Consultation" – The Second Lock-in

People's News[6] tells what happened:

> "More than 400 people packed into the inadequate church hall, many of them believing that at last there was to be discussion, real discussion about the future. They were badly disappointed. All the Council was prepared to do was to get a shorthand writer to take down comments, and to duck all questions about what they wanted to do in the area or pass them over to officers. The meeting swiftly became irritated with the farce, and the radical organisations of the people in the area became united, first to press home the demands that had been hammered out by local groups and people working in the area, and then in an attempt to get the Council representatives to show their good faith by dealing quickly with just one overcrowded family, whose future lay wholly in the Council's hands.
>
> "It was agreed that shorthand comments were no use to anyone, and votes were taken on 11 proposals. The first seven were the Housing Group demands which were supported by a majority of 400:16.
>
> "Unanimous votes were then passed:

8. FOR the *Electric Cinema* remaining;
9. AGAINST a *car park* being built on the site of the Electric block;
10. FOR the *Talbot Tabernackle* being opened up as a community centre with play facilities but not as a sports centre;
11. FOR local *secondary schools* remaining in the area.

"These last four demands all oppose the recommendations of the Colville Study.

"This part of the meeting was decided and finished by 9.15 p.m., only one hour after the start of the meeting. With the main business of the evening finished, the meeting decided to put the Council's good faith to the test. The Chippolina family was brought in, two parents and six children. They were about to be evicted by the Council and placed into a single room in a hostel. The Council members and officers present were asked to take action to ensure this family was provided with adequate accommodation before it was evicted, and so give a gesture of good faith to all at the meeting. But no one would admit to being able to do anything.

"They declined to send for the Director of Social Services, or for anyone who could be helpful. At 11.30, when it became clear that for them a real discussion only means 'we can't' or 'we haven't decided', a last effort was made by the meeting to make progress. Council representatives were sat around the table with representatives of the family, to agree on a statement and to pledge early action in the morning. Eighteen separate drafts were drawn up, but the result was so woolly that the meeting was unanimous that everyone should stay until the morning.

"The meeting settled down for the night in a relaxed manner. Food, drink and music were sent for and hard debate went on and on and on. If there is any interest in what people think, there will be no doubts left in Council minds."

Ned Gate (No. 4, May 1973), another local newspaper, fills out what happened:

"The Councillors sat around in their smart suits, with nervous grins, making cheap jokes and trying to fob people off with long-winded replies about what they couldn't do. But they weren't left in peace. Many people decided to give these fat-bellied councillors some of the harassment and repression they have experienced for years. People sat on the council table, shouted abuse at them. For the first time in their lives, the councillors were forced to listen. In the early morning, the councillors had only agreed to put off the eviction of the Chippolina family for two weeks while they consider the case.

"At about 10 a.m. the police, who had been circling all night, came to the building and Methuen ran to a window demanding, 'Get me out!'". The police announced that they would break in and 'release' the councillors if people did not leave peacefully. Most people thought that it would not be useful to give the police another opportunity to beat people up and make a lot of arrests. After a few minutes everybody made their demands once more to the councillors, and walked out singing, 'Power to the people: CPO!'.

"The frightened councillors were let out the back door."

The event was seized on by local and national press and front page headlines read "The siege of Notting Hill", "Mob rule". The meeting had succeeded in holding 22 councillors and officials in the meeting hall from 10.30 p.m. to 10.30 a.m. the next morning. These included the Deputy Leader of the Council and every senior officer except the Town Clerk. It provoked a row between the Council and the police. The police were accused of unnecessary delay in freeing the "hostages". But their argument was that Methuen had told the Chief Superintendent just before the meeting that he would be prepared "to talk all night if necessary" so that though the police knew the councillors were still in the hall, they did not know if they were there voluntarily or under duress. The police maintained "The doors were locked during the early hours simply to keep undesirables from getting in. There was no question of the people being kept there against their will" (*Evening News* 9.5.73).

But Methuen maintained he called the police at 7.00 a.m. and Crofton stated, "It was only after strenuous efforts were made by the Town Clerk that the police moved in some three hours later", despite the fact that Crofton had told the police to use "whatever force is necessary" to free the councillors (*West London Observer* 18.5.75).

The Council response was hysterical. Sir Malby Crofton announced his decision to ban any further Council public meetings in the north of the borough and declared, "It is impossible to have further consultation with the north. These are thugs. They don't want the voice of reason to be heard and they don't want public discussion" (*Kensington Post* 18.5.73). The story went on,

> "A gang of organised thugs and anarchists has moved into North Kensington with the specific intention of hampering the Borough Council's efforts to improve conditions there. They aim to prevent progress and to stifle public discussion. Already they have been so successful that they have created a general atmosphere of anarchy and terrorism in North Kensington. These are the views of Leader Sir Malby Crofton."

The morning after the lock-in, Crofton told the press, "I am not making any bargains with these bloody anarchists" (*Evening Standard* 9.5.73).

But the press also carried views of local residents wholeheartedly supporting the lock-in.

> "They are absolutely justified in what they did. Everybody in this area has got to stick together, otherwise we will not get anywhere. The Council

have got to know that the Notting Hill people are a fighting race and this is what we are going to do — fight."

(— *a local stall holder. West London Observer* 25.5.73.)

A local company director took issue with Crofton's allegations:

"In fact the whole population of North Kensington was fully represented, with numerous Council and private tenants, owner occupiers, shopkeepers and stall holders. The only people present from outside the area were the Borough Council platform party, none of whom either live in North Kensington or represent any part of it.

"The only people who stayed away were the very councillors who will decide the fate of the Council report which the meeting was called to discuss — the new Planning Committee Chairman and Council Leader Crofton himself!

"He also claims that not all viewpoints were given a hearing, and that there was organised disruption. In fact every single viewpoint was heard at length, including that of the platform party.

"The only disruptive element was the evasive and irresponsible attitude of the platform towards truthfulness, their statutory duties and the people of North Kensington."

(— *Kensington Post* 25.5.73)

A local adult education officer wrote:

"Did the night achieve anything?

1. It could be a reminder that the compulsion of a night is nothing compared with the compulsion experienced by families in similar and worse straights to the Chippolinas. Their need is decent housing provided at a rent they can afford. Such people are much more hemmed in than anyone was the other night — and get no reprieve in the morning.
2. Councillors who for one minute faced intimidation as the attempt was made to move them to the gallery to make way for the day nursery, might reflect that those with no capital and low incomes are under constant exposure to intimidation. Their movements-under-compulsion are to make way, not for children but for those to whom property is a money making game, not a human necessity.
3. I have a personal abhorrence of compulsion and intimidation and of exploitation too. But people like myself with a liberal background must avoid the trap of being more offended by the unrestrained anger and the style of controversy and disruption than by the quiet victimisation of people."

(— *Kensington Post* 18.5.73)

The main issues voted on almost unanimously early on in the meeting were also picked up in the press:

"The really significant aspect of the Notting Hill outrage was not so much the siege itself (which was sparked off by an individual case of bureaucratic insensitivity) as the evidence it provided of firm local approval for the chief principles set out in the Colville/Tavistock report.

"The use of compulsory purchase powers where necessary to rehabilitate old housing stock and then return it to the rented market to be run either by the Council or by housing associations (a policy the report advocates) has much to recommend it . . . Unless the Government is aware of the sort of grievances that led to the incident in Notting Hill, its expected White Paper in July on the problems of obsolescent housing will have little new to offer."

(*– Evening Standard* editorial 10.5.73)

Just three days later, *The Guardian* carried a story announcing a major shift in government housing policy:

"The Government now accepts that a much more widespread use of CPOs to deal with the housing problem is inevitable . . . The main purpose of the CPOs will be to ensure that:

- Old houses throughout the country which urgently need repairs and renovation can be swiftly acquired and improved by local authorities and thus saved for the housing stock.
- In areas such as London where traditional communities are being driven out by high prices and middle class invasions, houses can be municipally acquired and let at reasonable rents.

"It was this issue of middle class takeovers of communities and soaring rents which lay behind the siege of Notting Hill this week . . ."

The lock-in was the culmination of the struggle against profit in housing. It fused mass radical action with a clear set of alternative policies based on legal powers the Council admitted it had. The confrontation was sharp and clear between two very different sets of political assumptions.

FOOTNOTES

1. *People's News*, Vol. 1, No. 18, May 18, 1969.
2. *People's News*, Vol. 3, No. 30, Oct. 1971.
3. *People's News*, Vol. 4, No. 22, July 24, 1972.
4. *People's News*, Vol. 4, No. 24, Aug. 7, 1972.
5. *People's News*, Vol. 5, No. 8, Feb. 19, 1973.
6. *People's News*, Vol. 5. No. 18, May 22, 1973.

Chapter 9

Housing Shifts 1966-1974

These years spanned a wide range of local actions demanding changes in housing in North Kensington — from the early attempts to force the Council to intervene over 1-9 Colville Gardens, to the lock-in of the Council where compulsory purchase of the whole Colville/Tavistock area was the clear demand of all politically active local people, and almost all local organisations.

Over this period massive changes occurred in both the Golborne Triangle and Colville/Tavistock areas.

However, in assessing these changes both the electoral invulnerability of the Conservative Group on the Council and their firm commitment to a non-interventionist housing policy over the years, explained in the political economy section, must be borne in mind. It is only in the context of these very real political constraints that the significance of the housing shifts which did take place in the Colville/Tavistock and Golborne areas, can be fully understood.

An attempt to chart these changes will focus on these two areas, since these were two of the three study areas which the 1967 Housing Survey of the Notting Hill Summer Project had highlighted as areas of bad housing conditions for which the Council had no plans.

The third area in the 1967 Survey was the Lancaster Road West redevelopment area for which the Council had plans. This area will not be examined since no major attack was launched on the redevelopment plans as such by local people and the Council has just continued with the slow implementation of their original plan.

Since 1967 the weight of community activity has continued to focus on the two areas. Most of the housing activity and campaigns described in this study took place in the Colville/Tavistock area. The housing activity in Golborne concentrated on the need for a phased redevelopment programme which would allow all who wished, to be rehoused in new homes within the area. These activities have not been described here since others are better qualified to write them up. But this is not to imply that the conditions in

Golborne were not equally in the minds of those who were fighting campaigns in Colville. At times, squats and marches united the people from both areas.

The Golborne Triangle and Colville/Tavistock Areas

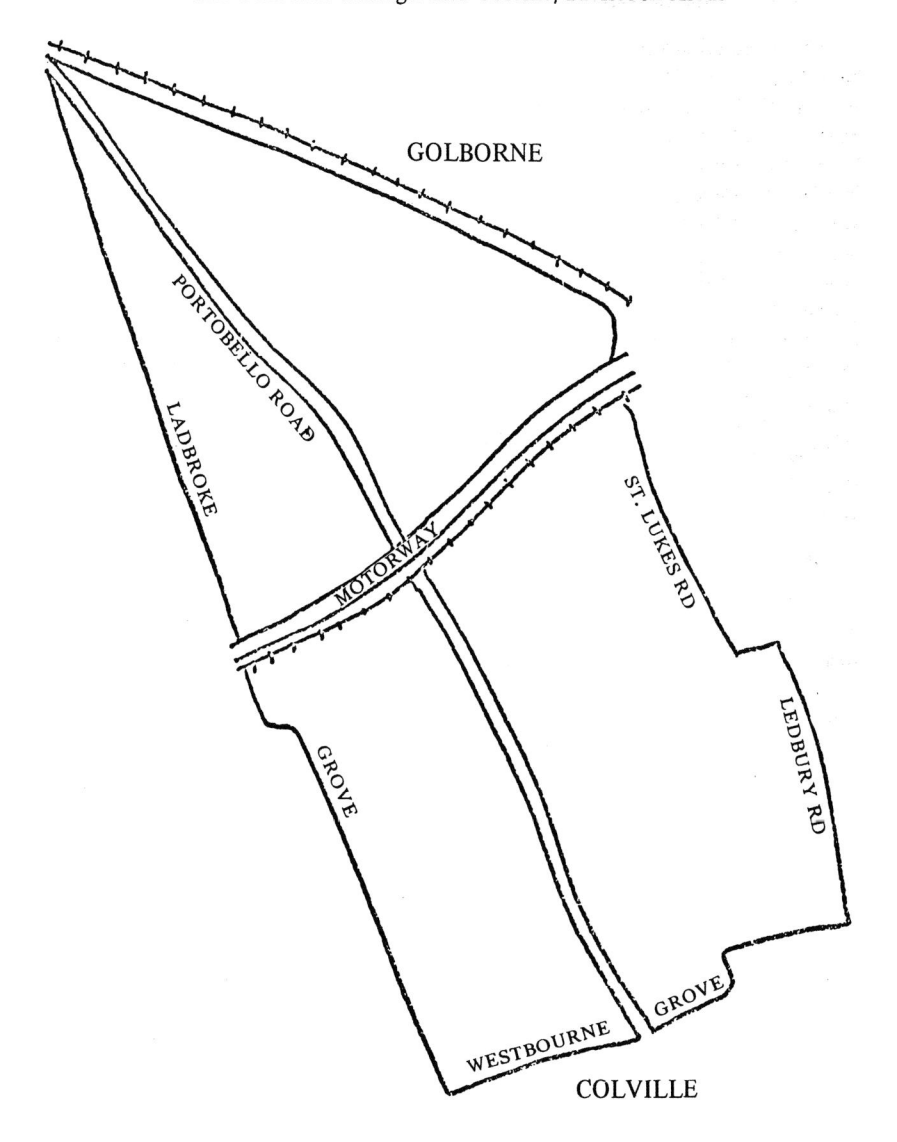

The map shows the boundaries of the two areas:

- The Golborne Area, enclosed by Ladbroke Grove, the Motorway and the Great Western Main Railway Line;
- The Colville Area, enclosed by the Motorway, Ladbroke Grove, Westbourne Grove and the Borough boundary.

The Council itself had recognised both Colville and Golborne as areas of bad housing in January 1963, when the Medical Officer of Health gave a report which pinpointed the 1900 houses in the two areas. He recommended that the best solution would be for the Council to demolish and redevelop both areas since all the houses were over 100 years old and not worth rehabilitating. However, the MOH went on, since the Council's present slum clearance commitment to the Lancaster Road West scheme made this impossible an inspection programme was recommended. This would aim at using the powers under the 1961 and 1957 Housing Acts to get the houses repaired and provided with the basic facilities like baths, toilets and hot and cold water. A team of six Public Health Inspectors was to be employed to work in the two areas. The Council accepted these recommendations and obviously hoped to get away with the cost of six Health Inspectors' salaries to solve the housing problems in these areas. The inspections were still going on in 1967.

However, by the beginning of 1974 there had been changes both in the Council's stance to housing in the two areas and in the actual plans for the areas.

A. The Council's Stance

In 1967 there were no grand statements made about the action the Council was going to take to improve housing in North Kensington. The inspection programme was still going on and thousands of visits and revisits clocked up by the Health Inspectors, but this was seen in terms of a "holding operation" aimed at "arresting the deterioration towards the conditions which could only have been dealt with by slum clearance". (Town Planning Committee Report, December 10th 1968).

But by 1969 the Council obviously felt under pressure to portray their housing programme in more dynamic terms. Sir Malby Crofton was the new Leader of the Council and the Interim Report of the Notting Hill Summer Project came out in May focussing the attention of the national press and the Ministry on the bad housing conditions in the north of the Royal Borough. The Minister of Housing, Anthony Greenwood, summoned representatives of the Council to meet him early in June and recommended that detailed schemes be prepared for redevelopment and rehabilitation schemes in North Kensington.

The Council obviously felt under pressure to justify its housing policies. They held a special press conference on June 24th, 1969, and prepared a thick folder for distribution, packed with reports from the Planning and Housing Committees, the Medical Officer of Health and the Leader of the Council, as well as diagrams and charts illustrating the Council housing policies.

Crofton's statement had a campaigning, pioneering introduction:

"We think the time has come to present the facts as we, the responsible authority, see them . . . What we are doing may be of wider interest in showing how bad conditions can be dealt with . . . so as to preserve rather than uproot and destroy an existing very lively and colourful community."

However, the only new element introduced into Council policy was a financial commitment to a substantial increase in ownership by the housing trusts.

In order to allow the housing trusts to purchase more properties in a highly competitive market, the Council announced a new deficit financing scheme for the trusts. A sum of £one-quarter million was to be set aside annually from the rates as a fund for bridging the gap between the high "cost rents" which the spiralling prices of houses bought by the trusts were producing, and the "actual" rents the tenants could afford. This was in fact introducing an open ended subsidy system to the trusts, allowing them to continue functioning by paying the high market prices and still cater for low income tenants. This subsidy shift was coupled with a new policy of allowing them to borrow from the Council the realistic market value of a property, including the cost of repairs and necessary charges. This replaced the previous policy of using the District Valuer's much lower valuations which corresponded more closely to what would be compulsory purchase price, which had resulted in the trusts being repeatedly outbid.

Crofton ended his speech with a messianic flourish:

"We are not attempting to wave a magic wand to change conditions overnight. We are proposing instead a long steady slog of clearance and improvement (involving a substantial change of ownership from private to other hands) which will preserve the character and vitality of our local community . . . We have a relatively young and enthusiastic Council, a first class team of officers, policies on which we are all in broad agreement and a real sense of compassion. We do care and we shall succeed".

There was certainly a change of style. Instead of talking in defensive terms of the inspection programme as a "holding operation" to stop further deterioration, Crofton has shifted to confident talk of "clearance and improvement" to "preserve the character and vitality of our local community" and of "a substantial change of ownership from private to other hands" introducing a new open ended subsidy system to the trusts to allow them to expand their operations. However, despite the change in style, the basic inconsistency between the policy of relying to a large extent on private

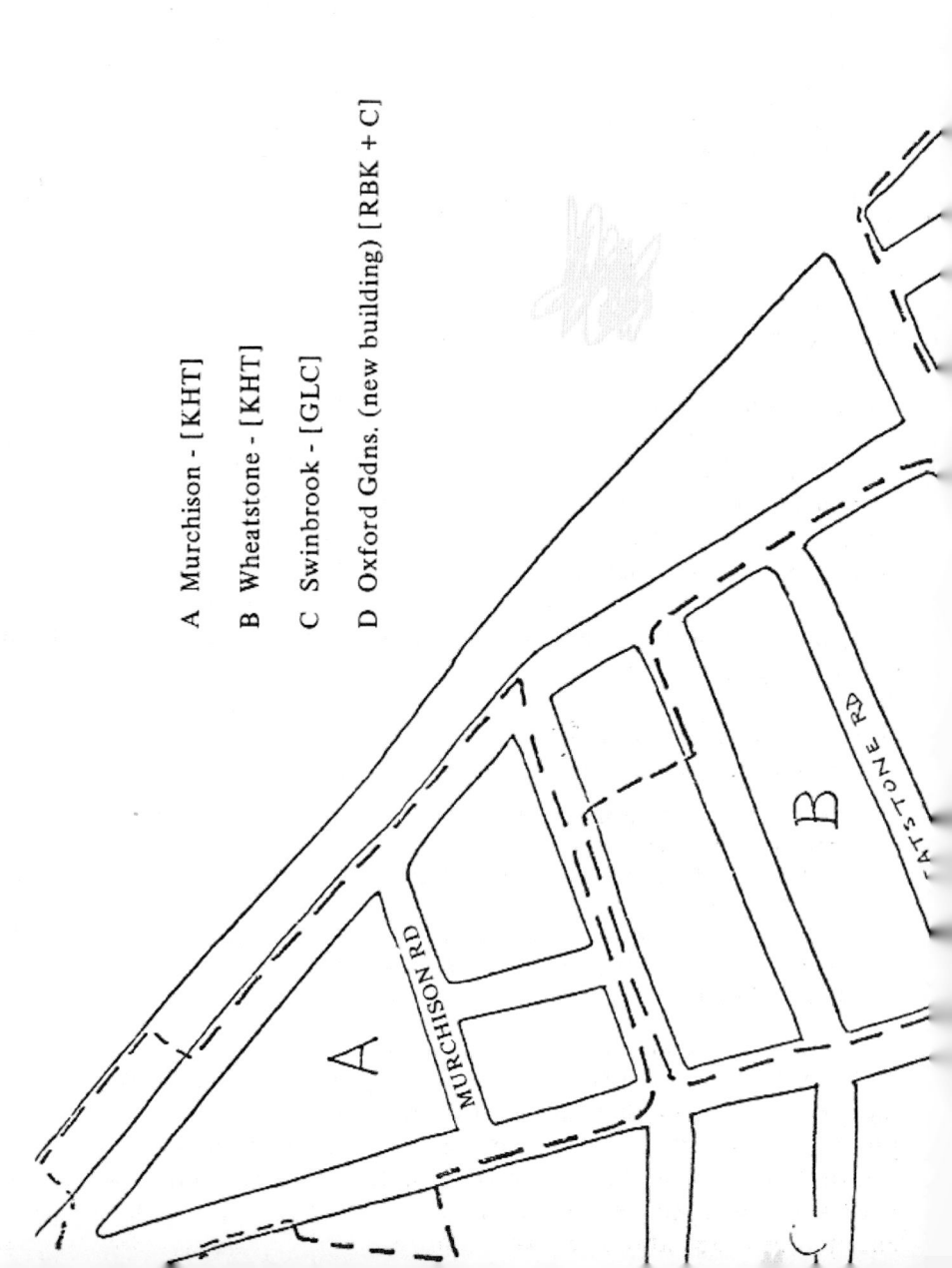

GOLBORNE REDEVELOPMENT

A Murchison - [KHT]
B Wheatstone - [KHT]
C Swinbrook - [GLC]
D Oxford Gdns. (new building) [RBK + C]

HOUSING SHIFTS 1966-1974

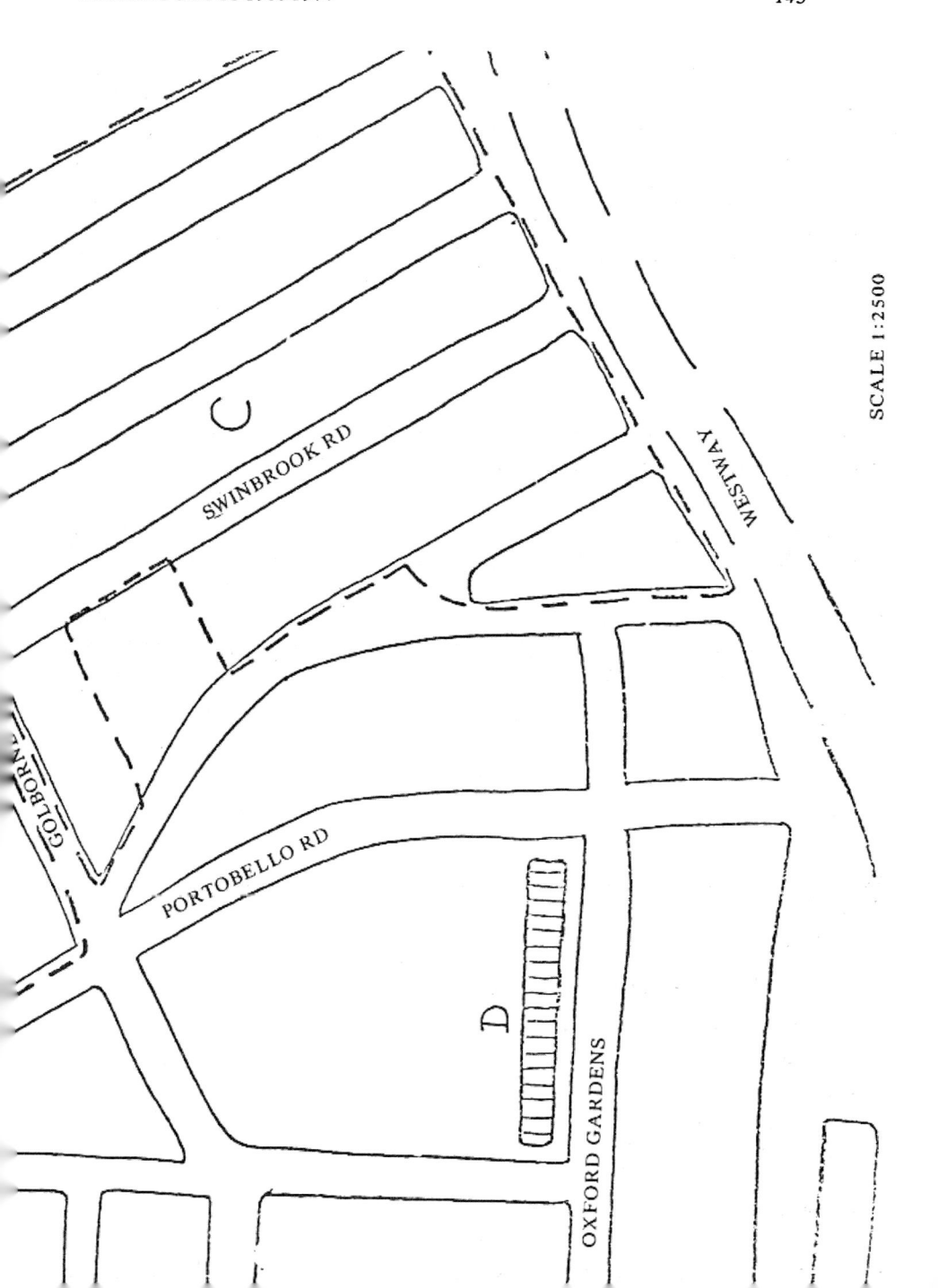

SCALE 1:2500

C

SWINBROOK RD

WESTWAY

GOLBORNE

PORTOBELLO RD

D

OXFORD GARDENS

improvement and the aim of preserving the local community, remained unresolved with the odds weighted heavily against the local community.

However, by 1974 the Tory Council believed they had set in motion a dynamic housing programme for all the areas of worst housing in North Kensington. Sir Malby Crofton, still leader of the Council, proclaimed:

> "We do now have a plan . . . Colville and Tavistock is the last piece in the jigsaw. Practically the whole of Golborne is to be rebuilt or rehabilitated, and Lancaster Road West is to go up. It means that bad housing will have gone by 1980 or maybe a little over that."
>
> *(West London Observer* 8.3.74)

B. The Council Plans

In *Golborne* by 1974, three redevelopment schemes were in progress.

1) The Wheatstone Redevelopment Area

The Council made a CPO on this area on December 9th 1969, and after this was thrown out by the Minister as inadequately prepared a second CPO was made on March 16th 1973. The public inquiry was held in June 1974. The Council never intended to carry out this redevelopment scheme themselves. After negotiations with various housing trusts they reached an agreement at the beginning of 1973 whereby the site once acquired and with the houses demolished would be handed over to the Kensington Housing Trust, who plan to build 191 dwellings. Building is not expected to start till the middle of 1976.

2) The Murchison Road Redevelopment Area

The Council made a CPO on this area on December 9th 1970 and this was confirmed in February 1972. This area was also to be acquired, cleared and handed over to the Kensington Housing Trust, though for both schemes the Council agreed to provide the loan finance. The scheme is to include 330 dwellings.

3) The Swinbrook Road Redevelopment Area

In April 1972 the GLC agreed to undertake the redevelopment of the Swinbrook Site with the aim of rehousing all who wished to remain in new housing on the site by carrying out the scheme in five phases. The CPO was put on the area and was confirmed by the Minister in May 1974. The GLC plan includes 848 dwellings.

What did all these plans mean in real terms to the people of Golborne?

In Wheatstone, the Kensington Housing Trust had continued to buy houses, but because of the impending redevelopment, major conversion works were not undertaken. The rejection of the initial CPO by the Minister meant longer in deteriorating conditions for tenants on the one hand, but on the other, it resulted in the Council shifting its policy on the rehousing of furnished tenants in redevelopment areas. In the past the Council had stuck out against any commitment to rehousing furnished tenants but as a result of Ministerial and local pressure their policy was shifted. In October 1972 it was agreed furnished tenants would be rehoused if they had been there since December 1969 when the first CPO was made. But this excluded single people and childless couples excepting pensioners. Still it was a beginning.

In Murchison the new building of 34 dwellings, the first phase of the redevelopment scheme, was begun by the Kensington Housing Trust in June 1972. This was nearing completion at the beginning of 1974. (Like the GLC scheme for Swinbrook the Murchison scheme was phased in such a way as to allow all who wished to be rehoused within the area to do so.) Demolition also started in preparation for the second phase of the scheme.

In Swinbrook, no new building began at all, though the Acklam Road houses were demolished by the GLC. The GLC started buying up houses by negotiation in advance of the CPO coming into force and this meant that basic maintenance work in the houses was done, that tenants wanting rehousing out of the area could move and that transfers within GLC properties in the area could be arranged for those who were living in very overcrowded conditions.

The rest of the Golborne triangle (about 230 houses) was left to private landlords and to the housing trusts wherever they could buy.

However, there was one bit of new building which local people did see completed in Golborne, and this was the Children's Home in Oxford Gardens with 40 flats above it. The site had been cleared back in the early 1960's and the building completed in 1970 by the Council.

In the *Colville/Tavistock* area, the changes in housing over the eight years have been of a very different nature. Whereas Golborne has remained an area of relatively low rent housing, in Colville/Tavistock, the larger size and more solid structure of the houses together with the position of the area just north of the rich, southern half of the Borough, have led to private luxury conversion activity on a large scale, unhampered by any major Council redevelopment plans.

a. Private and Housing Trust improvement

The Council policy has been to welcome both private landlord and housing trust improvement. In 1969 the Council selected the Notting Hill Housing Trust as the main trust responsible for rehabilitation in the Colville/Tavistock area, while Kensington Housing Trust was to concentrate on Golborne.

The Council decision in June 1969 to introduce a system of deficit financing to the major trusts, meant that the Notting Hill Housing Trust could expand its purchases to the Colville area, instead of confining its purchases to the cheaper properties in Tavistock. In October 1969 the Council declared a General Improvement Area in the southern part of Colville from Lonsdale Road to Talbot Road. The aim was to encourage landlords to make use of the increased grants under the 1969 Housing Act. The Council continued house-to-house inspections, revisiting 320 of the houses included in the 1963 inspection programme, urging and cajoling landlords to act in their own interests and convert their property. The rest of Colville/Tavistock outside the GIA was reinspected from 1970 onwards by the Council using the Direction Order procedure under the 1961 Act to fix the number of occupants of each house in relation to the facilities.

So in 1969 and in 1970 the Council embarked on two programmes covering exactly the same areas as the 1963 inspection programme was meant to have dealt with despite the fact that over the six years 34,211 reinspections in the 1,900 houses of Golborne and Colville had only resulted in work being completed in 42 per cent of them.

Then in 1971 the Council's decision to carry out the Colville Study meant another two years' grace for private landlords, to get stuck into the conversion business and use improvement grants to boost their profits and make the most of the spectacular rise in property prices. To help them on their way, in April 1972 the Council provided exhibitions on how to make the most out of improvement grants.

The Colville Study Report showed how private improvement could never provide homes for low income people and argued for unified non-profit ownership. But the Council chose to ignore this, and rejected any widespread use of compulsory purchase powers.

b. Council Building

During the seven years the Council had done a small amount of re-building in Colville.

1. **Elgin Mews**. In June 1968, 24 flats for old people were completed in Elgin Mews off Ladbroke Grove.

2. **Convent site**. In December 1968 the Council clinched a deal over the site of the Convent of the Poor Clares Colettines in Ladbroke Grove. The nuns moved out of the area and the Council was left an empty site with no rehousing responsibilities and a minimal amount of demolition before the new building could begin. By 1973 the scheme was completed and 115 households moved in.

This scheme epitomises the Council's approach to its housing responsibilities. If there is a clear site to be built on, and no rehousing obligations then they will not even consider inviting other agencies to consider it. However, anything more burdensome or complicated than this should always be put out for bids by other interested agencies. All the

COLVILLE REDEVELOPMENT

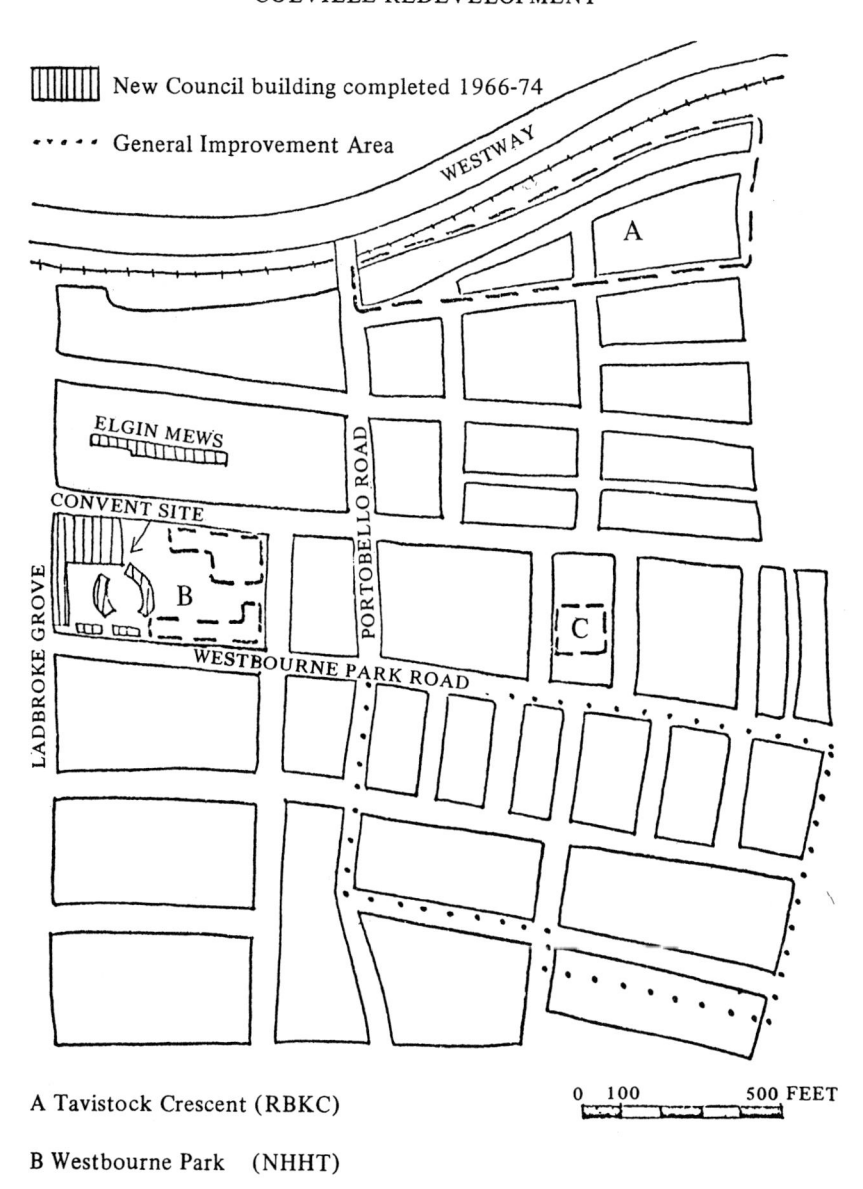

- ▥ New Council building completed 1966-74
- ····· General Improvement Area

A Tavistock Crescent (RBKC)

B Westbourne Park (NHHT)

C All Saints (NHHT)

redevelopment schemes in Golborne illustrate this, as does the Council's reliance on the housing trusts for almost all the rehabilitation work.

c. *Redevelopment Plans*

1. **The Westbourne Park Scheme.** This is a redevelopment scheme to be undertaken by the Notting Hill Housing Trust who plan to build 104 units, to be completed by December 1976. This assumes no delays in the CPO of July 1973 which the Council put on the few remaining properties not already in Trust ownership.

2. **The All Saints scheme.** The Notting Hill Housing Trust and the All Saints Church have plans to demolish the vicarage and church halls of All Saints Church and to build a new block including a new church hall together with housing units for 23 households. It is hoped to complete the scheme by December 1976.

3. **Tavistock Crescent redevelopment.** This is the only scheme for which the Council is planning to take responsibility. Though talked of by the Planning Department as a possibility for years before, it was only in the aftermath of the Colville Study (July 1973) that the Council made a CPO on this site - an area bounded by Tavistock Road, Portobello Road, Tavistock Crescent and St. Lukes Road. The current plans are to build 225 units of accommodation.

d. *Council response to Colville Study*

It is worth looking at the Council response to the Colville study in July 1973 more closely in order to clarify the Council's position at the end of this period of agitation.

The terms of reference of the study were:

"to organise a social and building survey and to incorporate its findings in a report including recommendations designed to improve housing conditions and the quality of urban life in the Colville/Tavistock area. A programme is to be presented which would lead to the achievement of the major objectives with the minimum disturbance of family and community life."

However, the inconsistency between such objectives and a continuation of the Council policy of relying on the private market and the housing trusts for the improvement of houses became most acute in the years leading up to 1973. The boom in property prices in the early 1970's together with the boost improvement grants had given to the luxury conversion process were the main causes of this. So glaring was the inconsistency that Clinch, who was appointed by the Council to write the Report, reached the conclusion that:

"The policy advocated for Colville/Tavistock is for the Council to use such powers as it has to secure that wherever possible terraces pass into the ownership of the Council or a housing trust for treatment as a whole".

P. 209 Sec. 5.8.29 Colville Study

In the Council's Coordinating and Policy Committee's report on the Study on July 25, 1973, they list the main housing recommendations: "the acquisition of whole terraces" for non-profit improvement; the two redevelopment schemes of the Tavistock and Westbourne Park sites, and "the compulsory purchase of properties in multi-occupation without self-sufficiency of dwelling units": (p. 10-11 Colville Study).

The Council report then goes on to state:

"We intend to use all our Housing Act powers in this area in order to achieve the aims outlined above, and we stress for the particular attention of bad landlords, that these include the making of CPO's and control orders."

It sounds fine and straightforward, but then come the actual decisions which are meant to back up and further this intention:

– "That the Council use all its powers under the Housing and Town Planning Acts to acquire or control, as may be deemed most appropriate in each case, substandard properties in the area, either for redevelopment, rehabilitation, improvement or for the retention of existing terraces, having due regard for owner occupiers".

– the CPO of the Tavistock and the Westbourne Park site (with a proportion of furnished tenants to be rehoused).

– "that a detailed survey of houses outside the Tavistock/Westbourne Park site but excluding the General Improvement Area be made to establish
   (i) those which need complete rehabilitation
   (ii) those to be included in CPO's
   (iii) the Council's rehousing obligations under such orders".

– "that empty properties in the area be acquired for overspill by agreement or by CPO".

However, Clinch had made much more specific recommendations as well: that 450 houses (1,800 households) needed to be acquired by the Council and improved in a crash programme over five years. But the Council chose to avoid any commitment to the actual number of substandard houses requiring Council control by inserting the sentence: "None of Clinch's figures should be taken as exact as they must arise from house to house inspection of the whole area by the Chief Public Health Inspector". Yet whatever these interminable inspections revealed, the Council made it clear that it was opposed to widespread use of compulsory purchase. The conclusion of the Council report on the Colville Study stated:

> "Having regard to the vast belt of single class low rented accommodation which we are creating immediately to the north, embracing as it will do some 15,000 people, we are not prepared to extend compulsory purchase over the entire Colville/Tavistock area."

Throughout there is no mention of timescales. The nearest the Council gets is in the July 25th report:

> "Owners of property outside the redevelopment areas face the option of speedily improving their properties or of becoming subject to acquisition or control by the Council".

However despite the absence of timescales, or details as to which property the Council is to acquire, the Council is already planning how they are to get rid of the responsibility for managing it. The Council report states: "We intend to provide as high a proportion of homes for sale as possible".

Crofton in concluding his presentation of his Council's plans for Colville and Tavistock reached the heights of messianic euphoria (with help from William Blake): "Nor shall my sword sleep in my hand till we have built Jerusalem in England's green and pleasant land"!

He obviously hoped that this would dull people's awareness of the fact that the basic inconsistencies between the Council's stated aims and their actual policies was still unresolved and as glaring as ever.

In the light of what happened after July 1973, the ten years that had passed since 1963 might in some ways never have been. The Council set about an inspection programme of the Colville area with the aim of improving the property just as they had in 1963. Four new Public Health Inspectors were appointed and by March 1974 a preliminary inspection of all the houses in the area had been completed. This concluded that 389 houses were unsatisfactory in that the households did not have exclusive use of toilet and washing facilities — and that was after 10 years of inspection programmes. A second more detailed inspection then started which involved serving notices on the owners. All the houses were not visited for a second time till the end of 1974. No compulsory purchase of bad properties was undertaken.

The only new element in the 1973 inspection programme was that the Council decided to buy by negotiation 30 empty units of accommodation in the area to help speed up the process of improvement. They agreed to offer alternative accommodation to families who could not be accommodated in their present house because the planned improvements would reduce the number of dwellings. They agreed to offer temporary accommodation to a family where it is necessary to clear the house before improvement work starts, on receipt by the Council of an undertaking from the owner to take the tenant back or a nominee of the Council once the work is completed. (Though no restriction was placed on the rent to be charged!) By March 1974, three houses had actually been bought by negotiation by the Council for this purpose. These ironically included a house which had been turned into luxury flats by a property company with the help of improvement grants, and two where the People's Association had fought unsuccessfully with the tenants to resist eviction. Again the Council had found yet another way of intervening in the housing market in such a way as to ease the problem of landlords wanting to improve property, by rehousing tenants they have failed to dislodge and by paying inflated market prices to the property companies for the individual properties the Council bought.

C. The Reality behind the Rhetoric

Despite the Council's heavy reliance on private landlords in the Colville area, there were significant shifts in the Council's style in its housing programme and in the plans for both Golborne and Colville. It is necessary to attempt to measure the effect of these shifts more closely.

Two measures will be examined in each of the areas, Colville and Golborne:
1. The shifts in ownership from housing for "profit" to "non-profit" housing;
2. The actual expenditure incurred on these schemes by the Council.

1. Ownership Shifts

Golborne

The major part of the shift from private to non-profit ownership in Golborne has resulted from the Kensington Housing Trust and the GLC buying up property in the areas covered by Compulsory Purchase Orders, in preparation for their redevelopment schemes. In addition to this, there has been the buying by the Notting Hill Housing Trust outside the redevelopment areas of half a street in one case and the small amount of Council redevelopment in Oxford Gardens.

The only demolition was of most of the houses in Acklam Road by the GLC following the opening of Westway, the elevated motorway directly in front of these houses.

There has been no evidence of large scale conversion of the houses in Golborne into high rent luxury flats as a result of the blight on much of the area from redevelopment proposals. No attempt has been made to measure the extent of this process within the privately rented sector, since it is not acting as an obvious break to the expansion of non-profit ownership.

The following table shows the ownership shifts which have taken place and which are likely to take place if current plans go ahead.

	1966	%	1974	%	1986	%
Owner occupier) Other private)	2653	85%	2050	68%	832	31.6%
Council	141	5%	261	8.6%	141	5.4%
GLC	–	–	188	6.2%	848	32.2%
Trust	324	10%	527	17.2%	807	30.8%
TOTAL	3118	100%	3026	100.0%	2628	100.0%

Households in the Golborne area - ownership

This table and those that follow are based on figures obtained from the 1966 Census, the Royal Borough of Kensington and Chelsea, the Greater London Council and the various housing trusts. The figure for households in private ownership was calculated as a residual. The projections were calculated in 1974 on the basis of the responsible authority's estimates of the completion dates and on the gains and losses of different types of ownership resulting from redevelopment schemes.

Colville

Ownership shifts in Colville must be seen in the context of the shifts within the private sector from low rent to high rent accommodation since this second process in fact limits the area of expansion of the non-profit sector. Once private housing has been converted to a high standard, sold as newly converted flats on long leases, it is extremely unlikely that the property would ever be taken into the non-profit sector. The purchase price would be too high for a housing association,* and the Council would exclude these properties from any redevelopment of rehabilitation schemes.

However, over the years between 1974 and 1986, the following assumptions are going to be made for the Colville area, as a basis for measuring the ownership shifts:

---

*However during 1974 both trust and Council started buying luxury converted houses in the Colville/Tavistock area, due to the drop in property prices, and new powers under the 1974 Housing Act.

- that the *letting* of private flats, unfurnished or furnished at or around "fair" rent levels no longer offers the return on capital that it previously did, because of the boom in property values in the early 1970's;
- that privately rented accommodation will either be converted into housing for a much higher income group, for sale, let at a very high rent, or for owner occupation or else will be bought up by the non-profit housing sector and let at subsidised rent levels.

Losing Out, the survey done by the People's Association Housing Group in May 1972, showed that between 1967-1972 in the Colville/Tavistock area, 40% of all privately owned houses covered in the 1967 Housing Survey had gone from "low" rent to "high" rent. so showing the rate at which this process within the private sector was operating.

The rents in the majority of the 40% of the houses increased as a result of being emptied, converted into smaller units with a higher standard of accommodation and relet. The average rent increase in such houses was from £4.80 in 1967 to £14.50 a flat a week in 1972. This contrasted with the rent increases in unconverted flats from £4.50 in 1967 to £5.40 in 1972. Since 50% of the households in Colville had incomes under £20 a week in 1967 (GLC Housing Occupancy Survey 1967) the rents in converted houses were obviously incompatible with the incomes of the majority of the original occupants. It was such rents which were put in the "high" rent category, while rents which were still compatible with the income levels of the original occupants were put in the "low" rent category.

Losing Out made the perhaps generous assumption that in 1967 there was no "high" rent private accommodation. However this was shown to be a fairly realistic assumption by the Building Survey carried out as part of the Colville/Tavistock Report which showed that of all residential properties (profit and non-profit) only three per cent had been converted to "modern standards" by 1967. The encroaching 40 per cent gradient line of "high" rent private accommodation has been expressed in diagramatic form together with the more gradual build up of non-profit ownership in Colville/Tavistock, both Council and Trust (see diagram). The 40 per cent gradient has been extended beyond 1972 since the Council has put no obstructions in the way of private developers, the only possible hindrance having been their shortage of capital funds and the resultant slump in the property market. It has proved difficult to measure this in any exact way, but it has been assumed that by 1975 private conversion to high income housing will have expanded to a sufficient extent to take over all the remaining private sector and so act as a barrier to non-profit expansion, other than through redevelopment. As a result of this, trust purchases for rehabilitation in the Colville area have been calculated on the basis that they will not be able to sustain their rate of purchase of 25 houses a year after 1975.

THE "GUILLOTINE" OF PROFIT – COLVILLE

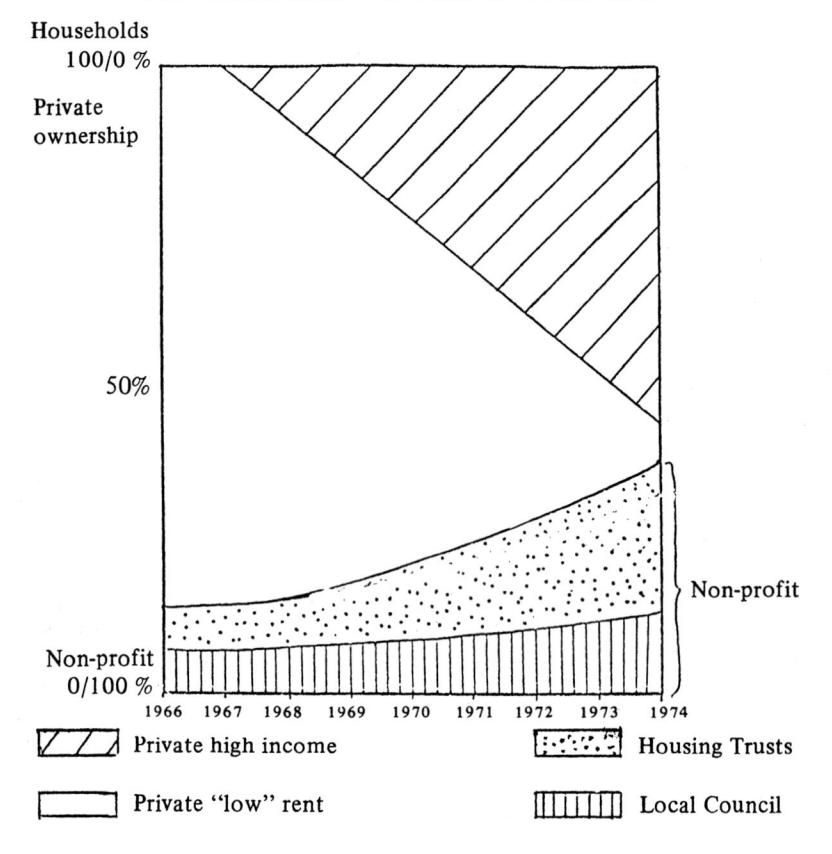

Households in Colville/Tavistock by ownership

	1966	%	1974	%	1986	%
Owner occupier	255	5.4	302	8.0	1709	50.6
Other private	3867	82.0	2050	54.4		
Council	344	7.3	503	13.4	755	22.0
Trust	249	5.3	911	24.2	930	27.4
TOTAL	4710	100.0	3766	100.0	3394	100.0

HOUSING SHIFTS 1966-1974

It is worth setting the ownership shift shown in the two areas in a longer time scale in order to understand their significance. If the forty year period 1946-1986 is taken, the ownership shifts for both areas would look like this:

OWNERSHIP SHIFTS FROM PRIVATE TO NON-PROFIT 1946-1986

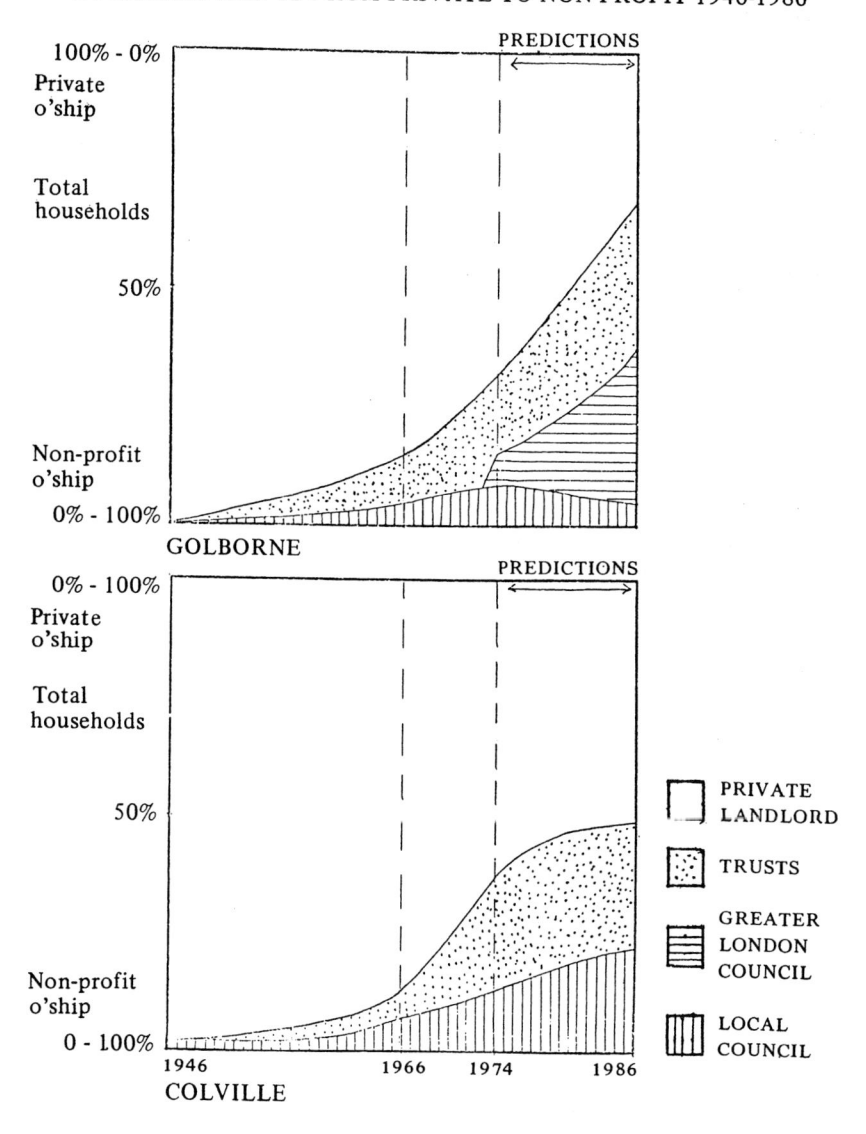

GOLBORNE

COLVILLE

PRIVATE LANDLORD
TRUSTS
GREATER LONDON COUNCIL
LOCAL COUNCIL

The actual percentages upon which these diagrams are based are:

Golborne   *% Households*

	1946	*1966*	*1974*	*1986*
Private-profit	100%	85%	68%	31.6%
Non-profit	0%	15%	32%	68.4%

Colville   *% Households*

Private-profit	98%	87.4%	62.4%	50.6%
Non-profit	2%	12.6%	37.6%	49.4%

These percentages are those of the two previous tables but simply expressed in terms of the two major categories of ownership: private-profit and non-profit.

So in both areas over this 40 year period there was the most marked increase in the shift from private to non-profit ownership in the eight year period 1966-1974, and this shift is likely to continue in both areas after 1974 though perhaps at a lesser rate.

(The categories of "profit" and "non-profit" have been used to distinguish between private owners who build a profit percentage into their calculations and the housing trust and local authority owners, who do not. However, of course, it must be recognised that there is still a profit element in the "non-profit" category in the form of interest charges paid.)

2. The Costs

What did these shifts in ownership mean in terms of expenditure? How much did they cost and on whom did the costs fall? The following table attempts to answer these questions:

Housing Expenditure 1 January 1967 - 1 January 1974
Area and Scheme

Golborne

Kensington HT	*RBKC*	*GLC*	*KHT*	*Total Expenditure*
Purchase and conversion	410,463		6,130	416,593
Major repairs			60,143	60,143
Wheatsone – fees	10,247			10,247
Murchison – fees	305,004			305,004

Greater London Council

Swinbrook, site purchase (estimate)		100,000		100,000

Notting Hill HT

Purchase and conversion	1,077,661			1,077,661

Council

Oxford Gardens – Building costs (Housing)	230,000			230,000

				2,199,548

Colville

Kensington HT

Purchase and conversion	12,925			12,925

Notting Hill HT

Purchase and conversion	2,844,748			2,844,748

Council

Convent site				
– site purchase	220,000			220,000
– building costs	805,000			805,000
Elgin Mews				
– building costs	62,000			62,000

				3,944,673

		Total	£6,144,221

So the total costs of the developments in housing in Colville and Golborne between 1.1.1967 and 1.1.1974 was £6,144,221, of which just under £6 million was Council expenditure, about £100,000 GLC expenditure and £60,000 Kensington Housing Trust expenditure.

There are two inadequacies in these figures: firstly the Notting Hill Housing Trust were unable to make available a figure for their own expenditure. Also it was hoped to calculate the expenditure which the Council and trusts were able to offset against government subsidy, but these have proved too difficult to obtain.

The relative importance of this level of expenditure in Colville and Golborne can only be gauged by setting it in the context of the Council's total capital expenditure on housing over the same period.

Kensington and Chelsea — Capital expenditure on housing

Year ended 31 March	Council Schemes	House Purchase Advances	Advances to Housing Associations	Improvement Grants	Total Capital expenditure
1966	714,443	251,221	185,726	6,769	1,158,159
1967	958,224	350,240	243,053	23,974	1,575,491
1968	1,816,063	220,025	366,246	52,421	2,454,755
1969	1,806,366	302,295	237,636	42,430	2,388,727
1970	2,038,821	258,792	525,375	82,514	2,905,502
1971	2,319,274	407,068	1,375,256	325,399	4,426,997
1972	2,801,458	970,286	1,487,316	761,714	6,020,774
1973	1,892,551	1,377,900	2,355,918	975,610	6,601,979

Source: Financial Digest RBK&C 1969, 1972, Capital Transactions A/c. Abstract of Accounts 1972/3.

This shows that in absolute terms the total capital expenditure on housing increased 470% from just over £1 million in 1966 to over £6½ million in 1973.

However, it must be remembered that over this period, between 31.12.1966 and 31.12.1973 property prices spiralled. In London and the South East the new house price index increased 144% and the prices of older existing houses sold with vacant possession increased 152% (Nationwide Building Society house price index). If the real increase in housing expenditure in terms of additional units of housing is to be measured, the total expenditure must be deflated by these amounts. This would mean that in real terms the total capital expenditure increased about 127% rather than 470% increase in absolute expenditure.

The figures also show that while just under £6 million was spent by the

Council in Colville and Golborne between the beginning of 1967 and 1974, just under £25 million was spent by the Council in total capital expenditure on housing in the whole of the Borough.

However, it is the General Rate Fund Revenue expenditure on housing which shows more clearly than the capital account, the Council's commitment to housing, since it shows how much of the Council's own locally raised rate revenue it is willing to spend net of any government grants.

CAPITAL EXPENDITURE ON HOUSING

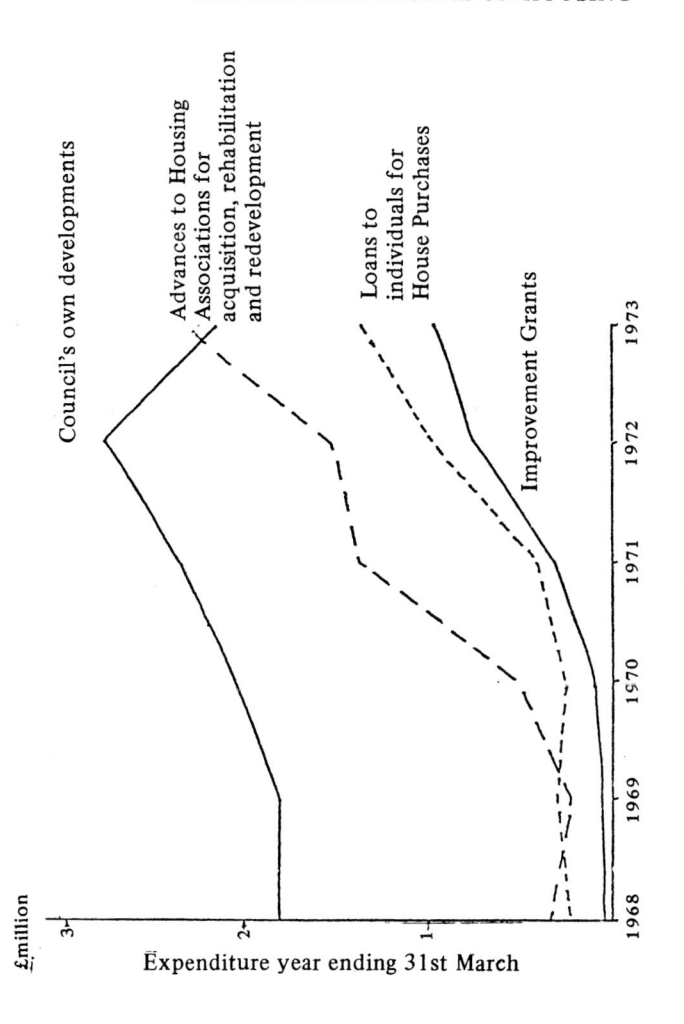

Source: RBK&C *Financial Digest* 1973

Kensington and Chelsea General Rate Fund Revenue Account

Year ended 31 March	Net expenditure on housing	Equivalent rate in £	% of total net expenditure
1966	144,639	1.44d	4.4%
1967	41,613	0.41d	–
1968	78,615	0.76d	–
1969	125,378	1.24d (0.51p)	3.1%
1970	199,826	0.79p	4.0%
1971	83,726	0.33p	1.0%
1972	71,552	0.28p	1.0%
1973	220,074	0.86p	2.9%

Source: Financial Digests RBK&C

These figures show that the percentage of Council total net expenditure of rate fund revenue on housing has decreased over the period, and has in no single year been higher than it was in 1966. This means Kensington comes bottom of all Inner London Boroughs in terms of the rate in the £ spent on housing.

So although all the housing action in North Kensington over the years may have increased the total amount of capital expenditure on housing, it did not result in any fundamental shift in terms of the Council's priorities as housing continued to get less of the total Council rate fund expenditure.

Conclusions

Over the eight years of housing agitation the Council has shifted from its own stated housing policy in Colville and Golborne of relying on the "holding operation" of the protracted inspection programme. In 1969 the Leader of the Council stated,

> "We are proposing a long steady slog of clearance and improvement (involving a substantial change of ownership from private to other hands) which will preserve the character and vitality of our local community. We do care and we shall succeed".

The deficit financing scheme for the trusts was introduced and redevelopment plans set in motion for most of Golborne. In Colville, the delays resulting from the Colville Study gave private capital the chance it needed to turn over half the area into high income houses at the height of the property boom. However, with a small block of new Council building and gradual increase in trust ownership, non-profit ownership increased to nearly 40% by 1974 in Colville.

So over the eight years households in non-profit ownership in Golborne more than doubled from 15% to 32% and in Colville increased threefold from 12.6% to 37.6%.

Seen in the context of the post war period, this eight years showed the most rapid increase in non-profit ownership and set in motion a process which is likely to continue over the next decade, though perhaps at a lesser rate. If the current plans go ahead, and the assumptions made are correct, by 1986 non-profit ownership will be 68.4% in Golborne and 49.4% in Colville — two areas for which a non-interventionist Council had no plans in 1967.

This will have cost the Council just under £6 million over the eight years, which may well have contributed to increasing the Council's total capital expenditure on housing by over 120% in the eight years.

So there have been changes: plans were produced where there were none before, together with the dramatic increase in non-profit ownership, but all this has been achieved without the Council altering its fundamental policy of relying on other agencies wherever possible, and resorting to compulsory purchase as little as possible.

However, outside the Royal Borough the housing agitation has contributed to a fundamental shift in national policy, from the emphasis on new Council building in the mid-60's, to the recognition of the need for compulsory purchase and improvement if houses are to be improved for those in greatest housing need. However, this shift towards greater public ownership in housing must be seen as just one step towards a housing system geared to need, not profit, and open to tenants control.

Chapter 10

Lessons for the Future

The weaknesses and the strengths experienced in the community struggles in Notting Hill over the eight years will be examined and an attempt will then be made, by taking full account of the weaknesses and by building on the strengths, to formulate some guidelines for future strategy in community struggle.

One of the most fundamental weaknesses of community based struggle is the limited range of sanctions which can be used in struggles against private capital and the local state. Whereas workers organised at their workplace can use the ultimate sanction of withdrawing their labour when all other channels have been tried to no avail, community based groups have no such powerful ultimate sanction. Though fully recognised theoretically from the start, this fact was brought home most acutely in the experience of the show-down with the Council over housing in 1973. Every means had been used to demonstrate the opposition of local people to the Council's housing policy of relying on private capital to "solve" the housing problem: squatting, auction-busting, reasoned research, mass meetings, and the lock-in of the Council. Despite all this the Council could ignore the alternative policy of compulsory purchasing the Colville/Tavistock area being demanded by the local people. Faced with this inaction of an electorally invulnerable Council, the local groups had reached the end of their period of resistance. A final attempt was made to gather together all the groups in the area to decide on joint action, and suggestions were made at this meeting about contacting the local unions to test the possibility of sympathetic strike action in the area, but this was all too late. People felt they had been kicked in the teeth by the Council and caught without a strategy when the Council decided to walk rough-shod over them.

A second important weakness was the failure to consolidate the structure of the People's Association when it was at its strongest and most expansive point in 1969. Attempts were made to structure and restructure the working groups within the People's Centre but the disciplined reporting back of the working groups was never systematised, partly because the role of Chairman was never taken seriously. Also the debate on the membership of the Centre or of the People's Association as a whole was never resolved. Taken together, these factors contributed to the working of the People's Centre being dominated by the shifting movement of cliques, and to the meetings being dominated by the most confident, those with the loudest voice, and the greatest capacity to interrupt and hold the floor. This must have produced a confusing impression to newcomers as it did to plenty of the long-term attenders.

The license to speak at meetings was both completely open and yet for many who lacked the confidence and capacity to interrupt, completely closed. The extreme tolerance to all kinds of attempts at disruption even when it took the form of infinite harangues and monologues and even physical assaults on others at the meeting, meant that no one was ever thrown out or physically excluded from the meetings, at least as long as they took place in the Church Hall. This was fine during expansive, energetic phases in the life of the organisation, but as time went on people grew weary of attending the political forum which they had valued since it was no longer a place to pool ideas and broaden perspectives. The purges and the exclusions began and it was not a political forum any longer. Instead it was the domain of one particular clique. So in the absence of a constitution which could be enforced and a fresh forum being set up, people withdrew to the working groups they believed in, and kept in touch with others in other working groups by *People's News* or by the friendship network in the area. However the forum had been destroyed, so forcing the working groups to operate in greater isolation than would otherwise have been necessary.

The idea of the "tyranny of structurelessness", developed within the women's liberation movement, is applicable to the workings of the People's Centre. In an article developing this idea, Jo Freeman explains how, in rejecting organisation and structure because of the danger that they can be misused, we deny ourselves tools for further development, and open ourselves up to fresh dangers[1]: "When informal élites are combined with a myth of 'structurelessness', there can be no attempt to put limits on the use of power. It becomes capricious".

Just as the first weakness examined was built into the very nature of community-based struggle, so perhaps was the third major weakness — the incoherence and impermanence of the national network of the groups involved in this type of struggle. The focus of each group on a relatively small locality meant that the danger of parochialism and isolationism was very real. An attempt was made by the Notting Hill Community Workshop to set up a regular dialogue between all the groups they knew of with a similar perspective on community struggle. This took the form of weekend conferences of neighbourhood agitators, the first of which was organised in January 1970.

There was an enthusiastic response to this type of conference and other groups undertook to organise future conferences. These took place in July, 1970, January and July, 1971, at Spode House in the Midlands, and at the fourth conference in July, 1971, it was decided to have a year's interval before the next conference. The aim was to leave enough time for groups to organise regional or city wide campaigns in the interim, as a way of building up the connections between different groups in a more real, meaningful way than simply meeting to discuss their own strategies and programmes at conferences. Information on landlords and property companies was to be pooled in the London area so that groups could begin to mount a London-wide attack on particular property companies which operated on a city-wide basis.

However, the work necessary to service such a flow of information and such record keeping was always more than any local group could mount and city-wide campaigns never developed any coherence.

The fifth and, as it turned out, the last conference of neighbourhood agitators took place in June, 1972. As a result of increasing concern at the wide range of political perspectives of groups which were coming to the conferences, a proposal was put that the conference should adopt a statement of position as a way of defining more precisely the kind of grouping they were. The statement of position read:

> "We, as groups involved in community organising, are opposed to the capitalist system and the inevitable exploitation this brings.
>
> We organise in the areas where we live, and therefore are separated from the traditional area of political organising, the place of work. However, the contradictions we seek to bring to the surface are vital, complementary ones, in the reproduction of wage labour, e.g. in housing, education, health and social security, play and leisure, and the position of women.
>
> With the present intensification of the class struggle and the deterioration of the economic situation we believe the time is now right to intensify our activities in all of these areas, developing whenever possible new, collective forms of power and developing the political consciousness of those who have come to feel themselves politically powerless.
>
> We seek contacts with and support from other groups such as women, claimants, blacks, new left groups and left political parties which share these aims and are engaged in similar struggles."

However, having agreed upon this statement, no further conferences were ever organised. This was to a large extent due to the fact that the Community Workshop groups which had been central to the organisation of the conferences and to the expansion of the contacts with other groups, were themselves in a state of flux. Some had already disbanded, others were on the point of doing so. Of the 20 or 30 groups which were involved in the conferences, the Community Workshop groups in Notting Hill, Wandsworth, Moss Side and Camden together with groups set up in Holloway and North Paddington by workers who had moved from Notting Hill, had been the core of the network. Within a year of the 1972 conference, the Camden Workshop had disbanded and many of its members had joined the Communist Party. In Wandsworth, the group split with some of the members joining International Socialists and the rest continuing with tenants work. The Moss Side group had disbanded because of political differences. The groups in Notting Hill, Holloway and Paddington continued but focussed on their own areas, and lacked the energy or the urgency to reconvene a national conference.

None of the Workshop groups had ever seen their own survival as an institution as crucial to the type of political work they were concerned to generate. There was a view that organisation in that form was only a provisional stage. This is well expressed by the Camden Community Workshop:-[2]

> "In a very crucial sense there is a tension built into community organising: the overall perspective is that of social revolution and yet the chosen site of activity, the localised neighbourhood, is far removed from such a possibility. This gives a provisional character to the Workshop as a form of political work. In fact it explains the adoption of the name Workshop: the word encapsulates the idea of experimentation, breaking new ground, developing projects provisional in nature — so the Community Workshop experiments with the elements of a new politics, encourages the mastering of the task of organising and presents itself in its practice without the overall political direction a revolutionary party provides."

In attempting to assess the strengths of community struggles in Notting Hill it is necessary to summarise the substantial changes produced as a result of local organisational initiatives.

In housing, the Council policy was opened up to public debate in the neighbourhood and nationally, and plans for two major areas of North Kensington were developed by the Council as a result. These involved the spending of over £6 million of public money and massive shifts from private to non-profit ownership in the two areas for which the Council had no plans at all at the beginning of this period of struggle.

However, it was not just the housing experts who were involved in all this pressurising of the Council. Hundreds, even thousands of local people had been involved in a real debate about the principles at stake in the housing struggle, and they came to see the struggle as a struggle between systems and not just as an individualised struggle between each tenant and his landlord. And as a result of all this, the active majority had come down firmly on one side. The profit-seeking motivation of the private landlord had proved itself inadequate to meet the housing needs of the area. Non-profit ownership and the elimination of private landlords was a crucial first step in the fight of local working class people for a decent home in the area. This shift in thinking was demonstrated in dozens of different ways, by attending mass meetings, and taking part in marches, by helping a squat, or locking-in the Council. It is fair to say that the majority of local people who were active politically, took part in all these events as channels for expressing their views on housing. There was an active minority who tried to rally people in support of an alternative view — the Colville Restoration Society — a tiny band of landlords and shopkeepers. A few years later a local estate agent claimed a Landlords' Protection Association had been formed to fight the attack on local landlords. However, neither of these groups ever managed to organise any public demonstration of their strength. The two central members in the Colville Restoration Society, a shopkeeper and a landlord, sold up and left the area. So far as the Landlords' Protection Association was concerned, the last that was heard of it was a grandiose offer of a £1,000 reward for anyone giving information which would lead to the prosecution of anyone trying to disrupt the local property market.

The whole idea of playspace was established in the area and space, resources and manpower were won for play for years to come. The bureaucracy controlling the motorway space was pierced, the non-decision to turn the space into a car-parking wilderness was effectively challenged, and a policy decision forced to use the space for community facilities.

It was not just local authority policies which were confronted and challenged, new institutions were also set up. The potential of neighbourhood centres as forums of political discussion and action was established, and all kinds of groups were formed through which local people challenged and changed some of the determining conditions of their lives. Children were being killed on the streets so local people took direct action to change the traffic system in the area. Playgroups were needed so local women trained as playgroup leaders, found money to pay themselves a wage and set up playgroups. Playspace for older children was needed, so private garden squares were opened up as play areas. People on social security needed to develop some collective strength, so a Claimants Union was set up. The actions of the police had to be scrutinised and challenged so a Police Group was set up to help organise collective defences in cases where the police had obviously picked off people not as individuals, but because they were part of a larger collective. Other kinds of institutions were also set up to act as community resources — the first Neighbourhood Law Centre and one of the first community printing presses.

So far as local organisation was concerned over these years, a live network of local people was built up and it was just this type of network which remained at the end of the eight years — a network which linked a dozen or so live working groups through which local people were still challenging the authorities and trying to control the decisions which determined how they lived in the area.

Seen in a wider socialist perspective, these years have shown ways in which working class struggle can and must be extended to include all those who are not at the point of production.

The Labour Party is unlikely to include them in its activities unless its constituency organisations transform themselves out of all recognition; unless they become the vanguard in the fight for better conditions ceaselessly campaigning, arguing, protesting and unifying the demands of all working people for a different kind of society. But with the impression of demoralisation and disintegration given by constituency party organisations, it would seem that scepticism as to whether such a transformation could still take place would be legitimate.

Most Marxist groups will also go on to neglect this large section of the population, focussing the bulk of their work on those at the point of production, and seeing all other struggles outside the workplace as secondary and so not worth the commitment of time, energy and resources.

So, in the absence of such community-based struggles as those experienced in Notting Hill, a huge section of the population would remain in a political wilderness, with no sense of what socialism could mean to them and so open to the insidious courting of the far right. As the crisis of profitability intensifies and redundancies increase, turning the waged into the wageless, it will become increasingly important that a theory of socialist struggle includes the wageless as well as the waged working population. Without this it will be impossible to obstruct capital's attempts to divide the working class.

> "At every stage of the struggle the most peripheral to the production cycle are used against those at the centre, so long as the latter ignore the former."[3]

However, as well as including a section of people in the struggle for socialism, this experience of community struggle in Notting Hill has important organisational lessons for the rest of the labour movement. It can be seen to add a fresh dimension to the kind of positive spontaneity Rosa Luxemburg described as "a series of great creative acts of the often spontaneous class struggle seeking its way forward" and as "the active untrammelled, energetic political life of the broadest mass of the people".

Parallels can be drawn between the "comités d'action" set up in France in 1968 and the kind of working groups spawned in one locality by the People's Centre over the years. Daniel Singer describes the nature of the political situation in which such groups develop:

> "A movement finding no ready channels for its expression is driven to seek its own new ways. The instruments for action it forges in the process

are improvised. They reflect the strength of the movement but also its weaknesses, difficulties and ambiguities as well as its deep aspirations."[4]

Just like the "comités d'action" the People's Centre groups were open to all on the left who wanted to use them as a base from which to organise action, as instruments of struggle.

Like them, their function was to intervene rapidly whenever required in their own area, to stir people into thinking and spur them to action. Both types of organisation owed their existence to the utter inadequacy of the traditional political parties in providing channels for the mass of people to take political action.

The importance of this type of working group as a base from which to organise struggle lies in the immediacy of politics which results. The thought becomes the action, with no organisational buffer to dull enthusiasm or imagination. Surely mistakes are made but because action and organisation are so directly related, confrontation with failure and mistake is equally immediate for all in the group, so increasing the likelihood of the lesson of the mistake being built into future thinking and action.

Political organisation through such groups produces a political rhythm very different from the steady state rhythms of more institutionalised political groups on the left. This was realised early on in Notting Hill.

"Throughout the struggle there will be a continual ebb and flow, bargaining to win concessions, alternating with sudden upsurges of direct action which fuse the energies of many different groups in united opposition to the injustices of the system."[5]

Both climaxes and lulls of these cyclical rhythms were in themselves stimuli to the generation of fresh ideas and fresh action. While at the climax of an action, or an intervention, the imagination soared with further political possibilities, in the lulls, the harsh reality of the constraints built into the system angered the spirits again.

Such political rhyrhms carry with them tactical advantages. They maximise the potential of the shock or surprise element in any action, since it may result in types of action being taken which the authorities least expect.

However, another important ingredient facilitating the relative frequency and scale of political climaxes and confrontations is the time and energy of people who can commit themselves to organising struggles full-time. The present political system has so many full-time paid maintenance engineers that if socialist struggles are to intensify and gain in strength, the number of full-time socialist engineers or anti-capitalist dam-busters must greatly increase. Only then will the political potential of each upsurge of anger be maximised. Only then will all the possible connections between those involved in struggle be built.

Both the type of activity and type of organisation through which working class struggle was expanded in the Notting Hill community are important in showing how an active socialist struggle in the here and now can be waged. In that many of the battles were over immediate decisions and policies, the danger of seeing a marginal shift as the solution was great.

However, from the start it was recognised that many of the concessions gained would be marginal, but despite this, what was thought to be important was that local people gained a wide experience of confronting the authorities and of all that this entailed — bureaucratic indifference, professional incompetence and open bullying. It was this experience of fighting for control in one area of life which was a vital political education for all involved and could well act as a spring board for challenging the controls over the other parts of one's life. As the Camden Community Workshop put it:

> "We have totally rejected the old economistic line that only material hardship and misery can politicise the working class, who will be bought off from engagement in the class struggle by any amelioration of their lot. On the contrary, every concession we win can contribute to increasing the pressure on contemporary capitalism; every victory can contribute to the climate of increasing demands. As long as we continue to bite the hand that feeds us and to avoid the constant danger of being bought off, and content ourselves with mere reformism."
> — Paper written in June, 1972

The basis of a revolutionary demand is that the demand is simultaneously within the scope of capitalism to grant but which also raises clearly the issues of exploitation within capitalism and the necessity of socialism.

A final way in which this experience is important is that it establishes a type of community action in its own right within a socialist tradition far removed from the non-directive community development tradition. Whereas the exponents of this tradition like Biddle talked of the community development process seeking "a local wholeness that includes all people, all factions" and of the "interrelatedness of all things within the common good"[6] the community activists involved with the People's Association fully recognise the class divisions and class conflicts within the present society.

> "In a class ridden society where the dice are loaded against the working class on every count, the Workshop makes no pretence to this so called 'neutrality' of the respectable community worker. Neutrality in such a situation could be nothing more than effective collusion with those forces which have an interest in preserving the status quo, collusion with the respectable manipulators, that is."[7]

It is because of this politically partisan view of society that such groupings have been looked down upon as beyond the pale of respectable community organising, as manipulative of the community. However, cynical manipulation would be no basis for the building of socialist struggle. It is only by starting with issues which people feel, only by starting wherever people are "touched, bitter, moved, frustrated, nauseated" that socialist struggle could expand, and gain its own momentum. It is because the partisan socialist community worker believes in working class people's capacity to take action to challenge the authorities and change the equations of power, that they can work with them on an egalitarian basis, discussing ideas as to the best strategy to adopt. There is no need for the socialist community worker to conceal his views and pretend to be value-free and neutral, since he believes that the local people he is working with have enough political judgment to reject ideas and plans for action which do not make sense, in terms of their own experience. The socialist community worker sees his role as feeding in ideas and opening up possibilities in such a way as to expand the political horizons of possible change so sustaining and inspiring the local working class to have confidence to expand the struggle into other areas of their lives.

In contrast, the "neutral" community worker has such a low opinion of working class organisational ability and political sophistication that they encourage the people they work with to pitch their expectations of achievement very low. For instance the workers in the North Kensington Family Study worked for 5 years with a group of women on the setting up and running of a playgroup. The workers had a very low level of expectation of the political development of the women they were working with. In June, 1967, Ilys Booker, the leader of the team, said to me, "If at the end of five years they can distinguish between the local Council and the Greater London Council, we will think we have succeeded."

So it would seem that the "neutral" "non-directive" community work is in much more danger of being both patronising and manipulative than the socialist community worker. Instead of socialist community work being seen as the lowest in the hierarchy of types of professional community work and part of the social work, welfare, group therapy tradition, it must be totally disentangled from that tradition.

The word "community" must no longer be used in a way to envelop all types of interventions into a single category of "community work". Rather, the political assumptions implicit in each type of intervention must be made explicit and used as the divisions between very different traditions. Once this is done then the kind of community action with which the Workshop and the People's Association groupings were involved is clearly seen to be part of a very different tradition — not of social work, but of socialist struggle.

So what does all this mean for future socialist strategy? There are those Marxist groups which have concentrated exclusively on the weakness built in to community struggle — the fact that community struggle is removed from the work place and therefore lacks the real political muscle, the sanctions which are inherent in industrial struggle. Focussing on this weakness and lacking the interest to explore the strengths, they reject community struggle as a worthwhile form of socialist struggle. Instead they concentrate exclusively on political organising with workers at the workplace.

One of the aims of this book has been to force socialists to take seriously the experience of community struggle described, and to see it as a fundamental way of expanding and enriching working class consciousness of their capacity to take action to challenge the different kinds of exploitation which determine their lives.

This is not to deny the crucial importance of industry based struggles, nor the intensification of militancy in industry in recent years. The days lost in strikes and lockouts per 100 union members have increased from 30 in the 1960-7 period to 113 in the years 1968-1972. The number of workers per dispute is increasing and the duration of strikes getting longer.[8] There has also been a change in the style of militancy with the sudden upsurge of factory occupations to over 100 in the period between March 1971 and mid 1974, leading up to the grand climax of direct action which liberated the five dockers from Pentonville.

However, there is also evidence that exclusively industry based struggles have serious limitations in terms of expanding the political horizons of the workers involved, beyond the factory walls. The experience of the workers' struggles within Ford's provides a clear example of this. Huw Beynon[9] in his extensive study of these struggles explains the limits to the political development of even the shop stewards in the Paint Shop at Ford's Halewood factory:

"Although the Halewood stewards were suspicious of both politics and politicians, they cannot be termed apolitical . . . they had quite a developed political understanding. The boundary of this politics however, was the factory floor. It knew about the bosses and the bureaucrats. About exploitation and being screwed. And this knowledge manifested itself in periods of sustained militancy. But it was a politics that was not easily transferable to other areas of class exploitation and power." (p.87).

"While 'politics' is contained within trade unionism, trade unions restrain rather than develop this political awareness. Fundamentally they are economic bargainers. Traditionally the British trade union movement has coped with the contradiction of opposing the employer while at the same time recognising him, through a dichotomy of the 'industrial' and 'political' wings of the Labour movement.

This tactic held some degree of conviction in the past, but holds little credence amongst working men after the last Labour government. In the absence of a party with any meaningful politics the lads at Halewood decided that they were on their own. They were thrown back upon the trade unions and their grassroots organisations within them." (p.230).

"Without the backing of a vigorous socialist movement, capable of relating particular sectional struggles to each other, and extending struggles beyond the particular factory, the radical trade unionist finds himself in an insoluble dilemma. He fights by the rules of a system that he hardly approves of, within an organisation that has proved itself manifestly incapable of changing those rules." (p.300).

Beynon ends by recalling the words of Marx in 1865 when addressing the General Council of the International Working Men's Association in London. Marx advised the workers that in their struggles in the factories they "ought not to forget that they are dealing with the effects, but not with the causes of those effects", and that they should extend the struggle beyond the factory and make demands other than purely economistic demands for better wages, For:

"Trade unions work well as centres of resistance against the encroachment of capital. They fail generally from limiting themselves to a guerilla war against the effects of the existing system, instead of simultaneously trying to change it, instead of using their organised forces as a lever for the emancipation of the working class, that is to say, the ultimate abolition of the wages system."[10]

Marx also made other clear statements showing the need to expand socialist struggle beyond the factory walls, to include and take account of factors affecting the consumption side of a worker's life.

"The important point to be emphasised here is that whether production and consumption are considered as activities of one or of separate individuals, they appear as aspects of one process in which production forms the starting point and therefore the predominating factor . . . consumption appears as a factor of production . . . the demands of consumption also influence production. A mutual interaction takes place between the various elements."[11]

Though under capitalism, production and consumption, work and the home, workmates and family appear as two separate spheres of social experience, they are indissolubly linked. It is as members of the community where they live that workers consume, so providing the market which capitalism requires. It is also within the community that the labour force upon which capitalism depends, is reproduced and serviced.

This interdependence of production and consumption is being reinforced by both recent and current developments in capitalism in Britain. The adoption of Keynesian policies by the government since the 1930's meant that in contrast to the pre-Keynesian response of cutting wages in times of slumps, the wage came to be used as a tool to boost capitalist expansion. The postwar boom was based on the development of mass consumption industries and for this to continue, expanding working class wages were essential. However, Keynesian economic policies had not removed the economic contraditions which had produced the booms and slumps. Instead, they just raised them to another level at which they appeared in a new form — inflation. This has resulted from full employment being sustained, so providing the basis for increasing working class strength and higher wage demands. Money wage increases have been won in excess of productivity rises, so putting pressure on profit margins, which can only be defended by price rises.

The productive mechanism has become less and less effective in operating by market means as it has had to deal both with increasing working class wage demands, and also with the increasingly large scale of productive units which subvert the effectiveness of the price mechanism in promoting competition. So the contradiction between the growing conscious public control of every aspect of the production process, and the private appropriation of production through the market, has intensified.

However, the removal of mass unemployment and the growth of persistent inflation have focussed attention on the distribution of resources rather than on the waste of human resources resulting from unemployment. Community struggles, the women's movement and environmental campaigns can all be seen as expressions of this shift of focus. It is the same pressures which have drawn into the arena of public debate the distribution and allocation of economic resources, which have also had a vital effect on areas of social life previously considered private or autonomous from the sphere of economic relationships. The state is not just concerned with the direct production process of goods and services, but also with the production of new modes of consumption, of new social wants and needs, the production and reproduction of labour power and of the social relations of capitalism. The state has become a collective capitalist.

This is not a static situation. Each new achievement in bending the market economy to conform with social needs does not relieve the social tensions, since successful attempts to expand conscious control over all aspects of their lives by the working class, diverts resources from market allocation, so encroaching further on the private market. This intensifies the economic crisis and leads in turn to the state attempting to pour resources into private industry, so leaving less money available for the public services.

Within this context, it is crucial that community and industrial struggles do not continue independently. Both must be integrated as much as possible. If this is taken as a starting point, then class struggle for greater control within the community must be seen as necessary and complementary to the struggle for greater control within the workplace. Only by closer integration will the maximum potential of working class action be realised.

In different parts of the world this integration of community and industrial struggle is beginning to take place.

In Australia there have been exciting developments within the New South

Wales branch of the Builders' Labourers Federation (BLF) since a radical leadership took over in 1969. The Builders' Labourers Federation is the largest union in the building industry, representing semi-skilled and unskilled workers. About 60% of its members are immigrants from Italy, Greece and Yugoslavia. Unlike its British counterparts, which are trying to outlaw the subcontracted labour working on the "lump", the Builders' Labourers Federation has got in amongst the subcontractors and organised their men. So no big building job can be done without the Builders' Labourers Federation's consent. Without letting up in the fight for better working conditions and pay for themselves, they have used their labour power to intervene wherever the interests of other working people were threatened. They have stopped developers from building on open bushland at Kelly's Bush which was much valued by the local people, by threatening the developers that all their other building projects would remain uncompleted if they went ahead. In January, 1972, they banned all demolition work of Sydney's Rocks area, where the State government was planning to demolish the working class homes and invite developers to build high rise luxury flats in their place. The ban was still in force 18 months later. The Builders' Labourers Federation have gone on to intervene to stop building developments wherever local groups asked them to in order to preserve amenities or buildings which the local people valued or needed: parks, theatres, swimming baths, pubs, churches, historic buildings, as well as working class homes. By July, 1973, there were 36 bans on development in force, worth a total of $3,000 million.

Jack Mundey, as Secretary of the New South Wales Branch in July 1973 explained the view of his branch of the Builders Labourers Federation.

> "In a modern society, the workers' movement, in order to play a really meaningful role, must engage in all industrial, political, social and moral struggles affecting working people as a whole."

> "More and more we are going to determine which buildings we will build. Those of us who build must be more concerned with what we build. The environmental interests of three million people are at stake and cannot be left to developers and building employers whose main concern is making profit."[12]

In all these actions the Builders' Labourers Federation are breaking new ground and showing the potential of working class power which can be released by a greater integration of community and industrial struggle.

There are also examples of the power of such integrated struggle in Italy in the years since 1969.

In the Via Tibaldi, Milan, in June, 1971, two weeks of continual occupations and street battles based on an alliance of workers, students and tenants resulted in victory. In six days of violence the people occupied everything — houses, the streets, the Town Hall, police wagons and the Architectural Faculty of the University. By the end of July the Council had allocated the 200 families who had squatted, new flats and each family had received 100,000 lire compensation. All evictions and rent arrears were to be frozen by the Council. The assembly of the families who had initially occupied the Via Tibaldi houses became a permanent organisation involving tenants and workers from every district of Milan, intent on expanding the struggle against rising rents, fares and prices.

In Via Alboccione, Rome, in 1973, building workers joined 205 families in the occupation of houses they had just built, and in the same year in Palermo building workers took over a block of luxury flats they had just built. When the police were called by the local Council, they failed to gain access through the professionally built barricades.

These are just a few of the militant struggles in Italy over this period, but they serve to show the power unleashed by the fusion of different sections of the working class in struggle.

As a result of the experience of struggle over the last few years Lotta Continua, one of the groups involved in the fusion of community and industrial struggle reached the following conclusion:

"The Italian working class have recognised that their needs for a freer, happier life cannot be realised by increasing the spending power of individual groups of workers. Any gains made inside the factories have been countered by the bosses' use of inflation and property speculation . . . In this situation the struggle in the community becomes crucial and working class people are forced to discover new forms of self organisation, tactics and demands."

— *Take over the City* 1973

There have been occasions in England as well where for a short time industrial and community struggles have fused. The St Pancras rent strike against the introduction of a differential rent scheme in September, 1960, is a good example. Two families, the Rowes and the Cooks, were evicted by the bailiffs and police acting for the Council, after barricading themselves in their Council flats for 25 days in defiance of eviction orders for non-payment of rent. Immediately, workers in different parts of London showed their support and solidarity for the tenants in different ways. Railway workers from the nearby Camden Goods Yard declared a 24-hour strike in support. Hundreds of building workers from the Shell Mex site on the south bank of the Thames, downed tools, walked off the site and marched to St Pancras with banners, meeting up with 200 workers from the Token building site in Southwark on the way. Drivers at the Independent Milk Supplies depot in Maida Vale declared a 24-hour sympathy strike, disrupting milk supplies in many areas of London.

Messages of support also came from Greenwich Trades Council, the building workers on the Science Museum building site, and the London District Committee of Plumbing Trade Unions. The federated shop stewards for the St Pancras Council building workers announced they would black all work on the two blocks from which Cook and Rowe had been evicted. The tenants displayed a "Roll of Honour" outside the blocks from which they had been evicted, listing all the trade union support they had received.

Such immediate sympathetic action was important as a final gesture of support, but was in the event too late in the day and not coordinated sufficiently to increase the political muscle of the tenants.

So there is experience of integrated struggle in Australia, Italy and England. But it is necessary to explore further ways in which a strategy of integrated industrial and community struggle could be further developed in England.

There is an increasing awareness that such integration is needed, especially on the part of community activists. For instance the network of 12 Community Development Projects set up by the government in 1969, has reached a common perspective on the need for integrated community and industrial struggle. They conclude in their Forward Plan for 1975/6:

> "Poverty is seen to be a consequence of fundamental inequalities in our present political and economic system, and the conditions which working class people experience are a consequence of these inequalities . . . To rectify this situation requires fundamental changes in the distribution of wealth and power."

The only cure for urban poverty is seen as lying "through the development of working class action and pressure on the widest possible front". The Projects see their contribution to this development as

> "bringing together all these interests — local organisations concerned with work, environment, housing — to deal with threats of redundancy, redevelopment proposals and other community issues in a unified way". [14]

Some projects, like the one in Canning Town, have been involved in bringing together local Action Committees set up at a rank and file level on a delegate basis, drawing in delegates from both the unions in industry and the community groups.

To get such action committees sponsored by a Trades Council was seen as a possible way of rejuvenating Trades Councils, which are traditionally the form of organisation that the labour movement has used to have a voice in local community affairs.

Trades Councils were set up in the mid-19th century with the following aims:
— to promote the interests of all affiliated organisations and to secure united action on all questions affecting those interests;
— to improve generally the economic and social conditions of workers;
— to help promote suitable educational, social and sports facilities for adult workers.

They are made up of delegates from any trade union branch which has members resident in the Trades Council area. Tenants associations and local organisations can send observers but they cannot speak or vote, so that local organisations can only raise proposals for action through their members who are there as trade union branch delegates.

With 500 Trades Councils throughout the country, their potential for uniting struggles is not to be dismissed till more efforts have been made to put energy into using them in this way. Before the formation of the Labour Party in 1906 and before the split between the industrial and political wings of the Labour movement was institutionalised, the Trades Council did act as the focus of working class political activity both in the community and at the work place. Now with the decline of the Labour Party there is no reason why the Trades Councils should not regain their former importance.

But there is still the very real problem in inner city areas that people do not live and work in the same area. To expect people to be active politically in both areas is a tall order. The more functional approach of the Builders' Labourers Federation in Australia may well be relevant in this context, since the workers, by taking responsibility for the social implications of their work combine community and industrial struggle within a single organisational framework.

In Notting Hill there is the additional problem that not only do most people not work in the area, but that most people work in the service sector, which is often poorly organised, and does not provide strong political muscle to back community struggles. However, organisation is developing even in sectors like the catering trade where it has never existed before.

Throughout the eight years in Notting Hill, efforts were made by the People's Association groups to ask for support for community struggles from local workers, and to give support to local workers in strike situations. The Trades Council was kept informed of the developments in the housing struggles with private capital and the Council, and the building workers gave very practical support in the form of stopping luxury conversions during their strike. However, the integration of these struggles was never given much time or energy and was not seen as an essential part of the struggle by either the local groups or the local trade unionists.

To attempt the integration of community and industrial struggles in a more structured way means confronting a very real organisational dilemma grounded in the long-standing debate over the value of spontaneity as against organisation. One of the strengths of community struggle is the political immediacy and non-hierarchical way of working, yet to gain the increased political power to be achieved through integration with industrial struggle means some kind of coordinating structure is necessary. Ways must be found of building a coordinating structure which does not destroy the political vitality of local or industrial groups, but which is geared to improving information of ongoing struggles so that it is accessible to both kinds of groups. A well-serviced network of groups involved in industrial and local issues throughout the area is the aim. This may well mean that a shared office with a manned telephone and an efficient information service paid for by all the groups involved, would be every bit as important as any more rigid institutionalisation.

All the pointers to a theory and practice of expanded working class struggle bridging community and industrial issues, are there. The Australian building workers' intervention in community struggles, and the mass occupations of Italian workers and tenants, together have shown some ways in which the theory can become a reality. The community struggles in Notting Hill have shown the real but limited potential of such struggles on their own. This experience was important in establishing such struggles as part of working class struggle, so that there is a body of experience to which workers in industry can refer and understand. Tentative attempts were made to build links between community and workplace struggles in Notting Hill, but it was perhaps true that the limitations of community struggle had to be experienced before the building of links with the workplace struggles could be recognised as a crucial part of an expanding socialist strategy. However, now a different stage has been reached. In England the crucial importance of integrating community and industrial struggles is being increasingly recognised in theory. What remains is to fuse these struggles in practice.

FOOTNOTES
1. Jo Freeman 'Tyranny of Structurelessness' in *Radical Feminism* 1972, Ed. by Anne Koedt, Ellen Levine.
2. Paper for June, 1972, conference. Camden Community Workshop.
3. *The Power of Women and the Subversion of the Community* Mariarose dalla Costa.
4. *Prelude to Revolution* Daniel Singer Pages 269, 272, 274.
5. "Community Action in Notting Hill 1969" — Notting Hill Community Workshop.
6. *The Community Development Process* Biddle.
7. Camden Community Workshop Paper June, 1972.
8. *Class in Contemporary Britain* Westergaard and Resler.
9. *Working for Ford* Huw Benyon, 1973.
10. *Wages, Prices and Profit* Karl Marx 1865.
11. *Grundrisse* Karl Marx.
12. *Taming the Concrete Jungle* Pete Thomas
13. 'Take Over the City' *Community Struggles in Italy,* Lotta Continua, 1973.
14. *Inter Project Report* CDP March, 1974.